HOLLY CLEGG'S
trim&TERRIFIC®

GULF COAST
FAVORITES

Over 250 easy, healthy and delicious recipes from my Louisiana kitchen!

Photographs by David Humphreys

Other Books by Holly Clegg:
Holly Clegg's trim&TERRIFIC® Too Hot in the Kitchen: Secrets To Sizzle At Any Age
The New Holly Clegg trim&TERRIFIC® Cookbook
Holly Clegg's trim&TERRIFIC® Home Entertaining The Easy Way
Holly Clegg's trim&TERRIFIC® Freezer Friendly Meals
Holly Clegg's trim&TERRIFIC® Diabetic Cooking
Eating Well Through Cancer: Easy Recipes & Recommendations Before & After Treatment

For more information, visit www.hollyclegg.com or call 1-800-88HOLLY

Interior Composition & Design: Rikki Campbell Ogden/pixiedesign llc
Cover Design: TILT
Creative Consultant: Pamela Clegg Hill
Nutritional Analysis: Tammi Hancock, Hancock Nutrition

Library of Congress Control Number:
ISBN-13   978-0-9815640-0-5
ISBN-10   0-9815640-0-3

Production, Manufacturing, and Distribution:
Favorite Recipes Press
An imprint of FRP
P.O. Box 305142, Nashville, TN 37230
800-358-0560

On the cover: *Barbecue Shrimp, pg. 122; Chocolate Pecan Pie, pg. 226; Greek Shrimp Scampi, pg. 128; Chicken and Sausage Gumbo, pg. 60*

Cover photography by Holly Clegg

Photograph opposite page courtesy of Louisiana Seafood Promotions Board

IN LOUISIANA, WE LOVE SEAFOOD, NOT ONLY BECAUSE OF THE DELICIOUS FLAVORS, BUT ALSO THE NUTRITIONAL BENEFITS. THROUGH HER COOKBOOKS, HOLLY CLEGG HAS HELPED LOUISIANA SEAFOOD LOVERS CREATE DISHES THAT ENHANCE THE NATURAL FLAVORS OF LOUISIANA SEAFOOD. BY ENCOURAGING READERS TO USE LOCAL INGREDIENTS SUCH AS LOUISIANA SEAFOOD, SHE ALSO HELPS SUPPORT OUR FISHING COMMUNITIES.

EWELL SMITH, EXECUTIVE DIRECTOR
Louisiana Seafood Promotion and Marketing Board

LOUISIANA FACTS

- Louisiana leads the nation in crawfish production; more than 90% of the crawfish we eat come from Louisiana.

- Louisiana leads the nation in production of both hard and soft-shell crabs.

- 69% of the domestic, US shrimp are harvested from the Gulf waters. One year's shrimp catch, strung end to end, would wrap around the Superdome 94,839 times.

- 70% of the oysters caught in the US are from the Gulf Coast.

- Louisiana produces 25-30 percent of the United States total seafood production.

- Louisiana produces 70 percent of Gulf of Mexico seafood production.

- The Louisiana yam (sweet potato) is the *official* state vegetable and #1 *vegetable* crop in Louisiana.

CONTENTS

Barbecue Chicken Bake with
Cornbread Crust p. 156

ACKNOWLEDGMENTS

MY FAMILY

MIKE—my husband, who begs me to prepare plain food and not make him try a different daily recipe, but after 29 years he still tastes whatever I give him. He is my confidante, advisor and my partner in life. **TODD**—working in New York at Onex, a private equity firm, your morning calls and our relationship are special, even though you don't cook! **SANA**—his lovely wife in fashion PR, and a great cook, I adore as my own daughter and treasure her fashion guidance, which I always need. And, of course, Georgia, the only non-Dachshund we love. **COURTNEY**—at Edelman PR, whose talent extends from my editor, to my recipe tester, and, hopefully, someday my sidekick in a mother-daughter cooking show (you remind me so much of my younger self). **CHAD**—her husband, in the scrap metal business, keeps her so happy in Dallas, never says I nag him, and instantly became my son, one that I would hand pick myself. Roux and Marley, their fantastic dachshunds. **HALEY**—my baby in her junior year at WashU keeps me smiling with her "Haley" stories. She calls for recipes as she exemplifies her cooking expertise to her college friends between all her time spent in the library. **ROBERT**—a great builder that's equally as good in the kitchen. I won't compete with him on the barbecue pit or with gumbo. **RUTH** and **JERRY**—my parents who have been my role models as parents and in life...I still want to grow up to be like ya'll. I'm so proud of my father's "One Man No Smoking Campaign" to educate children not to smoke. He turned his bout with larynx cancer into a positive giving experience, which isn't easy to do! **MAE MAE**—what would I do without you? In fact, all of Baton Rouge thinks you are my mother, as only a mother would do all you do for our family. **PAM** and **DR. JIM**—my books wouldn't be the same without you. Your talent in and out of the kitchen as my Clegg sis sounding board is invaluable. And, finally, I have a book about Jim's passion, besides just good food. **DR. ILENE**—a sister with many job descriptions who continues to fill each and every one of them, caringly, no matter what it is. **DR. BART**—much appreciation for all your advice at all hours, giving me more time to cook. I love our times together! **MICHAEL** and **KIM**—the family wine connoisseurs. Sure wish I lived closer to trade food for wine! **CANNON**—a restaurateur in Jackson, I will gladly share my kitchen with you anytime, as I am always guaranteed good food. **PAPA**—the one and only godparent to all my kids. **AUNT GARNEY**—my aunt with attitude who isn't settling down yet.

MY BOOK TEAM

Flip through my books and you'll notice I still work with the same "dream team." When you have perfection, it is hard to improve. **DAVID HUMPHREYS**—your talent as my photographer never ceases to amaze me. With each book, I am in awe of your food shots and what a fun time we manage to have working ten hour days. Thanks for the time, patience and talent you graciously bestow on me. **PAM**—there is not a proper title to describe everything you do for me. Your endless hours in the kitchen preparing the food for every shot, your dedication, and your invaluable coordination all wrapped up in one very special person...you! **TAMMI HANCOCK**—of Hancock Nutrition, for over ten years I have turned to you for your nutritional expertise. Your effort always goes way beyond the call of duty. **RIKKI**—your graphic design, layout and creative input is exceptional. I LOVE your work and respect your talent tremendously. Thanks for all the extra you do for me to create the best book! **AMANDA**—from my kitchen to my office, and even PR and proofreading for this book, you are invaluable to me. I enjoy you being here, especially since my daughters are away. Special thanks to **VAL MARMILLION**, **RANNAH GRAY** and

LISA NOBLES of Marmillion and Company for their dedication and commitment to this project to benefit America's Wetlands. SHEILA—at Favorite Recipes Press, I rely on you more than you know. Your opinion, guidance, and friendship in business, and life, is priceless to me. You make developing books a pleasurable experience and the end result is an outstanding cookbook. DAVE—thanks for your interest.

MY PROJECTS

GERALD MILETELLO, MD—my *Eating Well Through Cancer* coauthor and one of the finest oncologists and partners. This has been the most rewarding experience. Sharing it with you and MELINDA has been a true blessing. AL, DIANE, and NANCY—at Diane Allen & Associates, I enjoy representing Louisiana yams and value your creative input. Al, I still need your mentoring! JILL—at *Relish* magazine, my first foodie buddy and a friend forever. ROB, ABE, and HESCHEL, at the ADA, I am honored to partner with you for my *trim&TERRIFIC™ Diabetic Cooking* to help fight diabetes. It was truly a dream to come true. DIANA, MATTY, and JON—thanks for my Running Press Trim & Terrific™ books, the anchor to my series. PIER—at Plus Media, for ten years of SMT's, projects, and a dear friendship.

THE PEOPLE IN MY LIFE

To all my dear friends! FRANCINE and DOLL—a lifetime of friendship (and fish) and my biggest and most enthusiastic promoters. LOUANN and DR. RONNIE—my super couple and super friends, I count on you for everything from recipes and friendship to medical questions. Ya'll are always there! BILL and GRACIE—Gracie (sister in disguise), I always look forward to our times together dining, trading recipes, and traveling. Thanks for being my sidekick. Bill, always looking out for me...you made this book happen. KAREN and DR. ANTHONY—I spend more time with you exercising my jaw and you know how I treasure "our time" and your advice. Anthony, you are still my #1 doc on retainer. GAIL and LEWIS—over 20 years of the dearest friendship, as we say "from peaks to valleys," sharing it all together is what counts. LYNELL and JEFF—my first

and only groupies, love those special chats and you always make time for me. MARTY and JOHN—for years of fun times and closeness, and now as invaluable wild game advisors. MELANIE and DR. TOMMY—I value our unique, exceptional bond. (Thanks for graciously answering all my doctor calls, Tommy.) JOHN and PAULA— from laughs to tears, your family has been an extension of our family for almost 25 years. CAROL and GARY, and RITA and GARY—lifelong special friends forever. To BUD LIGHT and COKE! LOUISE and JIM— lifelong friends, my tennis partner and pal, even though I haven't played in 10 years. DALE and ANISA—for keeping my smile looking good and for being my resident PR friend. JANET and DOUG—years of friendship. Mydear college friends who I'm grateful to still have in my life. AMY and SCOTT—I wear my "Amy jewelry" with pride! And Scott, my new consultant! JOLIE—for a friendship that started with a toaster oven in college and is still going even as my kids get married...I love it! LESLIE—my college roommate who is now planning my son's honeymoon. How special! LILA—college roomie! I treasure our shopping and conversations, and my Atlanta visits. SHERRI—Denver stopovers and cheers to good skin. RENATE—over 30 years of love from London. MARCIA, SELMA, and JOYCE—my Fort Worth extended family for as long as I can remember. Marcia and Selma, I love getting your recipes and Joyce I still enjoy cooking for you. MISSY—the "Missy Hair" is a must. MARY—at my Thursday appointments, the chats are as good as my nails.

Also, a special thanks to all who helped me with the wild game recipes. I turned to my expert hunter friends and their wives for some of these incredible recipes—DEBBIE and RANDY, LOUANN and RONNIE, MARTY and JOHN, DANA and JIM, COLLEEN and PAUL, and HANK.

Finally, to all my trim&TERRIFIC™ supporters—this concept began as a way to help people enjoy eating healthier food. And, thanks to your continued support, here is the latest addition to my trim&TERRIFIC™ cookbooks! Keep on cooking trim&TERRIFIC™ so I can continue my passion of writing cookbooks.

INTRODUCTION

A WORD FROM HOLLY

Louisiana is known for its cuisine, therefore, a cookbook with recipes indigenous to Louisiana and the gulf sparked my taste buds. I have credited our great food to the accessibility of our fresh seafood and local ingredients. As you flip through the recipes in this book, my hope is for you to learn and understand the value of the Louisiana seafood and the wetlands while enjoying a repertoire of mouth-watering recipes.

In *trim&TERRIFIC® Gulf Coast Favorites*, I am excited to share with you regional specialties, home cooking, and many familiar favorites. As in my *trim&TERRIFIC®* book series, you can count on easy, everyday and healthier recipes designed for the busy person. This book includes Southern Biscuits and Gravy, Crawfish Enchiladas, Steak Tacos with Cucumber Avocado Salsa, Crab Nachos and Chocolate Pecan Pie...plus so much more. My philosophy is you never have to give up any food nor is there a forbidden food, as I trim the recipes down and keep them terrific! I have been deemed "the queen of quick" for a reason as I believe in time friendly and pantry friendly recipes, allowing you to prepare a healthier meal on those hectic days. As a mother, I am aware of time constraints and family pleasing recipes, so you can assure yourself this book will satisfy the cook and the family.

I have included popular symbols for quick reference to your cooking needs. For those that prefer delicious vegetarian recipes, look for the carrot symbol by the recipe. If you prefer make-ahead meals, look for the snowflake symbol to indicate freezer-friendly recipes. I believe a well stocked pantry is equivalent to a permanent shopping list so you will find a Pantry Stocking Guide which will enable you to prepare quick meals by pulling ingredients you already have at home. I am also including the popular Menu section to guide you for different holidays, themes or when you are in that cooking rut.

Each recipe includes the nutritional analysis and the diabetic exchange. The analysis is based on the larger servings. The nutritional analysis does not include any salt or pepper (since it is listed to taste) or any ingredient with "optional" after it. I am thrilled to present my *Gulf Coast Favorites* cookbook as now you can enjoy *trim&TERRIFIC®* regional specialties along with basic everyday recipes in hopes that you will have a trim & terrific kitchen!

Tomato and Goat Cheese Tarts pg. 16

APPETIZERS

Shrimp Remoulade	4		Baked Caramel Brie	14
Shrimp Cocktail Sauce	4		Brie Apricot Bites	14
Marinated Shrimp	6		Chicken, Brie and Cranberry Chutney Quesadillas	15
Marinated Crab Fingers	6		Exotic Shrimp Bundles	15
Ronnie's Venison Bites	7		Tomato and Goat Cheese Tarts	16
Hamburger Dip	7		Southwestern Shrimp Cups	17
Southwestern Guacamole	8		Simple Spicy Shrimp	17
Roasted Tomato Salsa	8		Mini Muffalettas	18
Southwestern Hummus Dip	9		Crab Nachos	18
Poor Man's Caviar	9		Stuffed Crab Poblano Peppers	20
Louisiana Red Bean Dip	10		Stuffed Pesto Mushrooms	20
Speedy Spinach Dip	10		Stuffed Crawfish Mushrooms	21
Crawfish Dip	11		Pork Picadillo Tortilla Cups	22
Smoked Gouda Crawfish	11		Marinated Duck Strip Skewers	23
Hot Crab Spinach Dip Baked in French Bread	12			
Oyster Rockefeller Dip	13			

The Mississippi basin is a major flyway for migratory birds. It is used by up to 40% of North America's duck, geese, swan and eagle populations.

Gulf of Mexico Alliance

WETLANDS FACT

SHRIMP REMOULADE

MAKES 8 (1/4-CUP) SERVINGS

You'll love my impressive, pantry-friendly version of this classic French sauce. Serve on a bed of lettuce for a light lunch or a fabulous first course.

1 pound medium peeled shrimp, seasoned and cooked

2 tablespoons light mayonnaise

2 tablespoons Creole or grainy mustard

1 tablespoon ketchup

1 tablespoon lemon juice

Dash hot sauce

1/4 cup chopped green onions

2 tablespoons finely chopped red onion

2 tablespoons chopped fresh parsley

1. Place shrimp in a bowl. In another small bowl, combine remaining ingredients and toss with shrimp. Refrigerate until serving.

NUTRITIONAL INFORMATION PER SERVING
Calories 74 | Calories from fat 22% | Fat 2 g
Saturated Fat 0 g | Cholesterol 112 mg | Sodium 243 mg
Carbohydrate 1 g | Dietary Fiber 0 g | Sugars 1 g | Protein 12 g

DIABETIC EXCHANGES
2 very lean meat

SHRIMP COCKTAIL SAUCE

MAKES 6 (1/4-CUP) SERVINGS

Shrimp is always a party favorite and cocktail sauce is the number one condiment to dress it up. One taste and you'll never be satisfied by a store-bought cocktail sauce ever again. Serve with shrimp in a martini glass and a lemon wedge.

1/2 cup chopped green bell pepper

1/4 cup chopped celery

1/2 cup ketchup

1/2 cup chili sauce

2 tablespoons prepared horseradish, or more if desired

1 tablespoon Worcestershire sauce

1 tablespoon lemon juice

Dash hot sauce

Salt and pepper to taste

1. In a food processor or blender, combine all ingredients. Pulse until mixture is smooth. Season to taste. Refrigerate until serving.

NUTRITIONAL INFORMATION PER SERVING
Calories 48 | Calories from fat 0% | Fat 0 g
Saturated Fat 0 g | Cholesterol 0 mg | Sodium 577 mg
Carbohydrate 12 g | Dietary Fiber 1 g | Sugars 10 g | Protein 1 g

DIABETIC EXCHANGES
1 carbohydrate

TERRIFIC TIDBIT

Shrimp counts with shells per pound:
Small 36/45
Medium 31/35
Large 21/30

trim&TERRIFIC™ **GULF COAST FAVORITES**

Shrimp Remoulade, pg. 4; Shrimp Cocktail Sauce, pg. 4

MARINATED SHRIMP

MAKES 16 (1/2-CUP) SERVINGS

Shrimp, artichokes, hearts of palm, and capers in a light, spunky vinaigrette are highlighted best when served in a glass bowl with frilled toothpicks or crackers. Leftovers may be used as a salad.

2 pounds medium peeled shrimp, seasoned and cooked

2 (14-ounce) cans quartered artichoke hearts, drained

1 (15-ounce) can hearts of palm, drained

3 tablespoons capers, drained

1 bunch green onions, chopped

2 tablespoons chopped parsley

1/4 cup red wine vinegar

2 tablespoons lemon juice

1/4 cup olive oil

2 tablespoons canola oil

3 tablespoons dry mustard

1 teaspoon minced garlic

Salt and pepper to taste

1. In a bowl, combine shrimp, artichoke hearts, hearts of palm, capers, and green onions.

2. In a small bowl, combine remaining ingredients and toss with shrimp mixture. Refrigerate until serving.

NUTRITIONAL INFORMATION PER SERVING
Calories 87 | Calories from fat 21% | Fat 2 g
Saturated Fat 0 g | Cholesterol 111 mg | Sodium 332 mg
Carbohydrate 4 g | Dietary Fiber 1 g | Sugars 1 g | Protein 13 g

DIABETIC EXCHANGES
2 very lean meat

MARINATED CRAB FINGERS

MAKES 8 SERVINGS

Take a shortcut using Italian dressing mix for a memorable—and easy—crab finger marinade.

2 tablespoons lemon juice

1 teaspoon Dijon mustard

1/4 cup balsamic vinegar

2 tablespoons cider vinegar

2 tablespoons olive oil

1 (.7-ounce) package Italian dressing mix

1 bunch green onions, chopped

1 pound crab fingers

1. In a bowl, combine all ingredients except crab fingers.

2. Toss crab fingers in mixture and marinate 1 hour, or overnight, in the refrigerator.

NUTRITIONAL INFORMATION PER SERVING
Calories 118 | Calories from fat 30% | Fat 4 g
Saturated Fat 1 g | Cholesterol 43 mg | Sodium 631 mg
Carbohydrate 6 g | Dietary Fiber 1 g | Sugars 4 g | Protein 13 g

DIABETIC EXCHANGES
1/2 carbohydrate | 2 lean meat

TERRIFIC TIDBIT

If you don't have balsamic vinegar, just use red wine vinegar.

RONNIE'S VENISON BITES

MAKES 1 SERVING

These easy and absolutely fantastic bites have become a signature recipe for our dear friend, Dr. Ronnie Bombet.

Slice of venison backstrap (1/2-inch thick)

1 sliced jalapeño (found in jar)

1/2 teaspoon reduced-fat cream cheese

1/2 strip center-cut bacon

Toothpicks

1. Place venison slice on a plate and pound slightly to flatten. Top with a jalapeño and cream cheese.

2. Roll up, wrap in the bacon, and secure with a toothpick. Grill about 5 minutes, or until done.

NUTRITIONAL INFORMATION PER SERVING
Calories 90 | Calories from fat 30% | Fat 3 g
Saturated Fat 1 g | Cholesterol 53 mg | Sodium 169 mg
Carbohydrate 1 g | Dietary Fiber 0 g | Sugars 0 g | Protein 14 g

DIABETIC EXCHANGES
2 lean meat

HAMBURGER DIP

MAKES 20 (1/4-CUP) SERVINGS

Just four simple ingredients create this satisfying, meaty dip in mere minutes, ideal for football season and last-minute company. Serve with chips.

1 pound ground sirloin

1/2 pound sliced mushrooms

1 (16-ounce) jar salsa

1 (8-ounce) package shredded, reduced-fat Monterey Jack or Mexican-blend cheese

1. In a nonstick pot, cook meat and mushrooms over medium heat for 5–7 minutes, or until meat is done. Drain any excess fat.

2. Add salsa and cheese, stirring over medium heat until cheese is melted.

NUTRITIONAL INFORMATION PER SERVING
Calories 82 | Calories from fat 48% | Fat 4 g
Saturated Fat 2 g | Cholesterol 19 mg | Sodium 175 mg
Carbohydrate 2 g | Dietary Fiber 0 g | Sugars 1 g | Protein 8 g

DIABETIC EXCHANGES
1 lean meat

TERRIFIC TIDBIT

Look for cuts of meat ending in "loin" or "round" for the leaner cuts.

SOUTHWESTERN GUACAMOLE

MAKES 8 (1/4-CUP) SERVINGS

Spicy jalapeños, red onion, corn, and cheese spruce up guacamole. This speedy dip makes an appetizing snack in a snap.

1 cup coarsely chopped avocados (about 2)

2–3 tablespoons lime juice

1/2 cup frozen corn, thawed

1/3 cup chopped red bell pepper

1/3 cup chopped red onion

1/3 cup shredded jalapeño Monterey Jack cheese

1 teaspoon chopped jalapeño (found in jar)

Salt and pepper to taste

1. In a bowl, combine avocados and lime juice. Stir in remaining ingredients.

NUTRITIONAL INFORMATION PER SERVING
Calories 62 | Calories from fat 62% | Fat 4 g
Saturated Fat 1 g | Cholesterol 4 mg | Sodium 42 mg
Carbohydrate 6 g | Dietary Fiber 2 g | Sugars 1 g | Protein 2g

DIABETIC EXCHANGES
1/2 carbohydrate | 1 fat

TERRIFIC TIDBIT

If you don't have chipotle chili powder, substitute chili powder. Chipotle powder adds a smoky flavor and is available in the spice section of your grocery store.

ROASTED TOMATO SALSA

MAKES 8 (1/4-CUP) SERVINGS

Give your salsa the kick it's been missing! Roasting the vegetables boosts the flavor for a fantastic, smoky five ingredient salsa.

3 large tomatoes, quartered

1/2 red onion, cut into thick slices

Salt and pepper to taste

1/4 teaspoon chipotle chili powder

3 tablespoons lime juice

1. Preheat broiler. Line a baking sheet with foil and coat with nonstick cooking spray.

2. Arrange tomatoes and onion slices in a single layer. Season to taste. Broil for 8–10 minutes, turning midway through, until skins are charred. Set aside to cool.

3. In a food processor, combine tomatoes, onions, and remaining ingredients. Purée until the mixture is smooth or slightly chunky.

NUTRITIONAL INFORMATION PER SERVING
Calories 17 | Calories from fat 0% | Fat 0 g
Saturated Fat 0 g | Cholesterol 0 mg | Sodium 5 mg
Carbohydrate 4 g | Dietary Fiber 1 g | Sugars 2 g | Protein 1 g

DIABETIC EXCHANGES
Free

SOUTHWESTERN HUMMUS DIP

MAKES 8 (1/4-CUP) SERVINGS

Middle Eastern flavor meets southwestern flair. Great served with pita or fresh veggies.

1/2 cup finely chopped onion

1 teaspoon minced garlic

1/2 teaspoon ground cumin

1/2 teaspoon chili powder

1 (15-ounce) can white beans (cannelloni), rinsed and drained

1 cup shredded, reduced-fat white Cheddar cheese

1/4 cup nonfat sour cream

1 tablespoon lemon juice

Salt to taste

Dash cayenne

3 strips center-cut bacon, cooked crisp and crumbled

1. Coat a nonstick skillet with nonstick cooking spray. Sauté onion and garlic over medium heat until tender, about 5 minutes. Add cumin and chili powder, stirring for one minute. Remove from heat.

2. In a food processor, pulse sautéed onion mixture with remaining ingredients, except bacon, until mixture is puréed.

3. Transfer to a serving dish and sprinkle with crumbled bacon.

NUTRITIONAL INFORMATION PER SERVING
Calories 105 | Calories from fat 30% | Fat 4 g
Saturated Fat 2 g | Cholesterol 11 mg | Sodium 248 mg
Carbohydrate 10 g | Dietary Fiber 2 g | Sugars 1 g | Protein 7 g

DIABETIC EXCHANGES
1/2 starch | 1 lean meat

POOR MAN'S CAVIAR

MAKES 12 (1/4-CUP) SERVINGS

One of those popular salsa-style dips you can whip up with little effort, This recipe has also been referred to as Texas Caviar. The longer it sits, the better it gets, so make it ahead of time.

1 (15-ounce) can black-eyed peas, rinsed and drained

1/4 cup finely chopped green bell pepper

1/3 cup finely chopped tomatoes

1/3 cup finely chopped red onion

1/3 cup finely chopped green onions

1/3 cup frozen or canned corn

1 tablespoon finely chopped jalapeños (found in jar)

3 tablespoons red wine vinegar or seasoned red wine vinegar

2 teaspoons olive oil

1. In a bowl, combine all ingredients. Cover and let sit at room temperature for 2–3 hours, stirring occasionally. Refrigerate after serving.

NUTRITIONAL INFORMATION PER SERVING
Calories 43 | Calories from fat 16% | Fat 1 g
Saturated Fat 0 g | Cholesterol 0 mg | Sodium 130 mg
Carbohydrate 7 g | Dietary Fiber 2 g | Sugars 1 g | Protein 2 g

DIABETIC EXCHANGES
1/2 starch

APPETIZERS

LOUISIANA RED BEAN DIP

MAKES 12 (1/4-CUP) SERVINGS

Reminiscent of the popular "red beans and rice," this speedy, spicy first-rate dip makes a statement.

1 cup chopped, reduced-fat sausage

2 (15-ounce) cans red kidney beans, rinsed and drained

1 (4-ounce) can chopped green chilies

3/4 cup salsa

1/2 cup nonfat sour cream

1 teaspoon chili powder

1 1/2 teaspoons ground cumin

1 1/2 cups shredded, reduced-fat Mexican-blend cheese, divided

1. Preheat oven 350°F.

2. Heat a nonstick skillet over medium heat and cook sausage until crisp brown. Set aside.

2. In a food processor, combine remaining ingredients, reserving 1 cup cheese. Process until mixture is smooth.

3. Transfer to a baking dish and sprinkle with remaining cheese and top with sausage. Bake until cheese is melted and dip is hot, about 15 minutes.

———

NUTRITIONAL INFORMATION PER SERVING
Calories 144 | Calories from fat 21% | Fat 3 g
Saturated Fat 2 g | Cholesterol 13 mg | Sodium 466 mg
Carbohydrate 16 g | Dietary Fiber 4 g | Sugars 3 g | Protein 10 g

DIABETIC EXCHANGES
1 starch | 1 1/2 very lean meat

SPEEDY SPINACH DIP

MAKES 16 (1/4-CUP) SERVINGS

Dip lovers of all ages will dig in to this hassle-free spinach dip. With reduced-fat cheeses, you won't have to feel guilty about going back for more.

2 (10-ounce) packages frozen, chopped spinach

1 cup salsa

4 ounces reduced-fat cream cheese

1 (5-ounce) can evaporated skim milk

1 cup shredded, reduced-fat Swiss or Alpine Lace cheese

1. Cook spinach according to package directions. Drain well.

2. In a medium nonstick pot, combine spinach with remaining ingredients. Cook over medium heat, stirring until cheese is melted

———

NUTRITIONAL INFORMATION PER SERVING
Calories 62 | Calories from fat 43% | Fat 3 g
Saturated Fat 2 g | Cholesterol 9 mg | Sodium 135 mg
Carbohydrate 4 g | Dietary Fiber 1 g | Sugars 2 g | Protein 5 g

DIABETIC EXCHANGES
1 lean meat

CRAWFISH DIP

MAKES 16 (1/4-CUP) SERVINGS

With a light tomato-white sauce and a touch of heat, this deliciously zesty crawfish dip is the perfect crowd pleaser.

2 tablespoons butter

1 tablespoon olive oil

1 cup chopped onion

1/2 teaspoon minced garlic

1/4 cup all-purpose flour

1 (10-ounce) can diced tomatoes and green chilies

1 cup skim milk

1 teaspoon Worcestershire sauce

Salt and pepper to taste

1 pound crawfish tails, rinsed and drained

1 bunch green onions, chopped

1. In large nonstick skillet, melt butter and oil. Sauté onion until tender, about 5 minutes. Add garlic and flour, stirring for 1 minute. Gradually add tomatoes and green chilies and milk, mixing well.

2. Bring mixture to a boil. Lower heat, stirring for about 5 minutes or until mixture thickens. Add Worcestershire sauce and season to taste.

3. Add crawfish and green onions, stirring until heated.

NUTRITIONAL INFORMATION PER SERVING
Calories 69 | Calories from fat 24% | Fat 3 g
Saturated Fat 1 g | Cholesterol 43 mg | Sodium 122 mg
Carbohydrate 5 g | Dietary Fiber 1 g | Sugars 2 g | Protein 6 g

DIABETIC EXCHANGES
1/2 carbohydrate | 1 lean meat

SMOKED GOUDA CRAWFISH DIP

MAKES 10 (1/4-CUP) SERVINGS

Simple to make, elegant to serve, and quick to disappear, this delightful dish combines crawfish and Gouda for a truly unique flavor. Serve with Melba rounds.

1 bunch green onions, chopped

1/2 cup chopped fresh parsley

1 teaspoon minced garlic

1/2 cup fat-free half-and-half

1 pound crawfish tails, rinsed and drained

4 ounces smoked Gouda cheese, rind removed and cut into small pieces

1/4 cup dry vermouth or cooking vermouth

Pepper to taste

1. In a nonstick skillet coated with nonstick cooking spray, sauté green onion, parsley, and garlic for about 3 minutes.

2. Add half-and-half and crawfish, stirring until well heated and bubbly. Add cheese and vermouth, stirring constantly, until cheese melts. Season to taste

---

NUTRITIONAL INFORMATION PER SERVING
Calories 103 | Calories from fat 33% | Fat 4 g
Saturated Fat 2 g | Cholesterol 75 mg | Sodium 155 mg
Carbohydrate 4 g | Dietary Fiber 1 g | Sugars 2 g | Protein 12 g

DIABETIC EXCHANGES
2 lean meat

APPETIZERS

HOT CRAB SPINACH DIP
BAKED IN FRENCH BREAD
MAKES 16 (1/4-CUP) SERVINGS

Don't miss this terrific spinach dip with creamy avocados, succulent crabmeat and a little kick. Baking it in French bread gives the dip style and finesse, with an easy clean up to boot. Cube the extra bread to serve with the dip, or serve with crackers

2 tablespoons butter

1/4 cup all-purpose flour

1/2 teaspoon minced garlic

1 cup fat-free half-and-half

1/2 cup skim milk

1/4 teaspoon cayenne

1 teaspoon dry mustard

Salt and pepper to taste

1 (10-ounce) package frozen chopped spinach, drained and squeezed dry

1 cup shredded, reduced-fat Monterey Jack cheese

1 pound lump or white crabmeat, picked through for shells

1 avocado, pitted and chopped

1 loaf French bread

1. In a nonstick pot, melt butter and add flour, stirring for about 1 minute. Add garlic and continue stirring. Gradually add half-and-half and milk, stirring constantly, until mixture comes to a boil.

2. Add cayenne, mustard, salt, pepper, spinach, and cheese, cooking and stirring until cheese is melted. Gently fold in crabmeat and avocado.

3. Slice a thin slice off the top of the French bread and scoop out the soft inside bread leaving a shell. Fill with crab-spinach mixture, and bake for 20–25 minutes or until bubbly. Cover top of bread with foil if it begins to brown.

NUTRITIONAL INFORMATION PER SERVING
(ANALYSIS FOR DIP ONLY)
Calories 111 | Calories from fat 41% | Fat 5 g
Saturated Fat 2 g | Cholesterol 29 mg | Sodium 194 mg
Carbohydrate 6 g | Dietary Fiber 1 g | Sugars 2 g | Protein 11 g

DIABETIC EXCHANGES
1/2 carbohydrate | 1 1/2 lean meat

TERRIFIC TIDBIT

Prepare the dip ahead of time, refrigerate, and transfer to the bread when ready to bake.

OYSTER ROCKEFELLER DIP

MAKES 12 (1/4-CUP) SERVINGS

If you are in the mood for oysters but don't want to go through the usual hassle of preparing them, take this easy, amazing dip out for a test drive. It has all the taste, and is virtually labor free.

36 oysters, drained, reserve 1/4 cup oyster liquid

3 tablespoons butter

1 (10-ounce) package frozen spinach, cooked and drained

1/2 cup chopped flat-leaf parsley (Italian)

1 bunch green onions, chopped

1/4 cup chopped green bell pepper

1 cup fat free half-and-half

1 cup skim milk

2 tablespoons cornstarch

1 tablespoon anise-flavored liqueur or Pernod (optional)

1. Preheat broiler. Coat baking sheet with nonstick cooking spray.

2. Place oysters in a single layer on prepared pan. Broil until oysters begin to curl, watching carefully. Drain any liquid, reserving 1/4 cup.

3. In a large nonstick pot, melt butter and add cooked spinach, parsley, green onion, and green pepper. Sauté until tender, about 5 minutes. Stir in half-and-half and milk.

4. In a small bowl, combine cornstarch with reserved oyster liquid. Add to spinach mixture, cooking until mixture comes to a boil and slightly thickens. Add anise, if desired.

NUTRITIONAL INFORMATION PER SERVING
Calories 99 | Calories from fat 36% | Fat 4 g
Saturated Fat 2 g | Cholesterol 30mg | Sodium 160 mg
Carbohydrate 10 g | Dietary Fiber 2 g | Sugars 4 g | Protein 6

DIABETIC EXCHANGES
1/2 carbohydrate | 1/2 very lean meat | 1 fat

TERRIFIC TIDBIT

I like the touch of anise-flavored liqueur suggesting the flavor but not overpowering the recipe. If freezing, freeze without oysters and add when serving.

APPETIZERS

BAKED CARAMEL BRIE

MAKES 12–14 SERVINGS

Splurge with this melt-in-your-mouth recipe.
Serve with crackers or gingersnaps.

1/2 cup water

1/3 cup light brown sugar

2 teaspoons cornstarch

1/4 teaspoon ground cinnamon

1 (5-ounce) can evaporated skim milk

1 teaspoon vanilla extract

1 (12-ounce) wheel Brie cheese

1/4 cup sliced almonds, toasted

1. Preheat oven to 225°F.

2. In a small pot, heat water and brown
   sugar over low heat until sugar dissolves.
   Increase heat and bring to a boil without
   stirring until mixture turns deep golden
   brown, about 2–4 minutes.

3. In a small bowl, combine cornstarch, cinnamon, and milk to make a thin paste.
   Stir into sugar mixture. Cook until sauce
   is slightly thickened and bubbly. Remove
   from heat and add vanilla.

4. Place Brie in a baking dish, remove the
   top rind, and top with sauce. Bake for
   15–20 minutes or until Brie softens. Remove
   from oven and sprinkle with almonds. Let
   stand 5 minutes before serving.

NUTRITIONAL INFORMATION PER SERVING
Calories 122 | Calories from fat 56% | Fat 8 g
Saturated Fat 4 g | Cholesterol 25 mg | Sodium 168 mg
Carbohydrate 7 g | Dietary Fiber 0 g | Sugars 7 g | Protein 6 g

DIABETIC EXCHANGES
1/2 carbohydrate | 1 high-fat meat

BRIE APRICOT BITES

MAKES 30 APPETIZERS

Rich velvety Brie, sweet apricots, and crunchy
almonds will tantalize your taste buds with
flavor. Also great for brunch.

30 frozen phyllo shells

1 (8-ounce) wedge Brie cheese, rind
   removed, cut into 30 pieces

1/2 cup spreadable apricot preserves

1/2 cup finely chopped dried apricots

1/4 cup sliced almonds

1. Preheat oven to 350°F.

2. Arrange phyllo shells on a baking sheet.
   Bake for 5 minutes. Remove from oven.

3. Spoon about 1/2 teaspoon apricot preserves into each shell. Place a piece of
   Brie on top of preserves.

4. Top with a small amount of chopped
   apricots and sprinkle with the almonds.
   Bake for 5–7 minutes or until Brie is
   melted. Serve warm.

NUTRITIONAL INFORMATION PER SERVING
Calories 68 | Calories from fat 47% | Fat 4 g
Saturated Fat 1 g | Cholesterol 8 mg | Sodium 60 mg
Carbohydrate 7 g | Dietary Fiber 0 g | Sugars 4 g | Protein 2 g

DIABETIC EXCHANGES
1/2 carbohydrate | 1 fat

TERRIFIC TIDBIT

For
a shortcut,
pick up a jar of
caramel sauce in-
stead of making
it at home.

trim&TERRIFIC™ **GULF COAST FAVORITES**

CHICKEN, BRIE, AND CRANBERRY CHUTNEY QUESADILLAS

MAKES 2 DOZEN WEDGES

Turn leftovers into a dinnertime delight with Brie and cranberry chutney in this easy and yummy quesadilla.

6 (8–10-inch) flour tortillas

1 (9-ounce) jar cranberry chutney

8 ounces Brie cheese, rind removed, cut into slices

2/3 cup chopped chicken breasts or turkey

1. Preheat oven to 425°F. Coat a baking sheet with nonstick cooking spray.

2. Spread one side of a tortilla with cranberry chutney, top with Brie and chicken. Fold in half, pressing edges together. Repeat for remaining tortillas.

3. Place on prepared pan and bake until cheese is melted and tortillas are golden, about 5 minutes.

NUTRITIONAL INFORMATION PER SERVING
Calories 85 | Calories from fat 31% | Fat 3 g
Saturated Fat 2 g | Cholesterol 13 mg | Sodium 149 mg
Carbohydrate 10 g | Dietary Fiber 1 g | Sugars 4 g | Protein 4 g

DIABETIC EXCHANGES
1/2 starch | 1/2 lean meat

TERRIFIC TIDBIT

Freeze unbaked bundles on a baking sheet. Then transfer to zip top freezer bags. Bake frozen bundles a little longer than directed.

EXOTIC SHRIMP BUNDLES

MAKES ABOUT 1 1/2 DOZEN

An outrageously delicious mixture of sweet, salty, spicy and crunchy.

12 sheets phyllo dough

1/3 cup nonfat plain yogurt

2 tablespoons flaked coconut

1/3 cup chopped cashews

1/4 cup mango chutney, chopped in pieces, if needed

1 teaspoon ground curry powder

1/2 teaspoon grated fresh ginger

1 cup small peeled shrimp, seasoned and cooked

1. Preheat oven to 350°F.

2. Place four layers of phyllo dough on top of each other, spraying each layer with nonstick cooking spray. Cut the stack into 6 squares.

3. In a small bowl, combine remaining ingredients. Place about 1 tablespoon of the mixture in the center of each square. Bring the four corners of each square together over the center of the filling, pinch and twist to enclose and form bundles.

4. Repeat with remaining phyllo and filling. Place on baking sheet and bake for 15–18 minutes or until golden brown.

NUTRITIONAL INFORMATION PER SERVING
Calories 59 | Calories from fat 25% | Fat 2 g
Saturated Fat 0 g | Cholesterol 19 mg | Sodium 58 mg
Carbohydrate 8 g | Dietary Fiber 0 g | Sugars 2 g | Protein 3 g

DIABETIC EXCHANGES
1/2 starch | 1/2 fat

APPETIZERS

15

TOMATO AND GOAT CHEESE TARTS

MAKES 1 1/2 DOZEN ROUNDS

A flaky crust topped with sautéed golden onions, goat cheese, tomatoes, and basil creates a bold-flavored snack. These tarts are also great served with soup or a salad.

1 tablespoon olive oil

4 cups thinly sliced onions, halved

1 teaspoon minced garlic

Salt and pepper to taste

3 tablespoons white wine or cooking wine

1/2 teaspoon dried thyme leaves

1 (17.3-ounce) package puff pastry sheet, thawed

3 ounces crumbled goat cheese (use Mediterranean if available)

3 Roma tomatoes, thinly sliced

3 tablespoons coarsely chopped fresh basil leaves or 1 tablespoon dried basil leaves

2 teaspoons grated Parmesan cheese

1. Preheat oven to 425°F.

2. In a large nonstick skillet, heat oil over medium heat and sauté onions and garlic for 15–20 minutes, stirring frequently, until onions are golden brown. Season to taste. Add wine and thyme. Continue cooking for another 5 minutes. Remove from heat.

3. Unfold each puff pastry sheet on a lightly floured surface and roll into a thin rectangle. Using a 3-inch cutter, cut circles from each sheet of pastry. (Save the scraps for reuse.)

4. Transfer pastry rounds onto prepared pan and prick each with a fork. Divide onion mixture evenly between each of the rounds. Sprinkle each with goat cheese and top with a tomato slice. Sprinkle with basil and Parmesan cheese. Season to taste.

5. Coat rounds with nonstick cooking spray. Bake for 15–20 minutes or until pastry is golden brown. Serve warm or at room temperature.

NUTRITIONAL INFORMATION PER SERVING
Calories 153 | Calories from fat 59% | Fat 10 g
Saturated Fat 3 g | Cholesterol 5 mg | Sodium 154 mg
Carbohydrate 12 g | Dietary Fiber 1 g | Sugars 3 g | Protein 4 g

DIABETIC EXCHANGES
1 carbohydrate | 2 fat

TERRIFIC TIDBIT

Use any extra pastry to pat into a round and top with cheese, tomatoes, spinach, or anything else to create your own pizza.

SOUTHWESTERN SHRIMP CUPS

MAKES 5 DOZEN CUPS

Won tons, found in the produce section, filled with a festive flavorful shrimp mixture make impressive party pick-ups. Chicken may be substituted for the shrimp, or leave both out for a vegetarian version.

5 dozen won ton wraps (squares)

2 cups shredded, reduced-fat Mexican-blend cheese

2 cups coarsely chopped peeled shrimp, seasoned and cooked

1 cup chopped roasted red pepper, drained (found in jar)

1 (11-ounce) can Mexicorn, drained

1 (4-ounce) can chopped green chilies, drained

1/2 teaspoon chili powder

1/2 cup chopped green onions

1. Preheat oven to 350°F. Coat mini muffin pans with nonstick cooking spray.

2. Press a won ton wrap into each muffin cup. Bake about 6–7 minutes or until lightly golden brown.

3. In a bowl, combine remaining ingredients. Divide shrimp mixture evenly into won tons. Return pan to oven and continue baking 6–8 minutes or until cheese is melted.

NUTRITIONAL INFORMATION PER SERVING
Calories 44 | Calories from fat 18% | Fat 1 g
Saturated Fat 1 g | Cholesterol 12 mg | Sodium 84 mg
Carbohydrate 6 g | Dietary Fiber 0 g | Sugars 0 g | Protein 3 g

DIABETIC EXCHANGES
1/2 starch

SIMPLE SPICY SHRIMP

MAKES 8 (1/4-CUP) SERVINGS

Whip up this simple and terrific stir-fry with shrimp and a few distinct seasonings. This versatile recipe may be served with toothpicks for an appetizer, used to top a salad, or tossed with pasta.

1 teaspoon sugar

Dash salt

1 tablespoon chili powder

1/2 teaspoon ground cumin

1/2 teaspoon dried oregano leaves

1 pound medium or large peeled shrimp

1 tablespoon canola oil

1. In a resealable plastic bag or bowl, combine all ingredients except oil. Mix well to coat shrimp.

2. In a large nonstick skillet, heat oil over medium heat. Add coated shrimp and cook, stirring occasionally, until the shrimp are done, about 4–6 minutes, depending on size.

NUTRITIONAL INFORMATION PER SERVING
Calories 63 | Calories from fat 30% | Fat 2 g
Saturated Fat 0 g | Cholesterol 84 mg | Sodium 107 mg
Carbohydrate 1 g | Dietary Fiber 0 g | Sugars 1 g | Protein 9 g

DIABETIC EXCHANGES
1 lean meat

TERRIFIC TIDBIT

By mixing the ingredients in a plastic bag, clean up is minimized.

MINI MUFFALETTAS

MAKES 32–40 MINI MUFFALETTAS

All it takes is four easy ingredients and 15 minutes to create my popular version of this Louisiana favorite Italian-style sandwich. Make them ahead of time and refrigerate or freeze until ready to bake.

2 (12-ounce) packages party-size rolls (16–20 to a package)

1/2 pound thinly sliced lean ham

1 1/2 cups shredded Italian five-cheese blend

1 (16-ounce) jar chopped Italian olive salad, drained

1. Preheat oven to 375°F.

2. Split rolls in half and lay on a baking sheet. Divide ham, cheese, and olive salad onto each roll.

3. Replace bread tops. Bake for 10–15 minutes or until cheese is melted.

NUTRITIONAL INFORMATION PER SERVING
Calories 107 | Calories from fat 48% | Fat 6 g
Saturated Fat 1 g | Cholesterol 9 mg | Sodium 260 mg
Carbohydrate 10 g | Dietary Fiber 1 g | Sugars 1 g | Protein 4 g

DIABETIC EXCHANGES
1/2 starch | 1 fat

TERRIFIC TIDBIT

Any combination of cheese may be used such as mozzarella, provolone, or Parmesan. Freeze muffalettas before baking.

CRAB NACHOS

MAKES 36 (2 NACHO) SERVINGS

Tortilla chips baked with a splendid southwestern-seasoned crab mixture and smothered with cheese is quick to prepare and quicker to disappear.

6 dozen baked tortilla flour chips

1/2 cup nonfat sour cream

3 tablespoons light mayonnaise

1/2 cup chopped green onions

1 (4-ounce) can chopped green chilies, drained

1/4 teaspoon ground cumin

1 pound lump, white, or canned crabmeat, picked through for shells

Salt and pepper to taste

2 cups shredded, reduced-fat sharp Cheddar or Mexican-blend cheese

Paprika, to sprinkle

1. Preheat broiler. Arrange tortilla chips in a single layer on a baking sheet.

2. In a bowl, combine sour cream, mayonnaise, green onions, green chilies, and cumin. Fold in crabmeat. Season to taste.

3. Spread mixture evenly over chips and sprinkle with cheese and paprika. Bake for 6–8 minutes or until cheese is melted.

NUTRITIONAL INFORMATION PER SERVING
Calories 57 | Calories from fat 29% | Fat 2 g
Saturated Fat 1 g | Cholesterol 14 mg | Sodium 143 mg
Carbohydrate 5 g | Dietary Fiber 0 g | Sugars 0 g | Protein 5 g

DIABETIC EXCHANGES
1/2 starch | 1/2 lean meat

Crab Nachos, pg. 18; Southwestern Guacamole, pg. 8

STUFFED CRAB POBLANO PEPPERS

MAKES 8 SERVINGS

Pablano peppers have a mild, sweet heat that complements the crabmeat and cheese.

1/2 cup nonfat sour cream

1/4 cup Italian or seasoned breadcrumbs

1/2 cup chopped red onion

1/3 cup finely chopped, roasted red peppers, drained (found in jar)

1 pound white crabmeat, picked through for shells or canned crabmeat

1/3 cup shredded, reduced-fat sharp Cheddar cheese

Salt and pepper to taste

4 poblano peppers, halved and seeded

1. Preheat oven to 375°F. Coat a baking sheet with nonstick cooking spray.

2. In a bowl, combine all ingredients except halved poblano peppers.

3. Spoon crab mixture into halved peppers and place on prepared pan. Cover with foil and bake for 30–35 minutes or until peppers are tender.

4. Remove foil and continue baking for 5–7 minutes or until top is crusty.

NUTRITIONAL INFORMATION PER SERVING
Calories 133 | Calories from fat 12% | Fat 2 g
Saturated Fat 1 g | Cholesterol 48 mg | Sodium 319 mg
Carbohydrate 12 g | Dietary Fiber 2 g | Sugars 4 g | Protein 17 g

DIABETIC EXCHANGES
1 vegetable | 1/2 carbohydrate | 2 very lean meat

STUFFED PESTO MUSHROOMS

MAKES ABOUT 24–30 STUFFED MUSHROOMS (DEPENDING ON MUSHROOM SIZE)

These trendy, tasty stuffed mushrooms may be prepared ahead of time. Refrigerate, and pop in the oven when ready to serve.

1 ounce (about 2/3 cup) packed fresh basil leaves, torn into pieces

2 tablespoons pine nuts, toasted

2 tablespoons grated Parmesan cheese

1 tablespoon minced garlic

1 tablespoon olive oil

Salt and pepper to taste

1/3 cup light ricotta cheese

1 pound fresh medium mushrooms or baby portabellas, washed and stems removed

1. Preheat oven to 425°F. Coat baking sheet with nonstick cooking spray.

2. Process basil leaves, pine nuts, Parmesan cheese, garlic, and oil in food processor until finely chopped. Add ricotta and season to taste. Process until mixed.

3. Place mushroom caps on baking sheet. Divide mixture evenly among mushroom caps. Bake for 10–13 minutes or until heated throughout.

NUTRITIONAL INFORMATION PER SERVING
Calories 15 | Calories from fat 60% | Fat 1 g
Saturated Fat 0 g | Cholesterol 1 mg | Sodium 8 mg
Carbohydrate 1 g | Dietary Fiber 0 g | Sugars 0 g | Protein 1 g

DIABETIC EXCHANGES
Free

STUFFED CRAWFISH MUSHROOMS

MAKES ABOUT 4 1/2–5 DOZEN MUSHROOMS

Stuffed mushrooms can be fussy to make, so I suggest making them ahead of time. Simiply refrigerate and pop in the oven when ready to serve. Crabmeat or cooked shrimp may be substituted for the crawfish.

2 pounds fresh medium mushrooms, washed

1 onion, chopped

1 teaspoon minced garlic

1/2 cup chopped green bell pepper

1 pound crawfish tails, rinsed and drained

1 cup breadcrumbs

1/2 cup chopped green onions

Salt and pepper to taste

Dash cayenne

2 tablespoons olive oil

4 tablespoons sherry or cooking sherry

1. Preheat oven to 350°F. Coat a large nonstick skillet and a baking sheet with nonstick cooking spray.

2. Remove and chop mushroom stems. In prepared skillet, sauté mushroom stems, onion, garlic, and green pepper over medium heat until tender, about 5–7 minutes. Add crawfish tails, stirring for one minute. Remove from heat and add remaining ingredients, stirring until combined.

3. Place mushrooms caps in a metal colander over a pot of boiling water. Cover and cook for about 5 minutes, or microwave for about 3–5 minutes, to slightly cook mushrooms.

4. Place mushroom caps on the prepared baking sheet, stuff with filling, and bake for 15 minutes, or until heated through.

NUTRITIONAL INFORMATION PER SERVING
Calories 23 | Calories from fat 26% | Fat 1 g
Saturated Fat 0 g | Cholesterol 10 mg | Sodium 22 mg
Carbohydrate 2 g | Dietary Fiber 0 g | Sugars 1 g | Protein 2 g

DIABETIC EXCHANGES
Free

TERRIFIC TIDBIT

Always keep cooking sherry available in your pantry for a dependable consistency in flavor.

PORK PICADILLO TORTILLA CUPS

MAKES 4–5 DOZEN TORTILLA CUPS

This zesty Spanish-influenced dish may be made with pork, beef, or veal. I use tortillas as the shell for this guaranteed great recipe.

1 pound ground pork

1 pound ground sirloin

1 teaspoon minced garlic

1/2 cup chopped onion

1 green bell pepper, cored and chopped

1 teaspoon ground cumin

1/2 teaspoon ground cinnamon

1 tablespoon chopped parsley

1/2 cup tomato paste

1/2 cup fat-free beef broth

Salt and pepper to taste

1/3 cup chopped pimento stuffed olives

1/4 cup golden raisins (optional)

12 large corn tortillas

1. Preheat oven to 350°F. Coat a large nonstick skillet and a miniature muffin pan with nonstick cooking spray.

2. In prepared skillet, cook pork and meat over medium heat for about 4 minutes. Drain any excess fat. Add garlic, onion, and green pepper and continue cooking until the meat is done and vegetables are tender, about 5–7 minutes. Add cumin, cinnamon, parsley, tomato paste, and broth. Season to taste.

3. Bring mixture to a boil, reduce heat, and continue cooking for 7–10 minutes. Stir in olives and raisins, and remove from heat.

4. Using a small round cookie cutter, cut out circles from tortillas. Place tortilla circles into cups of prepared muffin pan. Bake for about 7–10 minutes or until tortillas are crisp. Remove and fill with warm filling.

NUTRITIONAL INFORMATION PER SERVING
Calories 44 | Calories from fat 52% | Fat 3 g
Saturated Fat 1 g | Cholesterol 10 mg | Sodium 50 mg
Carbohydrate 2 g | Dietary Fiber 0 g | Sugars 0 g | Protein 3 g

DIABETIC EXCHANGES
1/2 medium-fat meat

TERRIFIC TIDBIT

To make ahead of time, prepare the meat mixture and bake the tortilla cups. Fill the cups when ready to serve. My family insists that I omit the golden raisins for a not-as-sweet version.

MARINATED DUCK STRIP SKEWER

MAKES 15 SKEWERS
(DEPENDING ON THE SIZE OF THE DUCK)

I think my friend Hank is a "chef at heart" and the proof is this easy recipe he shared with me. Skewer ahead of time, refrigerate, and pop on the grill when ready to serve.

3 to 4 duck breasts (depending on size)

1 cup apricot preserves

1/2 cup Jack Daniels Tennessee whiskey

1 teaspoon low-sodium soy sauce

1 tablespoon canola oil

1 tablespoon coarsely ground black pepper

Dash cayenne

1 red bell pepper, cored and cut into 1-inch squares

1 yellow bell pepper, cored and cut into 1-inch squares

3 bunches green onion stems, cut into 2-inch pieces.

15 toothpicks or wooden skewers (soaked in water for 1 hour)

1. Cut duck breasts into 1/2-inch wide strips and place in a shallow dish or resealable plastic bag.

2. In a bowl, combine all remaining ingredients (except toothpicks). Pour over duck breasts, cover, and refrigerate for 1–3 hours. Remove from refrigerator and bring to to room temperature before skewering. Reserve marinade.

3. With a skewer or wooden toothpick, skewer a pepper square, a duck strip, and an onion. Skewer the duck by folding the strip and sticking the skewer through both sides of the fold.

4. Place skewers on a hot grill and brush once with marinade. Cook approximately 1 1/2–2 1/2 minutes per side. Duck should be just barely firm to the touch. Do not overcook.

NUTRITIONAL INFORMATION PER SERVING
Calories 57 | Calories from fat 26% | Fat 2 g
Saturated Fat 0 g | Cholesterol 26 mg | Sodium 31 mg
Carbohydrate 3 g | Dietary Fiber 1 g | Sugars 2 g | Protein 7 g

DIABETIC EXCHANGES
1 lean meat

TERRIFIC TIDBIT
The skewers may be broiled inside or use longer skewers for a duck shish kebob entrée.

Fabulous French Bread Loaf pg. 27; Italian Pull Aparts pg. 27

BREADS, MUFFINS, & BRUNCH

Overall, more than half the grain exported from the United States is transported via barge down the Mississippi River and...through Gulf of Mexico waters.

Gulf of Mexico Alliance

WETLANDS FACT

BEER BREAD
MAKES 16 SERVINGS

Nothing can beat the wonderful aroma of freshly baked bread right out of the oven. With these four simple ingredients, bread making becomes a snap.

4 cups self-rising flour

1/4 cup sugar

1 (16-ounce) can light beer, room temperature

2 tablespoons butter, melted

1. Preheat oven to 400°F. Coat a 9 × 5 × 3-inch nonstick loaf pan with nonstick cooking spray.

2. In a large bowl, combine flour, sugar, and beer, mixing only until moistened.

3. Transfer batter into prepared pan. Bake for 50 minutes or until golden brown.

4. Remove from oven and pour melted butter over top.

NUTRITIONAL INFORMATION PER SERVING
Calories 144 | Calories from fat 10% | Fat 2 g
Saturated Fat 1 g | Cholesterol 4 mg | Sodium 407 mg
Carbohydrate 27 g | Dietary Fiber 1 g | Sugars 3 g | Protein 3 g

DIABETIC EXCHANGES
2 starch

TERRIFIC TIDBIT

You may substitute a mixture of 1 cup all-purpose flour, 1/2 teaspoon baking powder, and 1/2 teaspoon salt, per 1 cup self-rising flour (if needed).

QUICK WHOLE-WHEAT BREAD
MAKES 16 SERVINGS

Whip up this great-tasting bread in mere minutes! Whole-wheat flour gives the bread a grainy texture, buttermilk keeps it moist, and molasses adds a slightly sweet taste.

2 cups whole-wheat flour

1/2 cup all-purpose flour

1/2 cup yellow cornmeal

1 teaspoon baking soda

1 2/3 cups buttermilk

1/2 cup molasses

1. Preheat oven to 350°F. Coat a 9 × 5 × 3-inch nonstick loaf pan with nonstick cooking spray.

2. In a bowl, combine whole-wheat flour, all-purpose flour, cornmeal, and baking soda. Set aside.

3. In another bowl, combine buttermilk and molasses. Stir into dry ingredients only until combined.

4. Transfer mixture to prepared pan and bake for 40–45 minutes or until toothpick inserted in center comes out clean. Do not overcook.

NUTRITIONAL INFORMATION PER SERVING
Calories 120 | Calories from fat 5% | Fat 1
Saturated Fat 0 g | Cholesterol 1 mg | Sodium 110 mg
Carbohydrate 26 g | Dietary Fiber 2 g | Sugars 7 g | Protein 4 g

DIABETIC EXCHANGES
1 1/2 starch

trim&TERRIFIC™ **GULF COAST FAVORITES**

FABULOUS FRENCH BREAD LOAF

MAKES 12–16 SLICES

Hot out of the oven, this bread oozes with cheesy mouth-watering flavor. Try not to eat the whole loaf—we did!

1 loaf French bread, cut in half lengthwise

4 tablespoons butter, softened

1 (4-ounce) can chopped green chilies, drained

2 teaspoons minced garlic

2 tablespoons light mayonnaise

2 tablespoons chopped parsley

1 cup shredded Monterey Jack cheese

Paprika to sprinkle

1. Preheat broiler. Place bread loaf halves on a baking sheet or broiler pan.

2. In a small bowl, combine all ingredients, except paprika, and spread mixture over the top of each bread loaf half. Sprinkle with paprika.

3. Broil until puffy and brown, watching careful (about one minute).

NUTRITIONAL INFORMATION PER SERVING
Calories 140 | Calories from fat 37% | Fat 6 g
Saturated Fat 3 g | Cholesterol 14 mg | Sodium 293 mg
Carbohydrate 17 g | Dietary Fiber 1 g | Sugars 1 g | Protein 5 g

DIABETIC EXCHANGES
1 starch | 1 fat

TERRIFIC TIDBIT

Use kitchen scissors to make biscuit cutting easier.

ITALIAN PULL APARTS

MAKES 20 BISCUITS

Biscuits, Italian seasoning, and Parmesan cheese create this quick, easy, and unbelievably tasty pull-apart bread that adds to any meal.

2 tablespoons butter, melted

1 1/2 teaspoons dried oregano leaves

1 teaspoon dried basil leaves

1 1/2 teaspoons sesame seeds

1/3 cup grated Parmesan cheese

2 (10-ounce) cans refrigerated buttermilk biscuits

1. Preheat oven to 400°F. Pour melted butter into a 9-inch round pan coated with nonstick cooking spray.

2. Combine oregano, basil, sesame seeds, and Parmesan cheese in a resealable plastic bag.

3. Cut each biscuit into two pieces. Add biscuit pieces to bag and shake to coat. Arrange coated biscuit pieces in prepared pan, and sprinkle with any remaining mixture. Bake for 15–18 minutes or until golden.

NUTRITIONAL INFORMATION PER SERVING
Calories 89 | Calories from fat 37% | Fat 4 g
Saturated Fat 1 g | Cholesterol 4 mg | Sodium 259 mg
Carbohydrate 12 g | Dietary Fiber 0 g | Sugars 1 g | Protein 2 g

DIABETIC EXCHANGES
1 starch | 1/2 fat

BREADS, MUFFINS, & BRUNCH

POPPY SEED PULL-APART BREAD

MAKES 1 LOAF (10–12 SERVINGS)

Ordinary refrigerated biscuits are transformed into extraordinary, melt-in-your-mouth bread with the addition of four simple ingredients. Prepare ahead in the loaf pan, and refrigerate until ready to bake.

3 tablespoons butter, melted

1 tablespoon olive oil

2 teaspoons poppy seeds

4 tablespoons dehydrated onion flakes or minced dried onion

2 (12-ounce) cans refrigerated biscuits

1. Preheat oven to 350°F. Coat a 9 × 5 × 3-inch loaf pan with nonstick cooking spray

2. In a small bowl or resealable plastic bag, combine butter, oil, poppy seeds, and onion.

3. Separate each biscuit into 2 sections by pulling apart layers. Lightly dip each layer in butter mixture and place in prepared pan. Make two rows.

4. Bake for 25–30 minutes or until biscuits are golden and done.

———————

NUTRITIONAL INFORMATION PER SERVING
Calories 183 | Calories from fat 39% | Fat 8 g
Saturated Fat 3 g | Cholesterol 8 mg | Sodium 481 mg
Carbohydrate 25 g | Dietary Fiber 1 g | Sugars 3 g | Protein 4 g

DIABETIC EXCHANGES
1 1/2 starch | 1 fat

SPEEDY SAVORY DROP BISCUITS

MAKES 16 BISCUITS

These easy-to-make drop biscuits give the illusion of biscuits made from scratch with all the flavor but without the time commitment.

2 cups all-purpose baking mix

1/2 cup water

1/4 cup skim milk

2/3 cup shredded, reduced-fat sharp Cheddar cheese

2 tablespoons butter, melted

2 tablespoons chopped parsley

1 teaspoon garlic powder

1. Preheat oven to 450°F.

2. In a large bowl, combine baking mix, water, milk, and cheese until thoroughly mixed. Drop by tablespoonfuls onto a baking sheet.

3. In a small bowl, combine butter, parsley, and garlic powder. Brush or pour mixture on top of biscuits. Bake for 8–10 minutes or until tops are golden brown.

———————

NUTRITIONAL INFORMATION PER SERVING
Calories 89 | Calories from fat 46% | Fat 5 g
Saturated Fat 2 g | Cholesterol 6 mg | Sodium 231 mg
Carbohydrate 10 g | Dietary Fiber 0 g | Sugars 1 g | Protein 3 g

DIABETIC EXCHANGES
1/2 starch | 1 fat

SOUTHERN BISCUITS WITH SAUSAGE GRAVY

MAKES 1 DOZEN BISCUITS

These soft, flaky biscuits are a southern staple, great for breakfast or with any meal.

2 cups all-purpose flour

4 teaspoons baking powder

1/4 teaspoon baking soda

1/4 teaspoon salt

3 tablespoons butter

1 1/4 cups plus 2 tablespoons buttermilk, divided

Southern Sausage Gravy (recipe pg. 30)

1. Preheat oven to 425°F. Coat a baking sheet with nonstick cooking spray

2. In a bowl, combine flour, baking powder, baking soda, and salt. Using a pastry blender or a fork, cut in butter until combined. Make a well in the center of mixture and add 1 1/4 cups buttermilk.

3. Stir dry ingredients into the buttermilk, until a sticky dough forms. (Using your hands works well.) If necessary, add a little more buttermilk. Transfer dough to a lightly floured surface.

4. Flatten dough with the ball of your hand or roll out to 1/2 to 3/4-inch thick. Use a 2-inch round cookie cutter or glass to cut out biscuits. Gather dough scraps together and repeat rolling and cutting until all dough is used.

5. Transfer to prepared pan. Brush tops with remaining buttermilk. Bake for 12–15 minutes or until tops are lightly browned. Serve with Southern Sausage Gravy.

NUTRITIONAL INFORMATION PER SERVING
Calories 111 | Calories from fat 27% | Fat 3 g
Saturated Fat 2 g | Cholesterol 9 mg | Sodium 255 mg
Carbohydrate 17 g | Dietary Fiber 1 g | Sugars 1 g | Protein 3 g

DIABETIC EXCHANGES
1 starch

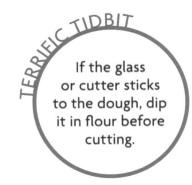

TERRIFIC TIDBIT

If the glass or cutter sticks to the dough, dip it in flour before cutting.

SOUTHERN SAUSAGE GRAVY

MAKES 12 (1/3-CUP) SERVINGS

Nothing is better than traditional southern sausage white gravy served over biscuits, mashed potatoes or rice. This recipe is trimmed down, without trimming tradition.

8 ounces reduced-fat ground sausage

1/4 cup finely chopped onion

1/4 cup all-purpose flour

3 1/4 cups skim milk

Salt and pepper to taste

1/2 teaspoon hot sauce

1. In a large nonstick skillet, cook sausage and onion until tender. Drain any excess fat. Add flour and stir for about 1 minute.

2. Gradually add milk. Cook over medium heat until mixture comes to a boil and thickens. Season to taste and add hot sauce.

NUTRITIONAL INFORMATION PER SERVING
Calories 57 | Calories from fat 10% | Fat 1 g
Saturated Fat 0 g | Cholesterol 11 mg | Sodium 138 mg
Carbohydrate 6 g | Dietary Fiber 0 g | Sugars 3 g | Protein 5 g

DIABETIC EXCHANGES
1/2 carbohydrate | 1 very lean meat

SWEET POTATO BISCUITS

MAKES 1–1 1/2 DOZEN BISCUITS

This no-fuss biscuit will be a breakfast hit! Best of all, the dough is incredibly easy to work with and may be pressed out by hand if you don't have a rolling pin.

4 cups all-purpose baking mix

1/2 teaspoon ground cinnamon

1 (15-ounce) can sweet potatoes (yams), drained and reserve 1/2 cup juice

1/2 cup skim milk

1. Preheat oven to 450°F.

2. In a large bowl, combine baking mix and cinnamon. In another bowl, mash sweet potatoes and add to dry mixture with reserved juice and milk. Mix well.

3. Transfer to a floured surface and roll out to 1-inch thick. Use a 2-inch round cookie cutter or glass to cut out biscuits. Place on baking sheet and bake for 10–12 minutes, or until golden.

NUTRITIONAL INFORMATION PER SERVING
Calories 129 | Calories from fat 27% | Fat 4 g
Saturated Fat 1 g | Cholesterol 0 mg | Sodium 343 mg
Carbohydrate 21 g | Dietary Fiber 1 g | Sugars 4 g | Protein 2 g

DIABETIC EXCHANGES
1 1/2 starch | 1/2 fat

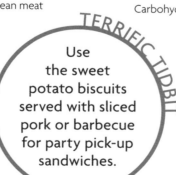

TERRIFIC TIDBIT

Use the sweet potato biscuits served with sliced pork or barbecue for party pick-up sandwiches.

SOUTHWESTERN CORNBREAD MUFFINS

MAKES 18–21 MUFFINS

Give basic cornbread muffins a southwestern kick. Great served with soups and barbecue.

1 1/2 cups yellow cornmeal

1/2 cup all-purpose flour

4 teaspoons baking powder

2 tablespoons sugar

1 1/2 cups skim milk

2 eggs

3 tablespoons canola oil

1 (4-ounce) can diced green chilies, drained

1 tablespoon finely chopped fresh jalapeño pepper

1/2 cup chopped green onions

1/2 cup shredded, reduced-fat Cheddar cheese

1. Preheat oven to 375°F. Line a muffin pan with papers.

2. In large bowl, combine cornmeal, flour, baking powder, and sugar. In a small bowl, whisk together milk, eggs, and oil. Add to dry ingredients with remaining ingredients and mix well.

3. Spoon batter into muffin cups filling each about 3/4 full. Bake for 17–20 minutes or until golden and firm to touch.

NUTRITIONAL INFORMATION PER SERVING
Calories 91 | Calories from fat 30% | Fat 3 g
Saturated Fat 1 g | Cholesterol 22 mg | Sodium 138 mg
Carbohydrate 13 g | Dietary Fiber 1 g | Sugars 2 g | Protein 3 g

DIABETIC EXCHANGES
1 starch | 1/2 fat

BEST CORNBREAD

MAKES 2 DOZEN SQUARES

It's hard to believe this out-of-this-world cornbread begins with a boxed mix. The cottage cheese keeps the cornbread moist. Great served with chili or soups.

2 (8.5-ounce) boxes corn muffin mix

1 teaspoon sugar (optional)

2 eggs

2 egg whites

1 onion, chopped

1/4 cup butter, melted

1 cup reduced-fat small curd cottage cheese

1 cup frozen corn, thawed

1. Preheat oven to 375°F. Coat a 13 × 9 × 2-inch baking pan with nonstick cooking spray.

2. In a bowl, combine all ingredients.

3. Pour mixture into prepared pan. Bake for 35–40 minutes, or until golden brown.

NUTRITIONAL INFORMATION PER SERVING
Calories 116 | Calories from fat 31% | Fat 4 g
Saturated Fat 2 g | Cholesterol 24 mg | Sodium 240 mg
Carbohydrate 17 g | Dietary Fiber 1 g | Sugars 5 g | Protein 3 g

DIABETIC EXCHANGES
1 starch | 1/2 fat

TERRIFIC TIDBIT

Alter the recipe to your tastes by adding green chilies and/or reduced-fat Cheddar cheese.

SEAFOOD CORNBREAD

MAKES 28 SQUARES

Corn, cheese, seafood, and just a bit of jalapeños unite for truly exceptional flavor in every bite. This is a great way to use any leftover seafood you may have.

1 1/2 cups yellow cornmeal

1/2 cup all-purpose flour

1/2 teaspoon baking soda

2 tablespoons sugar

1 cup skim milk

1 egg

1/4 cup canola oil

1 onion, chopped

1 green bell pepper, cored and chopped

1 (15-ounce) can cream-style corn

1 cup shredded, reduced-fat sharp Cheddar cheese

1/3 cup chopped green onions

2 tablespoons chopped jalapeño pepper slices (found in jar)

2 cups combination seafood (crawfish tails; small peeled shrimp, cooked; or claw crabmeat)

1. Preheat oven to 350°F. Coat a 13 × 9 × 2-inch pan with nonstick cooking spray

2. In a large bowl, combine cornmeal, flour, baking soda, and sugar.

3. In another bowl, combine milk, egg, and oil. Add remaining ingredients except seafood. Mix well. Stir into flour mixture. Gently stir in seafood.

4. Transfer mixture to prepared pan. Bake for 55–60 minutes or until golden brown.

NUTRITIONAL INFORMATION PER SERVING
Calories 87 | Calories from fat 33% | Fat 3 g
Saturated Fat 1 g | Cholesterol 27 mg | Sodium 130 mg
Carbohydrate 10 g | Dietary Fiber 1 g | Sugars 2 g | Protein 5 g

DIABETIC EXCHANGES
1/2 starch | 1/2 lean meat

TERRIFIC TIDBIT
If you have left-over seafood from a crawfish boil, peel the shrimp and crawfish as the seasoned seafood turns this into an extraordinary cornbread—a meal in itself.

SWEET POTATO, ORANGE, AND CRANBERRY MUFFINS

MAKES 1–1 1/2 DOZEN MUFFINS

Louisiana, known for its naturally sweet yams (sweet potatoes), and Florida, known for its tangy oranges, merge with tart cranberries to create the ultimate muffin.

2 cups all-purpose flour

1 1/2 teaspoons baking powder

1/2 teaspoon baking soda

1 teaspoon ground cinnamon

1 (15-ounce) can sweet potatoes (yams), drained and mashed, or 1 cup fresh cooked, mashed sweet potatoes

3/4 cup light brown sugar

1/4 cup canola oil

1/2 cup orange juice

1 egg, beaten

1 tablespoon grated orange rind

1/2 cup nonfat plain yogurt

1 1/2 cups fresh cranberries, coarsely chopped

1. Preheat oven to 400°F. Line a muffin pan with papers, or coat with nonstick spray.

2. In a bowl, combine flour, baking powder, baking soda, and cinnamon.

3. In another bowl, combine sweet potatoes, brown sugar, oil, orange juice, egg, and orange rind. Add with yogurt to dry ingredients, stirring just until dry ingredients are moistened. Fold in cranberries.

4. Spoon batter into muffin tins, filling each about 3/4 full. Bake for 20–25 minutes or until done.

NUTRITIONAL INFORMATION PER SERVING
Calories 153 | Calories from fat 20% | Fat 4 g
Saturated Fat 0 g | Cholesterol 12 mg | Sodium 91 mg
Carbohydrate 28 g | Dietary Fiber 2 g | Sugars 12 g | Protein 3 g

DIABETIC EXCHANGES
2 starch | 1/2 fat

TERRIFIC TIDBIT

Orange rind may be found dried in the spice section or may be freshly grated from the orange. Dried cranberries may be substituted for fresh.

BLUEBERRY MUFFINS WITH TROPICAL STREUSEL TOPPING

MAKES 1 DOZEN MUFFINS

Juicy plump blueberries and a crumbly, nutty, tropical topping make these hard to resist.

1/4 cup flaked coconut

2 tablespoons plus 3/4 cup all-purpose flour or whole wheat flour, divided

2 tablespoons plus 1/2 cup light brown sugar, divided

1/2 cup chopped walnuts, divided

1 teaspoon coconut extract, divided

4 tablespoons canola oil, divided

1 teaspoon baking powder

1/4 teaspoon baking soda

1/2 teaspoon ground cinnamon

1 egg

1 egg white

3/4 cup buttermilk

2 cups fresh blueberries

1. Preheat oven to 400°F. Line a muffin pan with papers, or coat with nonstick spray.

2. To make the topping: In a small bowl, combine coconut, 2 tablespoons flour, 2 tablespoons brown sugar, and 1/4 cup walnuts. Add 1/2 teaspoon coconut extract and 1 tablespoon oil. Mix well and set aside.

3. In a large bowl, combine remaining 3/4 cup flour and 1/2 cup brown sugar with baking powder, baking soda, and cinnamon.

4. In another bowl, whisk together egg, egg white, and buttermilk with remaining 1/2 teaspoon coconut extract and 3 tablespoons oil.

5. Make a well in the center of dry ingredients and add buttermilk mixture, stirring just until combined. Add blueberries and remaining 1/4 cup walnuts.

6. Spoon batter into muffin pans. Sprinkle with topping, gently pressing into batter. Bake for 20 minutes or until golden brown.

NUTRITIONAL INFORMATION PER SERVING
Calories 219 | Calories from fat 37% | Fat 9 g
Saturated Fat 1 g | Cholesterol 18 mg | Sodium 96 mg
Carbohydrate 31 g | Dietary Fiber 3 g | Sugars 15 g | Protein 5 g

DIABETIC EXCHANGES
2 starch | 1 1/2 fat

TERRIFIC TIDBIT

If using frozen blueberries, don't defrost before adding to the mixture. Try using whole wheat flour to boost nutrition while adding a rich nutty flavor.

Blueberry Muffins with Tropical Streusel Topping pg. 34;
Sweet Potato, Orange, and Cranberry Muffins pg. 33

BRAN OATMEAL MUFFINS

MAKES 5–6 DOZEN MUFFINS

Have a hot muffin on the spot whenever you want. This great basic batter makes a big batch that will keep in the refrigerator up to six weeks. Experiment by adding some dried fruit or nuts for different flavors and textures.

2 1/2 cups old-fashioned oatmeal	3/4 cup sugar
2 cups bran cereal	4 eggs
2 cups shredded wheat cereal	5 cups all-purpose flour
2 cups boiling water	5 teaspoons baking soda
2/3 cup canola oil	1 tablespoon ground cinnamon
3/4 cup light brown sugar	1 quart buttermilk

1. Preheat oven to 400°F. Line a muffin pan with papers, or coat with nonstick spray.

2. In a large bowl, combine oatmeal, bran cereal, and shredded wheat. Add boiling water and set aside to cool.

3. In a mixing bowl, whisk together oil, brown sugar, and sugar. Add eggs, mixing well. Stir in cereal mixture.

4. In another bowl, combine flour, baking soda, and cinnamon. Add dry ingredients to the oatmeal mixture, alternating with the buttermilk, stirring only until combined.

5. Pour batter into muffin tins. Bake for 20 minutes or until lightly browned. Any unused batter may be stored in a covered container in the refrigerator.

NUTRITIONAL INFORMATION PER SERVING
Calories 96 | Calories from fat 26% | Fat 3 g
Saturated Fat 0 g | Cholesterol 12 mg | Sodium 52 mg
Carbohydrate 16 g | Dietary Fiber 1 g | Sugars 5 g | Protein 2 g

DIABETIC EXCHANGES
1 starch | 1/2 fat

TERRIFIC TIDBIT

An ice cream scoop with a "sweeper" is great for filling muffin tins. One that measures 1/2 cup works best for most tins

TOASTED COCONUT BANANA BREAD

MAKES 16 SLICES

Looking for a different take on an old favorite? Coconut adds a smooth, sweet flavor to a moist banana bread. Try tossing in toasted walnuts or pecans for a bit of crunch.

1 egg

2/3 cup light brown sugar

1/4 cup canola oil

1 teaspoon vanilla extract

2 bananas, mashed

1 cup light canned coconut milk (shake before opening)

2 cups all-purpose flour

1 teaspoon ground cinnamon

1 teaspoon baking powder

1/2 teaspoon baking soda

1/2 cup flaked coconut, toasted, divided

1. Preheat oven to 350°F. Coat a 9 × 5 × 3-inch nonstick loaf pan with nonstick cooking spray

2. In a bowl, combine egg, brown sugar, oil, and vanilla. Add bananas and coconut milk.

3. In another bowl, combine flour, cinnamon, baking powder, and baking soda. Add to egg mixture, stirring just until moistened. Stir in 1/4 cup coconut and transfer batter into prepared pan.

4. Sprinkle top with remaining 1/4 cup coconut, gently pressing into batter. Bake for 50–55 minutes, or until a toothpick inserted into center comes out almost clean.

NUTRITIONAL INFORMATION PER SERVING
Calories 161 | Calories from fat 29% | Fat 5 g
Saturated Fat 1 g | Cholesterol 13 mg | Sodium 85 mg
Carbohydrate 26 g | Dietary Fiber 1 g | Sugars 12 g | Protein 2 g

DIABETIC EXCHANGES
1 1/2 starch | 1 fat

TERRIFIC TIDBIT

Slow down the ripening of bananas by putting them in the fridge. The skin may brown, but the bananas will stay the same for a few days. Ripe bananas also freeze.

MANGO BREAD

MAKES 16 SERVINGS

The whole-wheat flour adds a rich nutty flavor, and sweet mangos keep this magnificent bread moist. All purpose flour may also be used, if desired. To make this bread year-round, look for mangos in a can or jar.

1 cup whole-wheat flour

1 cup all-purpose flour

1 teaspoon baking soda

1/4 cup canola oil

1/2 cup applesauce

1 cup light brown sugar

2 eggs

1 teaspoon vanilla extract

2 cups chopped mango

1/2 cup chopped walnuts

1. Preheat oven to 350°F. Coat a 9 × 5 × 3-inch loaf pan with nonstick cooking spray

2. In a bowl, combine whole-wheat flour, all-purpose flour, and baking soda. Set aside.

3. In another bowl, whisk together oil, applesauce, brown sugar, eggs, and vanilla. Add dry ingredients, stirring just until combined. Stir in mango and walnuts. Transfer batter to prepared pan.

4. Bake for 40–45 minutes or until a toothpick inserted into center comes out clean.

NUTRITIONAL INFORMATION PER SERVING
Calories 187 | Calories from fat 31% | Fat 7 g
Saturated Fat 1 g | Cholesterol 26 mg | Sodium 94 mg
Carbohydrate 30 g | Dietary Fiber 2 g | Sugars 17 g | Protein 3 g

DIABETIC EXCHANGES
2 starch | 1 fat

TERRIFIC TIDBIT

I like the combination of all-purpose and whole-wheat flour in my quick breads, so give it a try in your favorite bread. The whole-wheat flour adds nutrition and flavor.

CHOCOLATE ZUCCHINI BREAD

MAKES 16 SLICES

Don't let the combination startle you, I promise this is one of my absolute favorite nutritious-and-delicious quick breads. Of course, chocolate perks up any recipe!

2 cups all-purpose flour

3 tablespoons cocoa

1 teaspoon baking soda

1/4 teaspoon baking powder

1 teaspoon ground cinnamon

3/4 cup sugar

2 eggs

3 tablespoons canola oil

1 cup applesauce

1 teaspoon vanilla extract

2 cups shredded zucchini

1/3 cup semi-sweet chocolate chips

1/2 cup coarsely chopped walnuts

1. Preheat oven to 350°F. Coat a 9 × 5 × 3-inch nonstick loaf pan with nonstick cooking spray.

2. In a large bowl, combine flour, cocoa, baking soda, baking powder, and cinnamon. Set aside.

3. In another bowl, whisk together sugar, eggs, and oil. Stir in applesauce and vanilla. Add dry ingredients, mixing just until moistened. Stir in zucchini, chocolate chips, and walnuts.

4. Transfer batter into prepared pan. Bake for 45–55 minutes, or until a toothpick inserted into center comes out clean. Don't overcook. Cool in pan.

NUTRITIONAL INFORMATION PER SERVING
Calories 187 | Calories from fat 34% | Fat 7 g
Saturated Fat 1 g | Cholesterol 26 mg | Sodium 96 mg
Carbohydrate 28 g | Dietary Fiber 2 g | Sugars 14 g | Protein 4 g

DIABETIC EXCHANGES
2 starch | 1 fat

TERRIFIC TIDBIT

Zucchini is grated by using a grater or the shredding blade on a food processor.

APPLE, BRIE, AND BROWN SUGAR PIZZA

MAKES 8 SLICES

A thin crisp crust topped with rich, creamy Brie and cinnamon apples, this pizza can be served for brunch, as a snack or even as a light dessert. It is hard to resist hot out of the oven. For a different and unique presentation, use miniature crusts.

1 (13.8-ounce) can refrigerated pizza crust

4 ounces Brie, rind removed and thinly sliced

1 large baking apple, peeled, cored, and thinly sliced

3 tablespoons chopped pecans

3 tablespoons light brown sugar

1/2 teaspoon ground cinnamon

1. Preheat oven to 450°F. Spread pizza crust onto a pan.

2. Top pizza crust with Brie and apple slices, arranged concentrically. In a small bowl, combine remaining ingredients and sprinkle on top.

3. Bake for 10–12 minutes or until cheese is melted and apples are tender. Slice and serve.

NUTRITIONAL INFORMATION PER SERVING
Calories 193 | Calories from fat 33% | Fat 7 g
Saturated Fat 3 g | Cholesterol 14 mg | Sodium 328 mg
Carbohydrate 26 g | Dietary Fiber 1 g | Sugars 10 g | Protein 6 g

DIABETIC EXCHANGES
1 1/2 starch | 1 medium-fat meat

BAKED COCONUT FRENCH TOAST

MAKES 8 SERVINGS

Love French toast? The mild coconut flavor pops out in a one-of-a-kind take on this exciting breakfast dish.

1 cup light canned coconut milk (shake before opening)

1 cup egg whites or egg substitute

1/3 cup sugar

1 teaspoon vanilla extract

1/3 cup flaked coconut

1 loaf French bread (whole wheat may be used), sliced in 1-inch thick slices

1. Preheat oven to 350°F. Coat a 13 × 9 × 2-inch baking pan with nonstick cooking spray

2. In a large bowl, whisk together the coconut milk, egg whites, sugar, and vanilla. Stir in the coconut. Soak the bread slices in the milk mixture for about 5 minutes.

3. Transfer the bread onto the baking pan in a single layer. Pour any remaining milk mixture over the bread. Cover and refrigerate as time permits, preferably overnight.

4. If making immediately, let sit at room temperature for about 15 minutes before baking. Bake for 30–35 minutes or until the bread is golden.

NUTRITIONAL INFORMATION PER SERVING
Calories 246 | Calories from fat 12% | Fat 3 g
Saturated Fat 2 g | Cholesterol 0 mg | Sodium 439 mg
Carbohydrate 43 g | Dietary Fiber 2 g | Sugars 12 g | Protein 10 g

DIABETIC EXCHANGES
2 starch | 1 carbohydrate | 1/2 lean meat

CINNAMON FRENCH TOAST WITH CARAMEL APPLES

MAKES 10 SERVINGS

This amazing one-dish breakfast tastes like apple pie and French toast combined in one bite. I created this scrumptious recipe when I needed a quick, impressive breakfast dish to serve company at a moment's notice.

1/2 cup plus 2 tablespoons sugar, divided

3 tablespoons butter

5 Granny Smith apples, peeled, cored, and thinly sliced

1/2 cup pure maple syrup

2 eggs

3 egg whites

1 cup skim milk

1 teaspoon vanilla extract

1/2 teaspoon ground cinnamon

8 slices cinnamon raisin bread

1. Preheat oven to 350°F. Coat a 3-quart oblong baking dish with nonstick cooking spray.

2. Place 1/2 cup sugar in a large nonstick skillet over medium heat, stirring constantly until sugar melts and begins to turn golden, about 6 minutes. Stir in butter until melted together. Fold in apple slices. If mixture hardens, keep stirring. It should dissolve again once apples have warmed.

3. When mixture and apples are well combined, gradually add maple syrup, cooking for about 6 minutes or until apples are tender. Set mixture aside.

4. In a mixing bowl, beat together eggs, egg whites, milk, vanilla, cinnamon, and remaining 2 tablespoons sugar, until well mixed.

5. Cover bottom of prepared dish with apple mixture. Lay bread slices on top of the apple mixture. Carefully top with egg mixture.

6. Let sit for 15 minutes, allowing bread to soak up mixture. Bake for 25–30 minutes. Serve immediately.

NUTRITIONAL INFORMATION PER SERVING
Calories 244 | Calories from fat 20% | Fat 6 g
Saturated Fat 2 g | Cholesterol 52 mg | Sodium 151 mg
Carbohydrate 44 g | Dietary Fiber 2 g | Sugars 35 g | Protein 6 g

DIABETIC EXCHANGES
1 starch | 2 carbohydrate | 1/2 very lean meat | 1 fat

Grillades and Cheese Grits pg. 43

GRILLADES AND CHEESE GRITS

MAKES 6–8 SERVINGS

This hearty dish of seasoned, seared, round steak cooked slowly in rich brown gravy with vegetables and tomatoes is usually served with grits. It is known as one of south Louisiana's finest breakfasts.

2 pounds lean, boneless, beef round steak, trimmed and cut into 1-inch strips

Salt and pepper to taste

4 tablespoons all-purpose flour, divided

1 onion, chopped

1 green bell pepper, cored and chopped

1/2 cup chopped celery

1 1/2 cups chopped tomatoes (drained canned tomatoes may be used)

1 teaspoon minced garlic

2 cups fat-free beef broth

1 tablespoon cider vinegar

1 teaspoon dried thyme leaves

1 tablespoon Worcestershire sauce

1 bunch green onions, chopped

Cheese Grits (recipe pg. 44)

1. Season steak strips to taste and coat with 3 tablespoons of flour, shaking off excess.

2. In a large nonstick skillet coated with nonstick cooking spray, brown meat over medium heat for 5–7 minutes on each side. Remove from skillet and set aside.

3. Add onion, pepper, celery, and tomatoes to same skillet and cook over medium heat about 5–7 minutes, stirring occasionally. Gradually add remaining 1 tablespoon flour, stirring for one minute. Add garlic, broth, vinegar, thyme, and Worcestershire sauce and bring to a boil.

4. Return meat to skillet. Reduce heat and cook, covered, for 1 1/2 hours, or until meat is very tender, stirring occasionally.

5. Add green onions, cook a few minutes longer, and serve with Cheese Grits.

NUTRITIONAL INFORMATION PER SERVING
Calories 190 | Calories from fat 18% | Fat 4 g
Saturated Fat 1 g | Cholesterol 64 mg | Sodium 292 mg
Carbohydrate 9 g | Dietary Fiber 2 g | Sugars 4 g | Protein 28 g

DIABETIC EXCHANGES
1 vegetable | 3 very lean meat

CHEESE GRITS

MAKES 6–8 SERVINGS

Don't limit cheese grits to breakfast only; they also complement meat and seafood dishes. If you are making it ahead of time or need to reheat, you may need to add more liquid to bring back the creamy texture.

2 cups fat-free chicken broth

2 cups skim milk

1 cup water

1 1/2 cups quick grits

1 1/2 cups shredded, reduced-fat, sharp Cheddar cheese (more if desired)

2 teaspoons Worcestershire sauce

1/2 cup chopped green onions

Salt and pepper to taste

Dash cayenne

1. In a medium pot, bring broth, milk, and water to a boil. Add grits, reduce heat, cover, and cook for about 5 minutes, or until grits are thickened and creamy.

2. Add remaining ingredients, stirring until cheese is melted. Serve immediately.

———————

NUTRITIONAL INFORMATION PER SERVING
Calories 200 | Calories from fat 21% | Fat 5 g
Saturated Fat 3 g | Cholesterol 12 mg | Sodium 428 mg
Carbohydrate 27 g | Dietary Fiber 1 | Sugars 4 g | Protein 11 g

DIABETIC EXCHANGES
2 starch | 1 lean meat

SOUTHWESTERN BREAKFAST BAKE

MAKES 10–12 SERVINGS

Go southwestern with this fantastic, crowd-pleasing easy morning meal.

1 (11-ounce) can Mexicorn, drained

1 (4-ounce) can chopped green chilies

1 bunch green onions, chopped

8 (6-inch) corn or flour tortillas, quartered

2 cups shredded, reduced-fat Mexican-blend cheese

4 eggs

6 egg whites

2/3 cup skim milk

1/2 teaspoon chili powder

1/2 teaspoon ground cumin

Salt and pepper to taste

1. Preheat oven to 350°F. Coat a 13 × 9 × 2-inch pan with nonstick cooking spray.

2. In a bowl, combine Mexicorn, green chilies, and green onions. Line bottom of pan with a layer of tortillas, top with half of the corn mixture, then half of the shredded cheese. Repeat layers.

3. In another bowl, whisk together remaining ingredients. Pour over layers in pan and let sit for 10 minutes. Bake for 30–35 minutes or until puffed.

———————

NUTRITIONAL INFORMATION PER SERVING
Calories 141 | Calories from fat 34% | Fat 5 g
Saturated Fat 3 g | Cholesterol 81 mg | Sodium 373 mg
Carbohydrate 12 g | Dietary Fiber 2 g | Sugars 3 g | Protein 11 g

DIABETIC EXCHANGES
1 starch | 1 lean meat

YAMCAKES

MAKES 16 PANCAKES

Start the morning off right with this bundle of flavor. Pancakes, sugar, spice, and everything nice—feel free to forget the syrup!

2 cups all-purpose baking mix

2 teaspoons ground cinnamon

1/2 cup mashed, cooked sweet potatoes (yams)

1 (12-ounce) can evaporated skim milk

1 egg

1 egg white

1 tablespoon canola oil

1 teaspoon vanilla extract

1. In a bowl, combine all ingredients just until combined. (The batter will be lumpy).

2. Heat a large nonstick skillet or griddle coated with nonstick cooking spray. Spoon 1/4 cup batter onto pan for each pancake. Cook pancakes 1–2 minutes on each side, or until lightly browned.

NUTRITIONAL INFORMATION PER SERVING
Calories 98 | Calories from fat 20% | Fat 2 g
Saturated Fat 0 g | Cholesterol 14 mg | Sodium 213 mg
Carbohydrate 15 g | Dietary Fiber 1 g | Sugars 4 g | Protein 4

DIABETIC EXCHANGES
1 starch

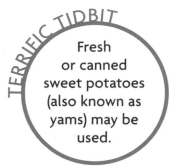

TERRIFIC TIDBIT

Fresh or canned sweet potatoes (also known as yams) may be used.

MILK PUNCH

MAKES 14–16 SERVINGS

An old, great classic New Orleans beverage typically served with brunch.

1/2 gallon fat-free vanilla ice cream

1 quart skim milk

1 cup bourbon or brandy (adjust to taste)

Nutmeg to sprinkle

1. Blend ice cream, milk, and bourbon in a blender. Pour into glasses and sprinkle with nutmeg.

NUTRITIONAL INFORMATION PER SERVING
Calories 153 | Calories from fat 0% | Fat 0 g
Saturated Fat 0 g | Cholesterol 0 mg | Sodium 91 mg
Carbohydrate 26 g | Dietary Fiber 0 g | Sugars 18 g | Protein 6 g

DIABETIC EXCHANGES
1 1/2 carbohydrate

TERRIFIC TIDBIT

To make ahead of time: Let ice cream soften, add the milk and bourbon, and mix well. Freeze. Remove from freezer about 1 hour before serving. Serve in a punch bowl or pitcher and sprinkle with nutmeg.

Shrimp, Tortellini, and Broccoli Soup pg. 49

SOUPS, STEWS, & CHILIS

70% of the oysters caught in the United States are found in the Gulf of Mexico.

Gulf of Mexico Alliance

Five of the top fifteen largest ports in the United States are located in Louisiana.

Gulf of Mexico Alliance

WETLANDS FACT

MANGO SOUP

MAKES 4 (1-CUP) SERVINGS

With just a hint of almond, this refreshing mango-orange summer soup goes great with a salad or sandwich, or even served in punch cups before a luncheon. Garnish with finely chopped mango and mint sprigs.

2 cups coarsely chopped mango (about 2)

1 1/2 cups orange juice

1–2 tablespoons lemon juice

2 tablespoons sugar

1/2 teaspoon almond extract

1 cup nonfat plain yogurt

1. In a food processor, combine all ingredients except yogurt. Purée until smooth.

2. Add yogurt and continue blending until well mixed. Refrigerate and serve chilled.

———————

NUTRITIONAL INFORMATION PER SERVING
Calories 156 | Calories from fat 3% | Fat 1 g
Saturated Fat 0 g | Cholesterol 1 mg | Sodium 50 mg
Carbohydrate 35 g | Dietary Fiber 2 g | Sugars 31 g | Protein 5 g

DIABETIC EXCHANGES
2 fruit, 1/2 fat-free milk

CUCUMBER SOUP

MAKES 4 (1-CUP) SERVINGS

This marvelous, simple-to-make cold soup lives up to the name "cool as a cucumber!" I like to serve it topped with 2 tablespoons of salsa verde (green salsa, found in the salsa section) for a little extra punch.

2 cups coarsely chopped seeded cucumbers (around 4)

1/2 cup chopped green onions

1 cup nonfat sour cream

1 cup buttermilk

1/4 teaspoon cayenne

1. In a bowl, combine all ingredients. Refrigerate until serving.

———————

NUTRITIONAL INFORMATION PER SERVING
Calories 98 | Calories from fat 6% | Fat 1 g
Saturated Fat 0 g | Cholesterol 12 mg | Sodium 120 mg
Carbohydrate 16 g | Dietary Fiber 1 g | Sugars 8 g | Protein 6 g

DIABETIC EXCHANGES
1 carbohydrate

TERRIFIC TIDBIT

To seed cucumbers, cut in half lengthwise and run a spoon or fork down the center to easily remove the seeds.

GAZPACHO WITH CORN AND GOAT CHEESE

MAKES 8 (1-CUP) SERVINGS

What better way to enjoy ripe, juicy, summer tomatoes than an invigorating chilled soup?

1 cup coarsely chopped red bell pepper

1/2 cup coarsely chopped red onion

1 1/2 cups coarsely chopped cucumbers, seeded and peeled

4 cups chopped tomatoes (about 2 1/2 pounds)

1/2 teaspoon minced garlic

1/4 cup lemon juice

2 tablespoons balsamic vinegar

Salt and pepper to taste

1 cup frozen corn, thawed

3 ounces crumbled goat cheese

1. In a food processor, process red pepper, onion, and cucumbers until finely chopped.

2. In a large bowl, combine tomatoes and garlic with chopped ingredients. Return half of the mixture to food processor and pulse until almost puréed.

3. Return puréed mixture to bowl and add lemon juice, balsamic vinegar, salt, and pepper. Refrigerate until serving. Serve topped with corn and goat cheese.

NUTRITIONAL INFORMATION PER SERVING
Calories 102 | Calories from fat 34% | Fat 4 g
Saturated Fat 3 g | Cholesterol 11 mg | Sodium 45 mg
Carbohydrate 13 g | Dietary Fiber 2 g | Sugars 6 g | Protein 5 g

DIABETIC EXCHANGES
1 1/2 vegetable | 1/2 starch | 1/2 high-fat meat

SHRIMP, TORTELLINI, AND BROCCOLI SOUP

MAKES 11 (1-CUP) SERVINGS

Talk about easy! This delicious broth-based soup with a subtle hint of ginger is cooked together in one pot, for a quick and easy dinner solution.

1 tablespoon olive oil

1/2 cup chopped red onion

1 teaspoon minced garlic

8 cups fat-free chicken broth

1 teaspoon ground ginger

1 (9-ounce) package cheese tortellini

3 cups broccoli florets

1 pound small peeled shrimp

Salt and pepper to taste

1. In a large nonstick pot, heat oil and sauté onion and garlic over medium heat until tender. Add broth and ginger, and bring to a boil.

2. Add tortellini, broccoli, and shrimp. Return to a boil, reduce heat, and cook until shrimp and tortellini are done, about 10–15 minutes. Season to taste.

NUTRITIONAL INFORMATION PER SERVING
Calories 135 | Calories from fat 25% | Fat 4 g
Saturated Fat 1 g | Cholesterol 71 mg | Sodium 443 mg
Carbohydrate 13 g | Dietary Fiber 2 g | Sugars 1 g | Protein 12 g

DIABETIC EXCHANGES
1 starch | 1 1/2 lean meat

SOUPS, STEWS, & CHILIS

EXOTIC SHRIMP SOUP

MAKES 8 (1-CUP) SERVINGS

A fusion of flavors in fantastic festive soup.

1 1/2 cups chopped Roma tomatoes

1 cup chopped onion

1 teaspoon minced garlic

4 cups fat-free chicken broth

2 cups peeled and chopped sweet potatoes
(yams)

1/2 cup chopped zucchini

1 pound medium peeled shrimp

1/2 teaspoon dried oregano leaves

1/2 teaspoon chipotle chili powder

1 teaspoon coconut extract

1/2 cup frozen pineapple juice concentrate,
thawed

1 cup frozen corn

Salt and pepper to taste

1. Coat a a large nonstick pot with nonstick
   cooking spray. Sauté tomatoes, onion,
   and garlic until tender, about 5–7 minutes

2. Add broth, sweet potatoes, and zucchini.
   Bring to a boil. Stir in shrimp, oregano, chili
   powder, coconut extract, and pineapple juice.

3. Cook over low heat until sweet potatoes
   are tender and shrimp are almost done.
   Add corn and continue to cook for about
   5 minutes. Season to taste.

NUTRITIONAL INFORMATION PER SERVING
Calories 150 | Calories from fat 5% | Fat 1 g
Saturated Fat 0 g | Cholesterol 84 mg | Sodium 315 mg
Carbohydrate 24 g | Dietary Fiber 3 g | Sugars 12 g | Protein 12 g

DIABETIC EXCHANGES
1 starch | 1/2 fruit | 1 1/2 very lean meat

QUICK SHRIMP AND CORN SOUP

MAKES 12 (1-CUP) SERVINGS

No time to cook? Open up cans of corn
and tomatoes, and toss in shrimp for this
simple yet superb tomato-based soup.

2 (15 1/2-ounce) cans cream-style corn

2 cups frozen corn

2 (10-ounce) cans diced tomatoes and
green chilies

1 (15-ounce) can tomato sauce

2 pounds medium peeled shrimp

1 bunch green onions, chopped

1. In a large nonstick pot, combine cream-
   style corn, corn, tomatoes and green
   chilies, and tomato sauce, until heated.

2. Add shrimp and bring to a boil. Lower
   heat and cook until shrimp are done,
   about 5–7 minutes. Sprinkle with green
   onions and serve.

NUTRITIONAL INFORMATION PER SERVING
Calories 162 | Calories from fat 8% | Fat 1 g
Saturated Fat 0 g | Cholesterol 112 mg | Sodium 825 mg
Carbohydrate 24 g | Dietary Fiber 3 g | Sugars 6 g | Protein 15 g

DIABETIC EXCHANGES
1 1/2 starch | 1 1/2 very lean meat

TERRIFIC TIDBIT
Chili powder may be substituted for chipotle chili powder. The chipotle adds a smoky flavor.

SHRIMP, CRAB, AND CORN SOUP

MAKES 14 (1-CUP) SERVINGS

If you prefer a creamier style seafood and corn soup that will wow your friends and not your waistline, you will enjoy this easy recipe.

1 onion, chopped

1 green bell pepper, cored and chopped

1 teaspoon minced garlic

2 tablespoons all-purpose flour

2 (10 3/4-ounce) cans cream-style corn

1 (10-ounce) can diced tomatoes and green chilies

2 cups fat-free chicken broth or vegetable broth

1 cup skim milk

1 (8-ounce) package reduced-fat cream cheese

2 pounds medium peeled shrimp

1 1/2 cups frozen corn

1 cup claw crabmeat, picked through for shells

1/4 cup chopped fresh parsley

1 bunch green onions, chopped

1. Coat a large nonstick pot with nonstick cooking spray. Sauté onion and green pepper until tender, about 5 minutes. Add garlic, sprinkle with flour, and stir for one minute.

2. Gradually add cream-style corn, tomatoes and green chilies, broth, and milk. Heat for several minutes. Add cream cheese and stir until melted.

3. Add shrimp and corn. Bring to a boil, reduce heat, and cook until shrimp are done, about 5–7 minutes.

4. Stir in remaining ingredients, cooking until well heated.

NUTRITIONAL INFORMATION PER SERVING
Calories 175 | Calories from fat 24% | Fat 5 g
Saturated Fat 2 g | Cholesterol 116 mg | Sodium 491 mg
Carbohydrate 17 g | Dietary Fiber 3 g | Sugars 5 g | Protein 17 g

DIABETIC EXCHANGES
1 starch | 2 lean meat

TERRIFIC TIDBIT

Claw crabmeat has a distinct sweetness and is a slightly brown color. It is less expensive and often used in soups, gumbos, and stuffings.

Crawfish and Sweet Potato Bisque pg. 53

CRAWFISH AND SWEET POTATO BISQUE

MAKES 8 (1-CUP) SERVINGS

This satisfying sweet potato based soup with a hint of sweetness and touch of curry highlights crawfish with a pleasing and unbeatable flavor.

2 tablespoons olive oil

1 cup chopped onion

1 cup chopped green bell pepper

1 cup chopped celery

1 teaspoon minced garlic

1/3 cup all-purpose flour

1/8 cup molasses

1/2 teaspoon ground curry powder

4 cups fat-free chicken broth

1 (15-ounce) can sweet potatoes (yams), drained and mashed, or 1 cup fresh sweet potatoes, cooked and mashed

1/2 cup fat-free half-and-half

1 pound crawfish tails, drained and rinsed

Salt and pepper to taste

1. In a large nonstick pot, heat oil and sauté onion, green pepper, celery, and garlic until tender, about 7–10 minutes.

2. Add flour and stir for one minute. Add molasses, curry, broth, and sweet potatoes. Bring to a boil, reduce heat and cook for about 10–15 minutes, stirring occasionally.

3. Add half-and-half and crawfish, season to taste. Continue cooking for about 5 more minutes or until heated thoroughly.

NUTRITIONAL INFORMATION PER SERVING
Calories 189 | Calories from fat 13% | Fat 3 g
Saturated Fat 0 g | Cholesterol 78 mg | Sodium 300 mg
Carbohydrate 27 g | Dietary Fiber 3 g | Sugars 8 g | Protein 14 g

DIABETIC EXCHANGES
1 1/2 starch | 1 1/2 very lean meat

TERRIFIC TIDBIT

Bisque is just a thick, creamy, rich soup. Don't let the name intimidate you.

CRAWFISH PUMPKIN SOUP

MAKES 8 (1-CUP) SERVINGS

Simple ingredients create a snappy smooth soup, perfect for fall. The crawfish may be omitted for an easy pumpkin soup.

1 onion, chopped

1 (15-ounce) can pumpkin purée

4 cups fat-free chicken broth

1/2 cup skim milk or fat-free half-and-half

1 (16-ounce) bag crawfish tails, drained and rinsed

Dash nutmeg

Salt and pepper to taste

1/4 cup chopped green onions

1. In a large nonstick pot coated with non-stick cooking spray, sauté onion over medium heat until tender, about 5 minutes.

2. Stir in pumpkin and broth, and bring to a boil. Reduce heat and simmer for about 10 minutes. Add milk, crawfish, and nutmeg. Season to taste.

3. Cook over low heat for 10 minutes. Serve sprinkled with green onions.

NUTRITIONAL INFORMATION PER SERVING
Calories 88 | Calories from fat 11% | Fat 1 g
Saturated Fat 0 g | Cholesterol 78 mg | Sodium 259 mg
Carbohydrate 7 g | Dietary Fiber 3 g | Sugars 4 g | Protein 13 g

DIABETIC EXCHANGES
1/2 starch | 1 1/2 very lean meat

CRAWFISH AND CORN SOUP

MAKES 8 (1-CUP) SERVINGS

On a busy night, use this quick version of a rich, velvety popular soup made with basic ingredients.

1/2 cup chopped onion

1/2 pound sliced mushrooms

1 (8-ounce) package reduced-fat cream cheese

2 (10 3/4-ounce) cans cream of potato soup

2 cups skim milk

2 cups frozen corn

1 (16-ounce) bag crawfish tails, rinsed and drained

Dash cayenne

1/2 cup chopped green onions

1. In a nonstick pot coated with nonstick cooking spray, sauté onion and mushrooms for 5 minutes or until tender.

2. Add cream cheese and potato soup, mixing until combined. Gradually add milk and corn, and cook over low heat until thoroughly heated.

3. Add remaining ingredients, cooking for about 10 minutes or until heated.

NUTRITIONAL INFORMATION PER SERVING
Calories 239 | Calories from fat 32% | Fat 9 g
Saturated Fat 5 g | Cholesterol 103 mg | Sodium 816 mg
Carbohydrate 23 g | Dietary Fiber 2 g | Sugars 8 g | Protein 18 g

DIABETIC EXCHANGES
1 1/2 starch | 2 lean meat

OYSTER ARTICHOKE SOUP

MAKES 6 1/2 (1-CUP) SERVINGS

The puréed artichokes give body to this perfectly blended creamy oyster soup.

2 (14-ounce) cans artichoke hearts, drained, divided

2 tablespoons butter

1 bunch green onions, chopped

1/2 teaspoon minced garlic

1/4 cup all-purpose flour

1 cup skim milk

1/4 cup chopped parsley

2 pints oysters, drained, reserve 1 cup liquid

1 cup fat-free half-and-half

1. In a food processor, purée one can artichoke hearts. Set aside.

2. In a nonstick pot, melt butter and sauté green onions and garlic for about 5 minutes. Add flour, stirring constantly, for one minute. Gradually add puréed artichoke hearts, milk, parsley, and oyster liquid.

3. Bring to a boil. Add oysters and remaining can of artichoke hearts, cooking until oysters curl around edges, about 10 minutes.

4. Stir in half-and-half, cooking until thoroughly heated.

NUTRITIONAL INFORMATION PER SERVING
Calories 174 | Calories from fat 27% | Fat 5 g
Saturated Fat 3 g | Cholesterol 47 mg | Sodium 449 mg
Carbohydrate 21 g | Dietary Fiber 2 g | Sugars 7 g | Protein 11 g

DIABETIC EXCHANGES
1 starch | 1 vegetable | 1 lean meat

CREAM OF POTATO AND BUTTERNUT SQUASH SOUP

MAKES 8 (1-CUP) SERVINGS

Potato soup fans will take pleasure in this full-bodied, smooth soup that packs a lot of flavor using few ingredients. Butternut squash boosts the soup with a rich orange color and a naturally slightly sweet flavor.

2 tablespoons butter

4 cups peeled, cubed butternut squash

3 cups peeled, cubed baking potatoes

4 cups vegetable or fat-free chicken broth

1 cup skim milk

Salt and pepper to taste

1/4 teaspoon ground nutmeg

Dash cayenne

1. In a large nonstick pot, melt butter and add butternut squash and potatoes. Cook for about 5 minutes, stirring continuously. Add broth and milk.

2. Bring to a boil. Reduce heat, cover, and cook for about 25–30 minutes or until potatoes are tender.

3. Transfer to a food processor, or use a hand blender, to purée the mixture. Season with salt, pepper, nutmeg, and cayenne.

NUTRITIONAL INFORMATION PER SERVING
Calories 142 | Calories from fat 20% | Fat 3 g
Saturated Fat 2 g | Cholesterol 8 mg | Sodium 235 mg
Carbohydrate 26 g | Dietary Fiber 4 g | Sugars 5 g | Protein 5 g

DIABETIC EXCHANGES
1 1/2 starch | 1/2 fat

SOUPS, STEWS, & CHILIS

CAULIFLOWER SOUP

MAKES 7 (1-CUP) SERVINGS

When my husband and daughter asked for seconds, I knew this nutritious, cheesy cauliflower soup, with a hint of roasted red peppers, passed the flavor test!

1 cup chopped onion

4 1/2 cups vegetable or fat-free chicken broth, divided

1 medium-large head cauliflower, trimmed and cut into florets

1/4 cup all-purpose flour

1 1/2 cups reduced-fat shredded Monterey Jack cheese or Mexian-blend cheese

1/3 cup chopped roasted red pepper (found in jar)

Hearty dash hot sauce

Salt and pepper to taste

1/3 cup chopped green onions

1. In a large nonstick pot coated with nonstick cooking spray, sauté onion for about 3–5 minutes or until tender.

2. Add 4 cups broth and cauliflower, and bring to a boil over medium heat. Reduce heat and cook for 10 minutes or until cauliflower is tender.

3. In a small bowl, whisk together remaining 1/2 cup broth and flour. Pour into the pot and cook, stirring constantly, until bubbly and thickened.

4. Transfer in batches to a food processor, or blender, and pulse until almost puréed.

5. Return to pot and add cheese, roasted pepper, and hot sauce, stirring until cheese is melted. Season to taste. Serve with chopped green onions.

NUTRITIONAL INFORMATION PER SERVING
Calories 128 | Calories from fat 33% | Fat 5 g
Saturated Fat 3 g | Cholesterol 13 mg | Sodium 433 mg
Carbohydrate 11 g | Dietary Fiber 3 g | Sugars 3 g | Protein 11 g

DIABETIC EXCHANGES
1/2 starch | 1 vegetable | 1 lean meat | 1 fat

TERRIFIC TIDBIT

Toss in claw crabmeat and substitute Brie for the cheese to create a truly divine, richer version of this soup!

QUICK BLACK BEAN SOUP

MAKES 8 (1-CUP) SERVINGS

Canned black beans turn a normally time consuming recipe into a tasty simple soup.

1 onion, chopped

1 green bell pepper, cored and chopped

1 teaspoon minced garlic

1 (14 1/2-ounce) can chopped tomatoes with juice

1 (4-ounce) can chopped green chilies

1 teaspoon ground cumin

1 teaspoon chili powder

4 (15-ounce) cans black beans, rinsed and drained

4 cups vegetable or fat-free chicken broth

Salt and pepper to taste

1. Coat a large pot with nonstick cooking spray. Sauté onion, green pepper, and garlic until tender, about 7 minutes.

2. Add tomatoes with juice, green chilies, cumin, and chili powder. Gradually add black beans and broth.

3. Remove 2 cups of mixture, and purée in a food processor until smooth. Return to pot and bring to a boil. Lower heat and simmer for 10–15 minutes. Season to taste.

———————

NUTRITIONAL INFORMATION PER SERVING
Calories 212 | Calories from fat 8% | Fat 2 g
Saturated Fat 0 g | Cholesterol 0 mg | Sodium 970 mg
Carbohydrate 34 g | Dietary Fiber 14 g | Sugars 3 g | Protein 13 g

DIABETIC EXCHANGES
2 starch | 1 vegetable | 1 very lean meat

TUSCAN CHICK PEA SOUP

MAKES 8 (1-CUP) SERVINGS

Take a quick trip to Tuscany with this easy earthy soup.

1 tablespoon olive oil

2 cups finely chopped onion

2 tablespoons minced garlic

4 cups vegetable or fat-free chicken broth

1/2 teaspoon dried rosemary leaves

3 (15 1/2-ounce) cans chick peas (garbanzo beans), rinsed and drained

1 (14 1/2-ounce) can chopped tomatoes with juice

Salt and pepper to taste

1 tablespoon balsamic vinegar

Grated Parmesan cheese (optional)

1. Coat a large nonstick pot with nonstick cooking spray. Heat oil and sauté onion and garlic over medium heat until tender, about 7 minutes

2. Add broth, rosemary, chick peas, and tomatoes with juice. Bring to a boil, reduce heat, and simmer for 15 minutes.

3. Remove 2 cups of mixture, and pureé in a food processor until smooth. Return to pot, and season to taste. Add vinegar and bring to a boil. Remove from heat. Sprinkle with Parmesan cheese, if desired.

———————

NUTRITIONAL INFORMATION PER SERVING
Calories 182 | Calories from fat 34% | Fat 4 g
Saturated Fat 0 g | Cholesterol 0 mg | Sodium 692 mg
Carbohydrate 28 g | Dietary Fiber 7 g | Sugars 8 g | Protein 10 g

DIABETIC EXCHANGES
1 1/2 starch | 1 vegetable | 1/2 lean meat

SOUPS, STEWS, & CHILIS

FRENCH ONION SOUP

MAKES 8 (1-CUP) SERVINGS

Red onions give the soup a sweet mild flavor, but any onion combination may be used. Whichever type of onion you use, it is most important to caramelize (brown) them. This does take time, but it brings out the onions' sweetness and gives the soup its unique rich flavor.

1 tablespoon olive oil

6 large red onions, peeled and thinly sliced

1 teaspoon sugar

1 teaspoon minced garlic

8 cups fat-free beef broth

1/2 cup white wine or cooking wine

1 bay leaf

1/2 teaspoon dried thyme leaves

Salt and pepper to taste

8 (1/2-inch thick) slices French bread, toasted

1 1/2 cups shredded light Swiss or Jarlsberg cheese

1. In a large nonstick pot, heat oil and sauté onions on medium heat until golden brown, but not burned, about 30 minutes. Stir in sugar about 10 minutes after onions begin to wilt.

2. Add garlic, stirring for 1 minute. Add broth, wine, bay leaf, and thyme, and bring to a boil. Cover, reduce heat, and simmer for about 30 minutes, allowing the flavors to blend. Season to taste. Remove and discard bay leaf.

3. Transfer soup to oven-proof soup bowls and arrange on a baking sheet. Top each with a slice of French bread. Sprinkle with cheese and broil several minutes, or until cheese is melted. Serve immediately.

NUTRITIONAL INFORMATION PER SERVING
Calories 236 | Calories from fat 22% | Fat 6 g
Saturated Fat 2 g | Cholesterol 10 mg | Sodium 610 mg
Carbohydrate 32 g | Dietary Fiber 4 g | Sugars 10 g | Protein 14 g

DIABETIC EXCHANGES
1 starch | 3 vegetable | 1 medium-fat meat

TERRIFIC TIDBIT

For a quick casual serving method, fill bowls with hot soup, top bread and cheese. The cheese will eventually melt from the soup's heat. If freezing, don't freeze with bread and cheese.

MINESTRONE

MAKES 12 (1-CUP) SERVINGS

This robust Italian vegetable soup with an assortment of fresh veggies, beans and pasta is first-class. Sprinkle with Parmesan cheese when serving, if desired.

1 tablespoon olive oil

1 green bell pepper, cored and chopped

1 medium red onion, chopped

1 teaspoon minced garlic

1 (28-ounce) can chopped tomatoes with juice

8 cups vegetable or fat-free chicken broth

1 teaspoon dried basil leaves

1 teaspoon dried oregano leaves

2 cups peeled carrots, cut into 1-inch slices

2 cups sliced zucchini

2 cups frozen lima beans

1 cup small penne or small tubular pasta

1 (15-ounce) can white cannellini beans, rinsed and drained

2 cups packed fresh baby spinach

Salt and pepper to taste

Grated Parmesan cheese (optional)

1. In a large nonstick pot coated with nonstick spray, heat oil and sauté green pepper, onion, and garlic, for about 5–7 minutes or until tender.

2. Add tomatoes, broth, basil, oregano, carrots, zucchini, and lima beans. Bring to a boil and cook over medium heat about 10 minutes.

3. Add pasta and continue cooking for another 5–7 minutes or until pasta is tender.

4. Add cannellini beans and spinach, stirring until spinach is wilted. Season to taste. If soup gets too thick, add more broth. Serve sprinkled with Parmesan cheese, if desired.

NUTRITIONAL INFORMATION PER SERVING
Calories 138 | Calories from fat 10% | Fat 2 g
Saturated Fat 0 g | Cholesterol 0 mg | Sodium 577 mg
Carbohydrate 24 g | Dietary Fiber 5 g | Sugars 5 g | Protein 7 g

DIABETIC EXCHANGES
1 1/2 starch | 1/2 very lean meat

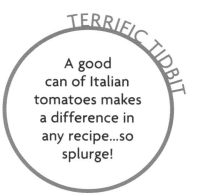

TERRIFIC TIDBIT

A good can of Italian tomatoes makes a difference in any recipe...so splurge!

SOUPS, STEWS, & CHILIS

CHICKEN AND SAUSAGE GUMBO

MAKES 14 (1-CUP) SERVINGS

A Louisiana favorite, chicken and sausage gumbo can be prepared easily and conveniently. Roux, the secret of good gumbo, gives it that nutty flavor and color without the fat. I use browned flour to create my roux. Gumbo is typically served over rice.

1/2 cup all-purpose flour

1 pound reduced-fat sausage, sliced in 1/4-inch pieces

2 pounds boneless, skinless chicken breasts, cut into pieces

1 onion, chopped

1 teaspoon minced garlic

1 green bell pepper, cored and chopped

2 stalks celery, chopped

8 cups fat-free chicken broth

1 (16-ounce) package frozen cut okra or fresh cut okra

1 teaspoon dried thyme leaves

1/4 teaspoon cayenne

Salt and pepper to taste

1 bunch green onions, chopped

1. Preheat oven to 400°F.

2. Place flour on a baking sheet and bake for 20 minutes, stirring every 7–10 minutes until a dark nutty brown color. Set aside.

3. In large nonstick pot coated with nonstick cooking spray, stir fry sausage over medium heat until crispy brown, and set aside. Remove any excess fat and recoat with nonstick cooking spray.

4. Add chicken and cook, stirring just until starting to brown. Add onion, garlic, green pepper, and celery, cooking until tender. Add browned flour and stir continuously.

5. Gradually add remaining ingredients, except green onions. Bring to a boil, reduce heat, and simmer for 30 minutes or until chicken is tender. Add sausage and green onions cooking for about 5 more minutes. Serve over rice.

NUTRITIONAL INFORMATION PER SERVING
Calories 160 | Calories from fat 11% | Fat 2 g
Saturated Fat 1 g | Cholesterol 49 mg | Sodium 550 mg
Carbohydrate 12 g | Dietary Fiber 2 g | Sugars 4 g | Protein 22 g

DIABETIC EXCHANGES
1 carbohydrate | 3 very lean meat

TERRIFIC TIDBIT

Gumbo is a quintessential recipe of both Creole and Cajun cooking.

CHICKEN TORTILLA SOUP
MAKES 13 (1-CUP) SERVINGS

Leftover chicken, southwestern seasonings and canned broth quickly turn into a mouth-watering one-pot meal. A cross between White Chicken Chili and Tortilla Soup, this chunky soup is filled with beans, corn, and southwestern flair.

4 (6–8-inch) flour tortillas, cut into 1/4-inch strips

1 cup chopped onion

1 teaspoon minced garlic

1 1/2 pounds boneless, skinless chicken breasts, cut into strips (4 cups cooked)

1 (28-ounce) can chopped tomatoes with juice

6 cups fat-free chicken broth

1 (4-ounce) can chopped green chilies, drained

1 (16-ounce) package frozen corn

1 (15 1/2-ounce) can Great Northern or navy white beans, drained and rinsed

2 tablespoons lime juice

1 1/2 teaspoons ground cumin

1 tablespoon chili powder

1/2 cup chopped green onions

1 cup shredded reduced-fat Mexican-blend or Cheddar cheese

1 small avocado, peeled and diced (optional)

1. Preheat oven to 350°F. Place tortilla strips on a baking sheet and bake for 10–15 minutes, or until crisp. Set aside. (This may also be done while soup is cooking in step 3.)

2. In a nonstick pot coated with nonstick cooking spray, sauté onion and garlic over medium heat until tender, about 7 minutes.

3. Add chicken and continue cooking until chicken is done, about 5–7 minutes. Add tomatoes with juice, broth, green chilies, corn, beans, lime juice, cumin, and chili powder. Bring to a boil, reduce heat and simmer for about 10–15 minutes.

4. Serve soup topped with tortilla strips, green onions, cheese, and avocado.

NUTRITIONAL INFORMATION PER SERVING
Calories 209 | Calories from fat 17% | Fat 4 g
Saturated Fat 2 g | Cholesterol 37 mg | Sodium 571 mg
Carbohydrate 24 | Dietary Fiber 5 | Sugars 4 | Protein 20 g

DIABETIC EXCHANGES
1 1/2 starch | 2 very lean meat

TERRIFIC TIDBIT

For any recipe calling for chicken, you may substitute skinless rotisserie or leftover chicken.

SOUTHWESTERN SOUP

MAKES 9 (1-CUP) SERVINGS

This hearty soup is a real family pleaser and stomach filler.

1 pound ground sirloin

1 cup chopped onion

2 cups water

1 (10-ounce) can diced tomatoes and green chilies

1 cup salsa

2 cups cubed, peeled, sweet or white potatoes

1/2 teaspoon chili powder

1 teaspoon ground cumin

1/2 teaspoon minced garlic

Salt and pepper to taste

2 cups frozen corn

1. In a large nonstick pot, cook meat and onion over medium heat until meat is done, about 5-7 minutes. Drain any excess fat.

2. Add remaining ingredients, except corn. Bring to a boil. Reduce heat, cover, and simmer for about 30 minutes.

3. Add corn and continue cooking, covered, for 15 minutes.

———————

NUTRITIONAL INFORMATION PER SERVING
Calories 149 | Calories from fat 17% | Fat 3 g
Saturated Fat 1 g | Cholesterol 28 mg | Sodium 289 mg
Carbohydrate 19 g | Dietary Fiber 3 g | Sugars 4 g | Protein 13 g

DIABETIC EXCHANGES
1 starch | 1 vegetable | 1 1/2 very lean meat

JANE'S "THROW IT IN" VEGETARIAN CHILI

MAKES 20 (1-CUP) SERVINGS

In Los Angeles, watching LSU football, my friend Jane shared her fantastic chili with secret ingredients. Makes tons so freeze extra.

1 (12-ounce) bottle light beer

1 (4-ounce) package chili mix (Shelby's), only chili seasoning packet

1 (28-ounce) can chopped tomatoes with juice

1 (12-ounce) can tomatillos, drained

4 (16-ounce) cans chili beans

1 (4-ounce) can chopped green chilies

1 (16-ounce) jar green salsa

1 (16-ounce) jar salsa

1 (2.25-ounce) can chopped black olives, drained

1 (2.25-ounce) can sliced green olives, drained

1 onion, chopped

1 red or yellow bell pepper, cored, chopped

1 bunch green onions, chopped

1/3 cup chopped fresh basil or 2 tablespoons dried basil leaves

1 (16-ounce) package frozen corn

1 (12-ounce) can frozen apple juice concentrate

1. In a large nonstick pot, combine all ingredients and bring to a boil. Cook for about 30 minutes to one hour, time permitting.

———————

NUTRITIONAL INFORMATION PER SERVING
Calories 205 | Calories from fat 9% | Fat 2 g
Saturated Fat 0 g | Cholesterol 0 mg | Sodium 1038 mg
Carbohydrate 39 g | Dietary Fiber 7 g | Sugars 12 g | Protein 6 g

DIABETIC EXCHANGES
2 starch | 1 vegetable

Jane's "Throw It In" Vegetarian Chili pg. 62

ULTIMATE CHILI
MAKES 12 (1-CUP) SERVINGS

Everyone seems to have their secret for the perfect chili, so I put all those secrets in one pot for the best chili ever. Serve topped with chopped red onions, cheese, and chips. This recipe makes a very large amount, so cut the recipe in half or freeze the extra for another time.

2 green bell peppers, cored and chopped

2 onions, chopped

4 pounds ground sirloin or ground sirloin chili meat

1 tablespoon minced garlic

1 (15-ounce) can tomato sauce

2 tablespoons molasses

1 tablespoon cocoa

1/2 cup chili powder

1 tablespoon ground cumin

1 teaspoon dried oregano leaves

1 (12-ounce) bottle light Mexican beer

2 (14-ounce) cans fat-free beef broth

2 (15-ounce) can pinto beans, rinsed and drained

1. In a large nonstick pot coated with nonstick cooking spray, sauté green pepper and onion until tender, about 5–7 minutes.

2. Add meat and garlic, cooking until meat is done, about 7 minutes, stirring continuously. Add remaining ingredients, except beans.

3. Bring to a boil. Reduce heat and simmer for 1 hour. Add beans and cook until well heated.

NUTRITIONAL INFORMATION PER SERVING
Calories 329 | Calories from fat 26% | Fat 10 g
Saturated Fat 3 g | Cholesterol 83 mg | Sodium 803 mg
Carbohydrate 22 g | Dietary Fiber 7 g | Sugars 6 g | Protein 39 g

DIABETIC EXCHANGES
1 starch | 1 vegetable | 5 lean meat

BEEF AND BARLEY STEW

MAKES 8–10 SERVINGS

Comfort-food flavors and powerful ingredients make this stew an amazing one-pot meal. Try serving it over couscous.

2 pounds extra lean stew meat, trimmed of excess fat, and cut into 1-inch pieces

Salt and pepper to taste

1/3 cup all-purpose flour

1 onion, chopped

1 teaspoon minced garlic

1/2 teaspoon dried thyme leaves

2 tablespoons finely chopped parsley

1 cup chopped carrots

6 cups fat-free chicken broth

2 cups (1-inch) chunks peeled potatoes

2 cups (1-inch) chunks peeled sweet potatoes (yams)

1 cup coarsely chopped Roma tomatoes

1/2 pound sliced mushrooms

1/2 cup medium barley

1 cup frozen peas

1. Season meat to taste and thoroughly coat with flour. In a large nonstick pot coated with nonstick cooking spray, cook meat over medium heat until browned, about 5 minutes.

2. Add onion and garlic, sautéing for several more minutes. Add thyme, parsley, and carrots, and sauté for 3–5 minutes. Add broth and bring to a boil, scraping bottom of the pan.

3. Reduce heat, cover, and simmer for about 30 minutes. Add potatoes, sweet potatoes, tomatoes, mushrooms and barley. Continue cooking, covered, over low heat for 45 minutes or until the barley is done. Add peas, stirring for one minute.

NUTRITIONAL INFORMATION PER SERVING
Calories 267 | Calories from fat 22% | Fat 7 g
Saturated Fat 2 g | Cholesterol 56 mg | Sodium 315 mg
Carbohydrate 28 g | Dietary Fiber 5 g | Sugars 5 g | Protein 23 g

DIABETIC EXCHANGES
2 starch | 2 1/2 lean meat

Crunchy Fruity Coleslaw pg. 78; Double Roasted Potato Salad pg. 79

Louisiana's coastal wetlands provide habitat for approximately 4.4 million migratory waterfowl.

Louisiana Department of Natural Resources

WETLANDS FACT

MIXED GREENS WITH APPLES, GOAT CHEESE, AND WALNUTS WITH MAPLE DIJON VINAIGRETTE

MAKES 4–6 SERVINGS

A subtle sweet Dijon vinaigrette perfectly complements apples, goat cheese, and toasted walnuts for a light refreshing salad.

6 cups mixed greens or fresh baby spinach (or combination)

1 green apple, cored, cut into small chunks

2 ounces crumbled goat cheese

1/3 cup chopped walnuts, toasted

Maple Dijon Vinaigrette (recipe below)

1. In a large bowl, combine all ingredients. Toss with Maple Dijon Vinaigrette. Serve.

MAPLE DIJON VINAIGRETTE

2 tablespoons cider vinegar

2 tablespoons pure maple syrup

1 tablespoon Dijon mustard

2 teaspoons canola oil

1. In a small bowl, whisk together all ingredients.

NUTRITIONAL INFORMATION PER SERVING
Calories 141 | Calories from fat 60% | Fat 9 g
Saturated Fat 3 g | Cholesterol 10 mg | Sodium 99 mg
Carbohydrate 11 g | Dietary Fiber 2 g | Sugars 7 g | Protein 5 g

DIABETIC EXCHANGES
1/2 carbohydrate | 1/2 lean meat | 1 1/2 fat

MARINATED AVOCADO, TOMATO, AND ONION SALAD

MAKES 4 (3/4-CUP) SERVINGS

This marinated mixture of household ingredients solves any salad dilemma instantly.

1 cup chopped tomatoes

1/3 cup chopped red onions

1 green bell pepper, cored and chopped

2 tablespoons chopped jalapeños (found in jar)

1 large or 2 small avocados, chopped

1 teaspoon minced garlic

2 tablespoons red wine vinegar

1 tablespoon olive oil

1/4 teaspoon hot sauce (or to taste)

Salt to taste

1. In a bowl, combine tomatoes, onions, green pepper, jalapeños, and avocado.

2. In a small bowl, whisk together remaining ingredients. Carefully toss with tomato mixture.

NUTRITIONAL INFORMATION PER SERVING
Calories 153 | Calories from fat 74% | Fat 13 g
Saturated Fat 2 g | Cholesterol 0 mg | Sodium 110 mg
Carbohydrate 11 g | Dietary Fiber 6 g | Sugars 3 | Protein 2 g

DIABETIC EXCHANGES
2 vegetable | 2 1/2 fat

PEAR AND BRIE MIXED GREEN SALAD WITH ORANGE VINAIGRETTE

MAKES 6 SERVINGS

The perfect merging of mild creamy Brie, fragrant walnuts, and the fresh bite of pears ensures this salad a permanent place in a salad-lovers arsenal of recipes.

1/3 cup orange juice

1/2 teaspoon dry mustard

1 teaspoon Dijon mustard

1/4 cup balsamic vinegar

2 tablespoons olive oil

6 cups mixed salad greens

1 pear, cored and cut into chunks

3 tablespoons chopped red onion

2–3 ounces Brie cheese, rind removed and cut into small chunks

3 tablespoons chopped walnuts, toasted

1. In a small bowl, whisk together orange juice, dry mustard, Dijon mustard, vinegar, and olive oil.

2. In a large bowl, combine remaining ingredients. When ready to serve, toss with dressing.

———————

NUTRITIONAL INFORMATION PER SERVING
Calories 140 | Calories from fat 61% | Fat 10 g
Saturated Fat 3 g | Cholesterol 9 mg | Sodium 94 mg
Carbohydrate 11 g | Dietary Fiber 3 g | Sugars 7 g | Protein 4 g

DIABETIC EXCHANGES
1/2 carbohydrate | 2 fat

FESTIVE SPINACH SALAD

MAKES 8 TO 10 SERVINGS

A tangy sweet dressing complements the tender spinach leaves punctuated with tart sweet cherries, crunchy onions, and crispy bacon. Make the dressing ahead of time and toss together when you're ready to serve.

1/4 cup raspberry vinegar

1 tablespoon sugar

1 teaspoon Dijon mustard

1/4 cup olive oil

1 (10-ounce) package fresh baby spinach

1/2 cup thinly sliced red onion

1/4 cup dried cherries or dried cranberries

1 (11-ounce) can mandarin oranges, drained

1/4 cup shredded carrots

4 strips center-cut bacon, cooked crispy and crumbled

1. In a small bowl, whisk together vinegar, sugar, mustard, and oil. Refrigerate until ready to toss salad.

2. In a large bowl, combine remaining ingredients. When ready to serve, toss with dressing

———————

NUTRITIONAL INFORMATION PER SERVING
Calories 100 | Calories from fat 57% | Fat 6 g
Saturated Fat 1 g | Cholesterol 2 mg | Sodium 87 mg
Carbohydrate 9 g | Dietary Fiber 1 g | Sugars 7 g | Protein 2 g

DIABETIC EXCHANGES
1/2 fruit | 1 fat

SPINACH SALAD WITH CANDIED SPICY PECANS

MAKES 10–12 SERVINGS

Seasonal fruit adds a touch of sweetness contrasting the salty prosciutto and candied spicy pecans for a sensational spinach salad.

2 (6-ounce) packages fresh baby spinach

2 peaches or nectarines, sliced (or kiwi, berries, or any seasonal fruit)

3 ounces thinly sliced prosciutto, coarsely chopped

Citrus Vinaigrette (recipe below)

Candied Spicy Pecans (recipe to the right)

1. In a salad bowl, combine all ingredients and toss with Citrus Vinaigrette.

2. Sprinkle with Candied Spicy Pecans. Serve immediately

CITRUS VINAIGRETTE

1/4 cup chopped red onion

3 tablespoons balsamic vinegar

2 tablespoons orange juice

1 teaspoon sugar

1 teaspoon lemon juice

1 tablespoon Dijon mustard

2 teaspoons canola oil

Salt and pepper to taste

1. In a small bowl, whisk together all ingredients

CANDIED SPICY PECANS

Use these pecans as a snack, in a salad, or as garnish around a cheese display.

1/4 cup confectioners sugar

1/4 teaspoon ground allspice

1/8 teaspoon ground cinnamon

1/8 teaspoon cayenne

Salt to taste

1/3 cup pecan halves, rinsed, drained

1. Preheat oven to 350°F. Coat a baking sheet with nonstick cooking spray.

2. In a small bowl, combine all ingredients, except pecans.

3. Add pecans, tossing to coat well. Transfer pecans to prepared pan and bake for 10–12 minutes, stirring occasionally.

4. Remove from oven and immediately scrape sugar mixture and pecans onto a plate to cool. Coarsely chop before serving.

NUTRITIONAL INFORMATION PER SERVING
Calories 77 | Calories from fat 48% | Fat 4 g
Saturated Fat 1 g | Cholesterol 6 mg | Sodium 176 mg
Carbohydrate 8 g | Dietary Fiber 1 g | Sugars 6 g | Protein 3 g

DIABETIC EXCHANGES
1/2 carbohydrate | 1 fat

SPINACH AND MELON SALAD WITH HONEY CITRUS VINAIGRETTE

MAKES 6 SERVINGS

Looking for a great summer salad that's refreshing, colorful, and jam-packed with flavor? Give your taste buds a thrill with this fruity spinach salad accented with Maple Pecans, if desired.

1 (6-ounce) package fresh baby spinach

1 cup cubed seeded watermelon

1 cup cubed cantaloupe

1 small cucumber, peeled and thinly sliced

1/2 cup thin red onion slices, halved

Honey Citrus Vinaigrette (recipe below)

Maple Pecans (optional, recipe below)

1. In a large bowl, combine all ingredients. Toss with Honey Citrus Dressing and Maple Pecans.

HONEY CITRUS VINAIGRETTE

2 tablespoons honey

1 tablespoon balsamic vinegar

1 tablespoon canola oil

2 tablespoons orange juice

1 tablespoon lime juice

Salt and pepper to taste

Dash hot sauce

1. In a small bowl, whisk together all ingredients.

———————

NUTRITIONAL INFORMATION PER SERVING
(NOT INCLUDING PECANS)
Calories 77 | Calories from fat 28% | Fat 3 g
Saturated Fat 0 g | Cholesterol 0 mg | Sodium 29 mg
Carbohydrate 14 g | Dietary Fiber 1 g | Sugars 11 g | Protein 2 g

DIABETIC EXCHANGES
1 carbohydrate | 1/2 fat

MAPLE PECANS

Simple to make and adds an enticing crunch and sweetness to any salad or snack.

1/4 cup pecan halves

1 tablespoon pure maple syrup

1. Preheat oven to 375°F. Coat a baking sheet with nonstick cooking spray.

2. In a small bowl, combine pecans and syrup. Spread on prepared pan. Bake for 10 minutes or until lightly browned.

———————

NUTRITIONAL INFORMATION PER SERVING OF PECANS
Calories 40 | Calories from fat 72% | Fat 3 g
Saturated Fat 0 g | Cholesterol 0 mg | Sodium 0 mg
Carbohydrate 3 g | Dietary Fiber 0 g | Sugars 2 g | Protein 0 g

DIABETIC EXCHANGES
1/2 fat

SALADS

HEARTS OF PALM SALAD

MAKES ABOUT 4 (1/2-CUP) SERVINGS

An interesting blend of hearts of palm, celery, cucumber, and feta, with a splash of lemon, presents an invigorating light salad option.

1 cup chopped hearts of palm

1/2 cup chopped celery

1 cup chopped, peeled cucumber

2 tablespoons lemon juice

1 tablespoon olive oil

Salt and pepper to taste

1/4 cup crumbled reduced-fat feta cheese

1. In a large bowl, combine all ingredients, except the feta, and mix well.

2. Toss with feta and serve.

NUTRITIONAL INFORMATION PER SERVING
Calories 65 | Calories from fat 63% | Fat 5 g
Saturated Fat 1 g | Cholesterol 3 mg | Sodium 292 mg
Carbohydrate 4 g | Dietary Fiber 1 g | Sugars 1 g | Protein 3 g

DIABETIC EXCHANGES
1 vegetable | 1 fat

TOMATO AND MOZZARELLA SALAD

MAKES 8 (1/4-CUP) SERVINGS

In this salad, the key ingredients are fresh basil and fresh mozzarella, so this is one time fresh ingredients are a must! Serve over thinly sliced toasted Italian or French bread for a bruschetta style snack.

2 cups cherry tomatoes, halved

6 ounces fresh mozzarella cheese, cut into small cubes

2 ounces thinly sliced prosciutto, chopped

3 tablespoons finely chopped fresh basil

1 tablespoon olive oil

1–2 tablespoons balsamic vinegar

Salt and pepper to taste

1. In a bowl, combine tomatoes, mozzarella, and prosciutto. Add remaining ingredients and toss well. Refrigerate until serving.

NUTRITIONAL INFORMATION PER SERVING
Calories 107 | Calories from fat 66% | Fat 8 g
Saturated Fat 4 g | Cholesterol 21 mg | Sodium 144 mg
Carbohydrate 3 g | Dietary Fiber 1 g | Sugars 2 g | Protein 6 g

DIABETIC EXCHANGES
1 lean meat | 1 fat

TERRIFIC TIDBIT

To thinly cut basil, roll up a stack of leaves and use a pair of sharp kitchen shears instead of a knife. Fresh mozzarella is higher in fat but makes such a difference in this salad!

SHRIMP, MANGO, AND AVOCADO SALAD

MAKES 6 SERVINGS

Sweet mangos, mild avocados, red onions, and shrimp in a slightly sweet vinaigrette characterize the subtle and bold flavors of Caribbean cuisine in this extraordinary salad.

1 cup chopped mango

1 cup chopped avocado

1/2 cup finely chopped red onion

1/2 cup finely chopped red bell pepper

1 pound peeled shrimp, seasoned and cooked

1 tablespoon honey

1/2 teaspoon minced garlic

1/4 cup lime juice

1 teaspoon Dijon mustard

2 tablespoons olive oil

3 cups baby spinach leaves

1. In a bowl, combine mango, avocado, red onion, red pepper, and shrimp.

2. In a small bowl, whisk together remaining ingredients, except spinach. Carefully toss mixtures together and serve over spinach leaves.

NUTRITIONAL INFORMATION PER SERVING
Calories 199 | Calories from fat 41% | Fat 9 g
Saturated Fat 1 g | Cholesterol 147 mg | Sodium 202 mg
Carbohydrate 13 g | Dietary Fiber 3 g | Sugars 9 g | Protein 17 g

DIABETIC EXCHANGES
1/2 fruit | 1/2 carbohydrate | 2 1/2 lean meat

CRISP SUMMER SALAD

MAKES 6 (2/3-CUP) SERVINGS

I started with leftover corn on the cob and created a dish bursting with color, crispness, and flavor. Perfect for summer!

1 1/2 cups fresh or frozen corn

1 cup chopped tomatoes

1 cup chopped peeled cucumber

1/3 cup shelled edamame, cooked according to directions and drained

1/2 cup chopped red onion

1/3 cup chopped avocado

2 tablespoons lime juice

1 tablespoon olive oil

Salt and pepper to taste

1. In a bowl, combine corn, tomatoes, cucumber, edamame, red onion, and avocado.

2. In a small bowl, whisk together lime juice and oil. Toss with corn mixture and season to taste.

NUTRITIONAL INFORMATION PER SERVING
Calories 92 | Calories from fat 42% | Fat 4 g
Saturated Fat 1 g | Cholesterol 0 mg | Sodium 9 mg
Carbohydrate 12 g | Dietary Fiber 3 g | Sugars 3 g | Protein 3 g

DIABETIC EXCHANGES
1/2 starch | 1 vegetable | 1/2 fat

TERRIFIC TIDBIT

Look for frozen shelled edamame in the frozen vegetables section.

SALADS

CREAMY CUCUMBERS WITH DILL

MAKES 4 (3/4-CUP) SERVINGS

Cucumbers and red onions in a creamy dill dressing are a natural combination.

1/3 cup nonfat sour cream

1 tablespoon lemon juice

1 teaspoon dried dill weed or 1 tablespoon fresh dill

3 cucumbers, peeled, halved lengthwise, cored, and thinly sliced (about 3 cups)

1/4 cup finely chopped red onion

Salt and pepper to taste

1. In a medium bowl, combine sour cream, lemon juice, and dill. Add remaining ingredients. Refrigerate until serving.

———————————

NUTRITIONAL INFORMATION PER SERVING:
Calories 44 | Calories from fat 0% | Fat 0 g
Saturated Fat 0 g | Cholesterol 3 mg | Sodium 21 mg
Carbohydrate 8 g | Dietary Fiber 1 g | Sugars 4 g | Protein 2 g

DIABETIC EXCHANGES
1/2 carbohydrate

BLACK BEAN AND MANGO SALAD

MAKES ABOUT 6 (1/2-CUP) SERVINGS

A colorful concoction bursting with fresh flavors tossed with a zingy vinaigrette hits the spot. I couldn't decide to serve this as a salsa with chips, with a grilled entrée, or as a side salad, so the choice is yours!

1 (15-ounce) can black beans, rinsed and drained

1 cup chopped mango

1/2 cup chopped red onion

1 avocado, chopped

2 tablespoons lime juice

1 teaspoon light brown sugar

Dash red pepper flakes

1. In a medium bowl, combine all ingredients. Serve or refrigerate until serving.

———————————

NUTRITIONAL INFORMATION PER SERVING
Calories 141 | Calories from fat 35% | Fat 6 g
Saturated Fat 1 g | Cholesterol 0 mg | Sodium 222 mg
Carbohydrate 19 g | Dietary Fiber 7 g | Sugars 6 g | Protein 5 g

DIABETIC EXCHANGES
1 starch | 1/2 fruit | 1 fat

TERRIFIC TIDBIT

For a variation, add 1/2 teaspoon ginger. If mangos aren't in season, they may be found in jars or cans in the grocery.

74

Black Bean and Mango Salad pg. 74; Chicken Orzo Salad pg. 82

BROCCOLI SALAD

MAKES ABOUT 10 (2/3-CUP) SERVINGS

This salad showcases crunchy broccoli, sweet red onion, tart cranberries, and toasty walnuts tossed in a tangy dressing.

6 cups broccoli florets, cut into small pieces

1/2 cup chopped red onion

1/2 cup shredded carrots

1/3 cup dried cranberries

1/4 cup light mayonnaise

2 tablespoons nonfat sour cream

1 tablespoon sugar

3 tablespoons raspberry wine vinegar

1/4 cup coarsely chopped walnuts, toasted

1. In a large bowl, combine broccoli, onion, carrots, and cranberries.

2. In a small bowl, combine remaining ingredients, except walnuts. Toss with broccoli mixture. Refrigerate. When ready to serve, toss with walnuts.

NUTRITIONAL INFORMATION PER SERVING
Calories 78 | Calories from fat 46% | Fat 4 g
Saturated Fat 1 g | Cholesterol 3 mg | Sodium 66 mg
Carbohydrate 10 g | Dietary Fiber 2 g | Sugars 6 g | Protein 2 g

DIABETIC EXCHANGES
1/2 carbohydrate | 1 fat

TERRIFIC TIDBIT

For a short cut, purchase bagged broccoli florets and bagged, shredded carrots.

BROCCOLI AND RED TIP LETTUCE SALAD

MAKES 4–6 SERVINGS

Healthy broccoli florets tossed with pecans, crunchy Ramen noodles, and a sweet-sour vinaigrette give this salad pizzazz.

1/4 cup chopped pecans

1 (3-ounce) package oriental Ramen Noodles, broken into pieces

4 cups broccoli florets, cut into small pieces

1 bunch green onions, chopped

1 small head red tip lettuce, washed and torn into pieces (about 4 cups packed)

1/2 teaspoon seasoning packet from Ramen Noodles

3 tablespoons light brown sugar

1/4 cup cider or seasoned rice vinegar

2 tablespoons olive oil

1. Preheat oven to 350°F. Spread pecans and Ramen pieces onto a baking sheet and bake for 8–10 minutes or until golden brown. Remove from oven and cool.

2. In a large bowl, combine broccoli, green onions, and lettuce with pecan-noodle mixture.

3. In a small bowl, whisk together remaining ingredients. Toss dressing with salad when ready to serve.

NUTRITIONAL INFORMATION PER SERVING
Calories 201 | Calories from fat 47% | Fat 11 g
Saturated Fat 2 g | Cholesterol 0 mg | Sodium 140 mg
Carbohydrate 23 g | Dietary Fiber 4 g | Sugars 9 g | Protein 4 g

DIABETIC EXCHANGES
1 starch | 2 vegetable | 2 fat

SOUTHWESTERN SLAW

MAKES 12 (2/3-CUP) SERVINGS

Ribbons of color and crunch personalize this fantastic slaw, loaded with a great range of ingredients and tossed with a spunky chili dressing.

1/2 cup coarsely chopped pecans

1 tablespoon sugar

Hearty dash cayenne

8 cups shredded green cabbage mixture

1 red bell pepper, cored and chopped

1/2 cup chopped red onion

1/2 cup finely chopped carrots

1/2 cup jicama, peeled and julienned (matchstick slices)

1/2 cup frozen or canned corn

Chili Dressing (recipe to the right)

1. In a small nonstick skillet coated with nonstick cooking spray, cook pecans over medium heat, stirring, until lightly browned. Add sugar and cook until melted.

2. Remove from heat and toss with cayenne. Transfer pecans into a bowl and break in pieces when cool. Set aside.

3. In a large bowl, combine remaining ingredients, mixing well. When ready to serve, toss with Chili Dressing and pecans.

CHILI DRESSING

Vinaigrette, southwestern style.

1 teaspoon minced garlic

1/2 teaspoon chipotle chili powder or chili powder

1/4 cup lime juice

1/4 cup vinegar or seasoned rice vinegar

1 tablespoon sugar

3 tablespoons olive oil

Salt and pepper to taste

1. In a small bowl, whisk together all ingredients.

NUTRITIONAL INFORMATION PER SERVING
Calories 101 | Calories from fat 62% | Fat 7 g
Saturated Fat 1 g | Cholesterol 0 mg | Sodium 18 mg
Carbohydrate 9 g | Dietary Fiber 2 g | Sugars 5 g | Protein 1 g

DIABETIC EXCHANGES
1/2 carbohydrate | 1 1/2 fat

TERRIFIC TIDBIT

Jicama is found in the produce section and should be peeled before using. It has a sweet nutty flavor and a crunchy texture. If it's not available, don't stress, just omit it.

SALADS

CRUNCHY FRUITY COLESLAW

MAKES 10–12 SERVINGS

A bag of pre-shredded cabbage makes for effortless preparation of a vibrant, crowd-pleasing salad, packed with sweet and savory ingredients.

4 cups shredded green cabbage

4 cups shredded red cabbage

1 red bell pepper, cored and thinly sliced into 1-inch pieces

2/3 cup chopped dried apricots

1 1/2 cups frozen corn, thawed

1 bunch green onions, chopped

1/4 cup slivered almonds, toasted

2 tablespoons sesame seeds, toasted

1/4 cup balsamic vinegar

1 tablespoon honey

2 tablespoons canola oil

1 teaspoon minced garlic

1. In a large bowl, combine green and red cabbages, red pepper, apricots, corn, green onions, almonds, and sesame seeds.

2. In a small bowl, whisk together remaining ingredients. Toss with salad and mix well.

NUTRITIONAL INFORMATION PER SERVING
Calories 118 | Calories from fat 34% | Fat 5 g
Saturated Fat 1 g | Cholesterol 0 mg | Sodium 18 mg
Carbohydrate 18 g | Dietary Fiber 3 g | Sugars 10 g | Protein 2 g

DIABETIC EXCHANGES
1 vegetable | 1 carbohydrate | 1 fat

MEXICAN COUSCOUS SALAD

MAKES 8 (1-CUP) SERVINGS

Fast cooking couscous enlivened with bold southwestern ingredients.

2 cups fat-free vegetable broth

1 1/3 cups couscous

1 cup chopped red onion

1 cup chopped, peeled, cucumber

1 (15-ounce) can black beans, rinsed and drained

1 (10-ounce) can diced tomatoes and green chilies, drained

1 cup shredded, reduced-fat, Mexican-blend cheese

1/4 cup lime juice

2 tablespoons olive oil

1/2 teaspoon ground cumin

1/2 teaspoon chili powder

Salt and pepper to taste

1. In medium pot, bring broth to a boil. Stir in couscous, cover, remove from heat and let stand for 5–7 minutes. Transfer to a large bowl and fluff with fork. Add onion, cucumber, beans, tomatoes and green chilies, and cheese.

2. In a small bowl, whisk together remaining ingredients. Toss with couscous mixture.

NUTRITIONAL INFORMATION PER SERVING
Calories 246 | Calories from fat 23% | Fat 7 g
Saturated Fat 2 g | Cholesterol 8 mg | Sodium 529 mg
Carbohydrate 34 g | Dietary Fiber 5 g | Sugars 1 g | Protein 11 g

DIABETIC EXCHANGES
2 starch | 1 very lean meat | 1 fat

COUSCOUS SALAD

MAKES 8 (3/4-CUP) SERVINGS

Sweet dried fruit, aromatic refreshing mint, crunchy almonds, and a unique dressing makes up this enticing and versatile salad.

1 1/2 cups orange juice

1 1/2 cups couscous

1/3 cup dried cranberries

1/3 cup dried apricots, cut into 1/4-inch strips

1 cup coarsely chopped fresh baby spinach

1/2 cup chopped fresh mint leaves

1/4 cup slivered almonds, toasted

2 tablespoons canola oil

2 tablespoons vinegar

1 tablespoon lemon juice

2 tablespoons honey

Salt to taste

1/4 teaspoon ground cinnamon

1/4 teaspoon ground cumin

1. In a medium pot, bring orange juice to a boil. Stir in couscous, cover, remove from heat and let stand for 5–7 minutes. Transfer to a large bowl and fluff with fork. Add cranberries, apricots, spinach, mint, and almonds.

2. In a small bowl, whisk together remaining ingredients. Toss with couscous. Serve at room temperature or chilled.

———————

NUTRITIONAL INFORMATION PER SERVING
Calories 259 | Calories from fat 21% | Fat 6 g
Saturated Fat 1 g | Cholesterol 0 mg | Sodium 15 mg
Carbohydrate 46 g | Dietary Fiber 3 g | Sugars 16 g | Protein 6 g

DIABETIC EXCHANGES
2 starch | 1 fruit | 1 fat

DOUBLE ROASTED POTATO SALAD

MAKES 12 HEAPING (1/2-CUP) SERVINGS

A tasty roasted potato assortment. Try simply serving the roasted potatotes alone as a side!

4 cups peeled sweet potato (yam) chunks

2 cups unpeeled red potato chunks

2 cups unpeeled Yukon Gold potato chunks

2 tablespoons olive oil

1 tablespoon dried rosemary leaves

1/2 teaspoon ground cumin

1/2 teaspoon ground ginger

1 cup chopped celery

1/2 cup chopped green onions

1/4 cup light mayonnaise

1 tablespoon Dijon mustard

1 tablespoon balsamic or red wine vinegar

1. Preheat oven to 425°F. Coat a baking sheet with nonstick cooking spray, or line with foil.

2. On prepared pan, toss together all potatoes with olive oil, rosemary, cumin, and ginger. Roast for 30–40 minutes or until potatoes are crisp and light brown. Cool and transfer to a large bowl. Add celery and green onions.

3. In a small bowl, combine remaining ingredients. Toss with potatoes. Refrigerate, if not serving within 2 hours,

———————

NUTRITIONAL INFORMATION PER SERVING
Calories 120 | Calories from fat 30% | Fat 4 g
Saturated Fat 1 g | Cholesterol 2 mg | Sodium 103 mg
Carbohydrate 19 g | Dietary Fiber 3 g | Sugars 3 g | Protein 2 g

DIABETIC EXCHANGES
1 1/2 starch | 1/2 fat

CHINESE CHICKEN SALAD

MAKES 4 (1/2-CUP) SERVINGS

Only six ingredients create this flavorful Asian chicken salad. Think of the crunchy won ton strips as Asian croutons. I tested two different dressings and couldn't decide which I liked better, so the choice is yours.

8 won ton wrappers

2 cups shredded, rotisserie, skinless white chicken

1 cup fresh baby spinach

1/3 cup shredded or chopped carrots

1/3 cup chopped green onions

1/4 cup chopped peanuts

Asian Vinaigrette or Satay Dressing (recipes to the right)

1. Preheat oven to 375°F. Coat a baking sheet with nonstick cooking spray

2. Cut each won ton wrapper into 1/2-inch wide strips and place them on prepared pan. Scrunch each strip to make it wavy. Bake for 7 minutes or until golden brown and cool. Set aside.

3. In a bowl, combine remaining ingredients and toss with your choice of dressing, either Asian Vinaigrette or Satay Dressing. Top with won ton strips.

ASIAN VINAIGRETTE

MAKES 1/2 CUP DRESSING

1/4 cup seasoned rice vinegar

1 tablespoon low-sodium soy sauce

1/2 teaspoon minced garlic

1 tablespoon sweet Asian chile sauce

2 teaspoons minced fresh ginger or 1/2 teaspoon ground ginger

1 tablespoon sesame oil

1. In a small bowl, whisk together all ingredients.

NUTRITIONAL INFORMATION PER SERVING
Calories 217 | Calories from fat 35% | Fat 9 g
Saturated Fat 1 g | Cholesterol 39 mg | Sodium 438 mg
Carbohydrate 14 g | Dietary Fiber 2 g | Sugars 2 g | Protein 21 g

DIABETIC EXCHANGES
1 carbohydrate | 3 lean meat

SATAY DRESSING

MAKES 1/2 CUP DRESSING

1/4 cup peanut butter

2 tablespoons honey

2 tablespoons low-sodium soy sauce

1 tablespoon lime juice

1 tablespoon sesame oil

1. In a small bowl, whisk together all ingredients.

NUTRITIONAL INFORMATION PER SERVING
Calories 343 | Calories from fat 43% | Fat 17 g
Saturated Fat 3 g | Cholesterol 39 mg | Sodium 606 mg
Carbohydrate 26 g | Dietary Fiber 3 g | Sugars 11 g | Protein 25 g

DIABETIC EXCHANGES
1 1/2 carbohydrate | 3 1/2 lean meat | 1 1/2 fat

GREEK SALAD WITH OREGANO MARINATED CHICKEN

MAKES 4–6 SERVINGS

This amazing salad with tasty chicken strips has all the elements of a Greek-style chef salad.

3 tablespoons lemon juice

1 tablespoon olive oil

1 teaspoon dried oregano leaves

Salt and pepper to taste

1 1/2 pounds boneless, skinless chicken breasts

4 cups mixed greens

1 cup peeled, cubed, cucumber chunks

1 cup cherry or grape tomatoes, halved

1/2 cup coarsely chopped red onion

1/3 cup pitted coarsely chopped kalamata or black olives

1/4 cup crumbled reduced-fat feta cheese

3 tablespoons pine nuts, toasted

Greek Vinaigrette (recipe to the right)

1. In a resealable plastic bag or glass container, combine lemon juice, oil, oregano, salt, and pepper. Add chicken breasts and thoroughly coat.

2. Marinate in refrigerator for at least 30 minutes, and up to 4 hours. Discard marinade and cook chicken on a nonstick grill pan or skillet coated with nonstick cooking spray for about 4–5 minutes on each side, or until done. Remove from pan and slice. Set aside.

3. In a large bowl, combine remaining ingredients and toss with Greek Vinaigrette. Top with chicken strips and serve.

GREEK VINAIGRETTE

MAKES ABOUT 2/3 CUP DRESSING.

3 tablespoons red wine vinegar

3 tablespoons lemon juice

2 teaspoons Dijon mustard

1 teaspoon minced garlic

1 teaspoon dried oregano leaves

1/4 cup plain nonfat yogurt

2 tablespoons olive oil

Pinch sugar

1. In a small bowl, whisk together vinegar, lemon juice, mustard, garlic, and oregano. Stir in yogurt and then add oil, mixing well. Add sugar, if desired.

NUTRITIONAL INFORMATION PER SERVING
Calories 271 | Calories from fat 42% | Fat 13 g
Saturated Fat 2 g | Cholesterol 68 mg | Sodium 328 mg
Carbohydrate 9 g | Dietary Fiber 2 g | Sugars 4 g | Protein 30 g

DIABETIC EXCHANGES
1 vegetable | 3 1/2 lean meat | 1/2 fat

TERRIFIC TIDBIT

The greener the lettuce the more nutrition. Toss in some baby spinach, or purchase bags of mixed greens for ease.

SALADS

CHICKEN ORZO SALAD

MAKES 10 (1-CUP) SERVINGS

Featuring chicken, peas, sun-dried tomatoes, and feta, this fantastic, marinated light pasta salad combines bold flavors with great ingredients.

2 cups orzo pasta

2 cups diced, rotisserie, skinless white chicken

1 cup frozen peas, thawed, or shelled edamame

1/2 cup chopped green onions

1/2 cup crumbled reduced-fat feta cheese

1 cucumber, peeled and chopped

8 ounces sun-dried tomatoes, sliced, reconstituted, reserving 1/3 cup water from reconstituting tomatoes

2 teaspoons dried dill weed leaves

3 tablespoons lemon juice

2 tablespoons olive oil

1 teaspoon minced garlic

Salt and pepper to taste

1. Cook orzo according to package directions. Drain.

2. In a large bowl, combine orzo, chicken, peas, green onions, feta, cucumber, tomatoes, and dill.

3. In another bowl, whisk together reserved sun dried tomato water with remaining ingredients.

4. Toss with orzo mixture. Refrigerate for at least 1 hour before serving.

NUTRITIONAL INFORMATION PER SERVING
Calories 300 | Calories from fat 18% | Fat 6 g
Saturated Fat 2 g | Cholesterol 26 mg | Sodium 148 mg
Carbohydrate 42 g | Dietary Fiber 5 g | Sugars 6 g | Protein 19 g

DIABETIC EXCHANGES
2 starch | 3 vegetable | 1 1/2 lean meat

TERRIFIC TIDBIT

To reconstitute the tomatoes, pour 1 cup boiling water over them and let sit for 15 minutes or until soft.

MARINATED CRABMEAT MIXED GREEN SALAD

MAKES 6 SERVINGS

Light Dijon vinaigrette, herbs, capers and sun-dried tomatoes provide a supporting cast of ingredients to the lump crabmeat.

3 tablespoons olive oil

2 tablespoons balsamic vinegar

2 tablespoons lime juice

1 teaspoon Dijon mustard

Salt and pepper to taste

1/4 teaspoon dried basil leaves

2 tablespoons chopped parsley

1/2 cup chopped red onion

2 tablespoons capers, drained

2 tablespoons sun-dried tomatoes, chopped, reconstituted in water

1 pound lump or white crabmeat, picked through for shells

6 cups mixed greens

1. Combine all ingredients except crabmeat and mixed greens. Add crabmeat, tossing gently. Refrigerate until ready to serve.

2. Before serving, gently toss with mixed greens. Serve immediately.

NUTRITIONAL INFORMATION PER SERVING
Calories 169 | Calories from fat 42% | Fat 8 g
Saturated Fat 1 g | Cholesterol 57 mg | Sodium 405 mg
Carbohydrate 6 g | Dietary Fiber 2 g | Sugars 2 g | Protein 18 g

DIABETIC EXCHANGES
1 vegetable | 2 1/2 lean meat

TERRIFIC TIDBIT

Serve with a cup of soup and you have a light meal.

SALADS

Marinated Shrimp Edamame Salad pg. 85

MARINATED SHRIMP EDAMAME SALAD

MAKES 6 (2/3-CUP) SERVINGS

Shrimp and edamame tossed with an Asian-infused vinaigrette bring a burst of fabulous flavors to this quick, easy salad.

1 pound medium peeled shrimp, seasoned, cooked, and coarsely chopped

1 cup shelled edamame, cooked according to directions

1 cup halved cherry tomatoes

1 bunch green onions, chopped

2 tablespoons lime juice

1 tablespoon olive oil

1 teaspoon wasabi paste

1 teaspoon grated fresh ginger or 1/2 teaspoon ground ginger

1. In a medium bowl, combine shrimp, edamame, tomatoes, and green onions.

2. In a small bowl, whisk together remaining ingredients and toss with shrimp mixture. Refrigerate until serving.

NUTRITIONAL INFORMATION PER SERVING
Calories 153 | Calories from fat 26% | Fat 4 g
Saturated Fat 1 g | Cholesterol 147 mg | Sodium 198 mg
Carbohydrate 8 g | Dietary Fiber 3 g | Sugars 4 g | Protein 19 g

DIABETIC EXCHANGES
1/2 carbohydrate | 2 1/2 lean meat

SHRIMP POPPY SEED PASTA SALAD

MAKES 6–8 SERVINGS

This simple six-ingredient salad will please even the most picky palate.

1 (12 ounce) package tri-colored rotini

1 pound medium peeled shrimp, cooked

1/3 cup pine nuts, toasted

2 cups fresh baby spinach

1/3 cup reduced-fat poppy seed dressing

1/4 cup balsamic vinegar

1. Cook pasta according to package directions and drain well. In a large bowl, combine pasta, shrimp, pine nuts, and spinach.

2. In a small bowl, whisk together poppy seed dressing and balsamic vinegar. Toss with pasta mixture before serving.

NUTRITIONAL INFORMATION PER SERVING
Calories 282 | Calories from fat 21% | Fat 7 g
Saturated Fat 1 g | Cholesterol 111 mg | Sodium 205 mg
Carbohydrate 36 g | Dietary Fiber 1 g | Sugars 4 g | Protein 19 g

DIABETIC EXCHANGES
2 1/2 starch | 2 lean meat

TERRIFIC TIDBIT

Make your own poppy seed dressing by whisking together 1/4 cup orange juice, 1/2 teaspoon lemon juice, 1 tablespoon honey, 2 tablespoons canola oil, 1 teaspoon poppy seeds, 1/4 teaspoon dry mustard, and salt.

SOUTHWESTERN SHRIMP SALAD

MAKES 6 SERVINGS

This salad sizzles with southwestern seasoned shrimp, corn, and black beans tossed with greens in a light salsa dressing. Serve with chopped avocados, if desired.

2 tablespoons chili powder

1/2 teaspoon garlic powder

1 teaspoon ground cumin

1 tablespoon lime juice

1 1/2 pounds medium peeled shrimp

1 cup frozen corn

1 (15-ounce) can black beans, rinsed and drained

1 cup salsa

1 cup plain nonfat yogurt

6 cups coarsely chopped Romaine lettuce or mixed greens

Avocado (garnish)

1. In a small bowl or resealable plastic bag, combine chili powder, garlic powder, cumin, and lime juice. Add shrimp and toss to coat.

2. In a large nonstick skillet coated with nonstick cooking spray, cook shrimp over medium heat until done, about 5 minutes. Add corn and beans. Remove from heat.

3. In a small bowl combine salsa and yogurt. Pour over shrimp mixture in skillet, stirring and scraping pan to get bits into sauce.

4. When ready to serve, place lettuce in a large bowl and spoon shrimp mixture over it, tossing gently to coat. Garnish with avocado, if desired. Serve immediately.

NUTRITIONAL INFORMATION PER SERVING
Calories 224 | Calories from fat 10% | Fat 3 g
Saturated Fat 0 g | Cholesterol 169 mg | Sodium 631 mg
Carbohydrate 24 g | Dietary Fiber 7 g | Sugars 6 g | Protein 26 g

DIABETIC EXCHANGES
1 1/2 starch | 3 very lean meat

TUNA AND AVOCADO SALAD WITH WASABI VINAIGRETTE

MAKES 4–6 SERVINGS

Seared ahi tuna paired with mild velvety avocado and tossed with a fiery vinaigrette is the ideal blend of flavors. Try using this salad as a dip with pitas or crackers.

2 pounds fresh ahi tuna fillets, 1-inch thick

Salt and pepper to taste

1/4 cup chopped green onions

1/4 cup chopped red onion

2 tablespoons olive oil

1 teaspoon wasabi powder

1/4 cup lime juice

2 teaspoons low-sodium soy sauce

1/2 teaspoon hot sauce

1–2 ripe medium avocados, chopped

1. Season tuna to taste. Heat a nonstick skillet coated with nonstick cooking spray over medium heat. Add tuna and sear for only 1–2 minutes on each side, depending on thickness. (Tuna should remain rare inside.)

2. Cut tuna into small chunks and place in a large bowl. Add green and red onion, and mix well. Set aside.

3. In a small bowl, combine the remaining ingredients, except avocados. Add avocados and gently toss. Pour over tuna and carefully toss together.

NUTRITIONAL INFORMATION PER SERVING
Calories 319 | Calories from fat 44% | Fat 16 g
Saturated Fat 2 g | Cholesterol 68 mg | Sodium 134 mg
Carbohydrate 8 g | Dietary Fiber 5 g | Sugars 1 g | Protein 37 g

DIABETIC EXCHANGES
1/2 carbohydrate | 5 lean meat

TERRIFIC TIDBIT

Wasabi powder is found in the Asian section of the grocery store and is the Japanese version of horseradish. Water is added to the powder to make wasabi. If you have wasabi paste, it may be used.

SALADS

Stuffed Louisiana Potatoes pg. 98; Sweet Potato Fries pg. 97; Spinach Gratin pg. 105

VEGETABLES & SIDES

WETLANDS FACT

The Gulf of Mexico provides a critical transportation link to move our trading products worldwide. It also provides essential habitat for migrating waterfowl, other birds, and many other species such as bullfrogs, alligators, dolphins and whales.

Gulf of Mexico Alliance

ASPARAGUS WITH LEMON CAPER VINAIGRETTE

MAKES 6 SERVINGS

Lemon Caper Vinaigrette turns asparagus into an amazing side. Also try splashing pesto-seasoned rice vinegar over asparagus for a quick snappy taste.

1 1/2 pounds asparagus spears, trimmed
Salt and pepper to taste
Lemon Caper Vinaigrette (recipe below)

1. Cook asparagus in a nonstick skillet coated with nonstick cooking spray, or heat in microwave, until crisp tender. Season to taste.

2. Transfer to serving platter and drizzle with Lemon Caper Vinaigrette.

LEMON CAPER VINAIGRETTE

1/4 cup lemon juice
1 tablespoon olive oil
3 tablespoons capers, drained
2 tablespoons finely chopped parsley
1 teaspoon minced garlic

1. Combine all ingredients.

NUTRITIONAL INFORMATION PER SERVING
Calories 49 | Calories from fat 40% | Fat 2 g
Saturated Fat 0 g | Cholesterol 0 mg | Sodium 128 mg
Carbohydrate 6 g | Dietary Fiber 3 g | Sugars 3 g | Protein 3 g

DIABETIC EXCHANGES
1 vegetable | 1/2 fat

BARLEY PILAF

MAKES 10 (1/2-CUP) SERVINGS

The earthy flavor of barley, with a hint of sweetness, perfectly complements wild game or meat.

1 cup medium pearl barley
3 1/2 cups vegetable or fat-free chicken broth
1 tablespoon butter
1/2 pound sliced mushrooms
1 bunch green onions, chopped
1/4 cup dried cherries or dried cranberries
1/4 cup sherry or cooking sherry
Salt and pepper to taste

1. In a pot, bring barley and broth to a boil. Reduce heat, cover, and cook for about 45–50 minutes, or until liquid is absorbed.

2. In a large nonstick skillet coated with nonstick cooking spray, melt butter and sauté mushrooms until tender, about 5 minutes. Add green onions and continue stirring.

3. In a small bowl, combine cherries and sherry, and let sit for 5 minutes. Add with barley to skillet, stirring continuously until well combined. Season to taste.

NUTRITIONAL INFORMATION PER SERVING
Calories 115 | Calories from fat 12% | Fat 2 g
Saturated Fat 1 g | Cholesterol 3 mg | Sodium 151 mg
Carbohydrate 21 g | Dietary Fiber 5 g | Sugars 3 g | Protein 4 g

DIABETIC EXCHANGES
1 1/2 starch

MAPLE BAKED BEANS

MAKES 10 (1/2-CUP) SERVINGS

Take a short cut with canned beans and add the rich sweetness of maple syrup. Omit the bacon for a vegetarian version.

1 onion, chopped

1/2 teaspoon minced garlic

1/4 cup pure maple syrup

1/4 cup molasses

1 cup chopped tomatoes

1/4 cup tomato sauce

1 teaspoon dry mustard

1 teaspoon ground ginger

2 tablespoons cider vinegar

3 (15-ounce) cans white navy or Great Northern beans, rinsed and drained

Salt and pepper to taste

2 strips center-cut bacon, cooked crispy and cut into pieces

1. Preheat oven to 300°F. Coat a large non-stick pot with nonstick cooking spray.

2. Sauté onion until tender, about 5 minutes. Add garlic and stir 30 seconds. Add remaining ingredients, except beans and bacon. Cook until well heated, about 5 minutes. Add beans, season to taste. Stir in bacon.

3. Transfer to a 1 1/2-quart baking dish. Cover and bake for about 35–45 minutes or until bubbly.

NUTRITIONAL INFORMATION PER SERVING
Calories 207 | Calories from fat 5% | Fat 1 g
Saturated Fat 0 g | Cholesterol 1 mg | Sodium 592 mg
Carbohydrate 40 g | Dietary Fiber 7 g | Sugars 13 g | Protein 10 g

DIABETIC EXCHANGES:
2 1/2 starch | 1/2 very lean meat

WHITE BEANS

MAKES 20 (1/2-CUP) SERVINGS

Leftover ham makes great white beans! This slow cooking recipe works well in a crock pot.

1 tablespoon canola oil

1 cup chopped celery

1 onion, chopped

2 teaspoons minced garlic

1 (16-ounce) package dried navy beans

8–10 cups low-sodium fat-free chicken or vegetable broth

2 bay leaves

1 teaspoon dried thyme leaves

1 (14 1/2-ounce) can chopped tomatoes with juice

1 pound leftover ham on bone or ham hocks

Salt and pepper to taste

1. In a large nonstick pot, heat oil and sauté celery, onion, and garlic until tender.

2. Add remaining ingredients and bring to a boil. Lower heat, cover, and simmer for 2 1/2 to 3 hours or until beans are tender.

3. Discard bay leaves and remove ham from the bone. Discard bone. Season to taste.

NUTRITIONAL INFORMATION PER SERVING
Calories 110 | Calories from fat 12% | Fat 2 g
Saturated Fat 0 g | Cholesterol 6 mg | Sodium 195 mg
Carbohydrate 16 g | Dietary Fiber 6 g | Sugars 2 g | Protein 9 g

DIABETIC EXCHANGES
1 starch | 1 very lean meat

VEGETABLES & SIDES

CAULIFLOWER AU GRATIN
MAKES 8 (1/2-CUP) SERVINGS

Cauliflower in a velvety white sauce topped with toasty walnuts makes an alluring side. Broccoli may also be used.

1 large head cauliflower, cut into florets
1/2 cup chopped onion
3 tablespoons all-purpose flour
2 cups skim milk
4 ounces Chavrie goat cheese (creamy)
Dash cayenne
Salt and pepper to taste
1/3 cup coarsely chopped walnuts

1. Cook cauliflower in a steamer, or in microwave, until tender. Arrange in a 1 1/2-quart baking dish.

2. In a nonstick pot coated with nonstick cooking spray, sauté onion until tender, about 5 minutes. Add flour and gradually stir in milk.

3. Bring to a boil, stirring. Boil for one minute, or until bubbly and thickened. Reduce heat and add cheese, stirring until melted. Add cayenne and season to taste.

4. Pour cheese sauce over cauliflower in baking dish and sprinkle with walnuts. Broil until walnuts are golden brown.

NUTRITIONAL INFORMATION PER SERVING
Calories 132 | Calories from fat 41% | Fat 6 g
Saturated Fat 2 g | Cholesterol 8 mg | Sodium 110 mg
Carbohydrate 13 g | Dietary Fiber 3 g | Sugars 6 g | Protein 8 g

DIABETIC EXCHANGES
1 vegetable | 1/2 carbohydrate | 1 medium-fat meat

BROCCOLI AND PECANS WITH CREAMY HORSERADISH SAUCE
MAKES 8 SERVINGS

Basic broccoli gets a makeover with toasty pecans and a spunky horseradish sauce.

6 cups broccoli florets
1/4 cup pecan halves
Salt and pepper to taste
1/4 cup light mayonnaise
3 tablespoons skim milk
1 tablespoon prepared horseradish
1/4 cup breadcrumbs
1 tablespoon grated Parmesan cheese

1. Preheat oven to 350°F.

2. In a covered microwave-safe container, microwave broccoli in 1/4 cup water for about 5 minutes, or until tender. Drain and transfer to a baking dish. Sprinkle with pecans. Season to taste.

3. In a small bowl, whisk together mayonnaise, milk, and horseradish. Pour over broccoli. Sprinkle with breadcrumbs and Parmesan cheese. Bake for 20–25 minutes until golden.

NUTRITIONAL INFORMATION PER SERVING
Calories 82 | Calories from fat 59% | Fat 5 g
Saturated Fat 1 g | Cholesterol 3 mg | Sodium 117 mg
Carbohydrate 7 g | Dietary Fiber 2 g | Sugars 1 g | Protein 3 g

DIABETIC EXCHANGES
1/2 carbohydrate | 1 fat

Broccoli and Pecans with Creamy Horseradish Sauce pg. 92

BUTTER PECAN BRUSSELS SPROUTS STIR-FRY

MAKES 4 SERVINGS

Many people don't like Brussels sprouts because they've never tasted fresh ones! Try them with this innovative preparation of shredding and stir frying with butter pecans.

1 pound fresh Brussels sprouts

1 tablespoon butter

1 tablespoon olive oil

3 tablespoons chopped pecans

Salt and pepper to taste

1. Cut ends off Brussels sprouts and slice into shreds with a knife.

2. In a nonstick skillet, heat butter and oil. Add pecans and cook over medium heat, stirring constantly, until lightly brown, about one minute.

3. Add shredded Brussels sprouts, stir, and cook for about 15 minutes or until tender. Season to taste.

NUTRITIONAL INFORMATION PER SERVING
Calories 112 | Calories from fat 51% | Fat 7 g
Saturated Fat 2 g | Cholesterol 8 mg | Sodium 49 mg
Carbohydrate 11 g | Dietary Fiber 5 g | Sugars 3 g | Protein 4 g

DIABETIC EXCHANGES
2 vegetable | 1 1/2 fat

CORN AND RICE

MAKES 10 (1/2-CUP) SERVINGS

Two family-pleasing sides join together for a quick and satisfying recipe. Use quick-cooking brown rice for a speedier dish.

1 cup chopped green onions

1 (16-ounce) package frozen corn, thawed

Salt and pepper to taste

1/2 cup vegetable or fat-free chicken broth

3 cups cooked brown rice (any rice may be used)

1/4 cup finely chopped parsley

1. In a large nonstick skillet coated with nonstick cooking spray, sauté green onions for several minutes.

2. Add corn, salt, pepper, and broth. Continue cooking until corn is done, about 2 minutes. Stir in rice and parsley, cooking until heated through, about 3 minutes.

NUTRITIONAL INFORMATION PER SERVING
Calories 115 | Calories from fat 6% | Fat 1 g
Saturated Fat 0 g | Cholesterol 0 mg | Sodium 29 mg
Carbohydrate 25 g | Dietary Fiber 3 g | Sugars 2 g | Protein 3 g

DIABETIC EXCHANGES
1 1/2 starch

TERRIFIC TIDBIT

When purchasing fresh Brussels sprouts, look for a bright green color, without yellow leaves.

CORN MAQUE-CHOUX

MAKES 8 SERVINGS

When sweet fresh summer corn is available, this is a time-honored southern favorite. For a short cut, you can use frozen corn and canned tomatoes.

8–10 ears fresh sweet corn (6 cups), cleaned and rinsed

2 onions, chopped

1 green bell pepper, cored and chopped

2 cups chopped tomatoes

2 teaspoons sugar

1/4 cup skim milk

Salt and pepper to taste

2 tablespoons canola oil

1. In a large bowl, use a sharp knife to shave kernels from cob, lengthwise down ear of corn. Scrape to extract any corn milk from the cob. Add remaining ingredients, except oil, and combine.

2. In a large nonstick pot, heat oil over medium heat. Add corn mixture, stirring to coat, then lower heat.

3. Cover and cook about 20–30 minutes or until corn is tender, stirring frequently. If mixture becomes too dry, add more milk.

NUTRITIONAL INFORMATION PER SERVING
Calories 159 | Calories from fat 25% | Fat 5 g
Saturated Fat 0 g | Cholesterol 0 mg | Sodium 24 mg
Carbohydrate 29 g | Dietary Fiber 5 g | Sugars 9 g | Protein 5 g

DIABETIC EXCHANGES
1 1/2 starch | 1 vegetable | 1/2 fat

SOUTHERN OKRA SUCCOTASH

MAKES 8 (1/2-CUP) SERVINGS

I raided my pantry one evening and made this fantastic one skillet dish in a snap.

1 tablespoon olive oil

1 pound fresh or frozen cut okra

1 cup frozen corn

1 (10-ounce) can diced tomatoes and green chilies

1 (15-ounce) can white navy beans, rinsed and drained

Salt and pepper to taste

1. In a nonstick skillet, heat oil over medium heat and stir-fry okra for several minutes. Add remaining ingredients, mixing well.

2. Cover and cook over low heat for 15 minutes or until okra is tender, stirring occasionally. Season to taste.

NUTRITIONAL INFORMATION PER SERVING
Calories 118 | Calories from fat 16% | Fat 2 g
Saturated Fat 0 g | Cholesterol 0 mg | Sodium 367 mg
Carbohydrate 21 g | Dietary Fiber 5 g | Sugars 2 g | Protein 6 g

DIABETIC EXCHANGES
1 starch | 1 vegetable

TERRIFIC TIDBIT

Easy okra: Microwave whole okra in shallow dish with 3 tablespoons seasoned rice vinegar and 1 tablespoon canola oil, covered for 4–5 minutes or until tender.

VEGETABLES & SIDES

ONE STEP MACARONI AND CHEESE

MAKES 10–12 SERVINGS

No boiling pasta for this all-in-one recipe which easier than using a box mix. My aunt always added sugar for a touch of sweetness, so I do too.

5 cups skim milk

1 egg

3 tablespoons sugar

1 tablespoon butter, melted

1 (16-ounce) package small sea shell pasta or macaroni

Salt and pepper to taste

2 cups shredded reduced-fat Cheddar cheese

1. Preheat oven to 350°F.

2. In a bowl, whisk together milk, egg, and sugar.

3. In a 2-quart oblong baking dish, combine remaining ingredients. Pour milk mixture over macaroni and stir well.

4. Bake, covered, for 60-65 minutes or until all liquid is almost absorbed. Uncover, and continue baking 10 minutes more.

NUTRITIONAL INFORMATION PER SERVING
Calories 255 | Calories from fat 19% | Fat 5 g
Saturated Fat 3 g | Cholesterol 32 mg | Sodium 178 mg
Carbohydrate 37 g | Dietary Fiber 1 g | Sugars 10 g | Protein 14 g

DIABETIC EXCHANGES
2 starch | 1/2 fat-free milk | 1 lean meat

GREEN BEAN CASSEROLE

MAKES 6 SERVINGS

An old classic gets a face lift!

1 small onion, finely chopped

1/2 pound sliced mushrooms

1/2 teaspoon minced garlic

1/4 cup all-purpose flour

2 cups skim milk

1/4 cup nonfat sour cream

Salt and pepper to taste

2 (9-ounce) packages frozen green beans

1/2 cup breadcrumbs (fresh preferred)

1. Preheat oven to 425°F. Coat a large non-stick pot and a 2-quart baking dish with nonstick cooking spray

2. Sauté onion, mushrooms, and garlic for 3–5 minutes or until tender. Sprinkle with flour and cook for 1 minute. Gradually add milk, whisking constantly.

3. Bring to a boil, reduce heat, and cook, stirring until thickened. Remove from heat. Whisk in sour cream and season to taste. Add green beans and mix well.

4. Transfer to prepared baking dish and sprinkle with breadcrumbs. Bake for 15–20 minutes or until bubbly.

NUTRITIONAL INFORMATION PER SERVING
Calories 114 | Calories from fat 12% | Fat 2 g
Saturated Fat 1 g | Cholesterol 7 mg | Sodium 166 mg
Carbohydrate 19 g | Dietary Fiber 3 g | Sugars 9 g | Protein 7 g

DIABETIC EXCHANGES
1 starch | 1 vegetable

SOUTHWESTERN ROASTED VEGETABLES

MAKES 6–8 SERVINGS

A simple package of taco seasoning gives roasted vegetables a kick of flavor.

4 cups peeled sweet potatoes (yams), cut in 1-inch chunks

1 1/2 cups zucchini slices, halved

1 cup yellow squash slices, halved

1 small red onion, cut into small chunks

1/2 pound mushrooms, halved

2 tablespoons olive oil

3 tablespoons taco seasoning mix

Salt to taste

1. Preheat oven to 425°F. Coat a baking sheet with nonstick cooking spray or line with foil.

2. In a large bowl, combine sweet potatoes, zucchini, squash, onion, and mushrooms. Coat with oil and toss with taco seasoning, coating well.

3. Spread onto prepared baking sheet and bake for 40 minutes, or until tender and roasted, shaking pan every 15 minutes. Season to taste.

NUTRITIONAL INFORMATION PER SERVING
Calories 113 | Calories from fat 28% | Fat 4 g
Saturated Fat 1 g | Cholesterol 0 mg | Sodium 210 mg
Carbohydrate 19 g | Dietary Fiber 3 g | Sugars 5 g | Protein 3 g

DIABETIC EXCHANGES
1 starch | 1 vegetable | 1 fat

SWEET POTATO FRIES

MAKES 4–6 SERVINGS

A fantastic, healthier alternative to greasy fries, and they're just as good!

4 sweet potatoes (yams), peeled

2 tablespoons olive oil

Salt and pepper to taste

Chopped parsley (optional)

1. Preheat oven to 400°F. Coat a baking sheet with nonstick cooking spray or line with foil.

2. Cut sweet potatoes into 1/2-inch thick lengthwise strips and toss with oil. Arrange in a single layer on baking sheet and bake for 15–20 minutes.

3. Turn potatoes over and bake for 15–20 minutes or until golden brown all over. Season to taste and sprinkle with parsley.

NUTRITIONAL INFORMATION PER SERVING
Calories 142 | Calories from fat 29% | Fat 5 g
Saturated Fat 1 g | Cholesterol 0 mg | Sodium 71 mg
Carbohydrate 23 g | Dietary Fiber 4 g | Sugars 7 g | Protein 2 g

DIABETIC EXCHANGES
1 1/2 starch | 1 fat

TERRIFIC TIDBIT

For a sweeter version, omit parsley and sprinkle with cinnamon and nutmeg before baking.

VEGETABLES & SIDES

STUFFED LOUISIANA POTATOES

MAKES 6–8 SERVINGS

These seafood filled spuds make a super side, or a light lunch. Use your choice of cheese or seafood depending on availability. Great to make ahead and refrigerate or freeze, before baking, to pull out on those busy days.

6–8 small or medium baking potatoes (about 4 pounds)

Olive oil

2 tablespoons butter

1 cup nonfat sour cream

Dash hot sauce

Salt and pepper to taste

1 pound crawfish tails, small peeled shrimp, seasoned and cooked, or crabmeat (or combination)

1 bunch green onions, chopped

1 cup shredded reduced-fat Cheddar cheese

Paprika to sprinkle

1. Preheat oven to 400°F. Wash potatoes and rub with oil. Place directly on oven rack, and bake for about one hour or until soft when squeezed.

2. Cut a thin slice off the top of each potato lengthwise. Scoop out insides and place in a bowl, leaving a thin shell. With a mixer, or by hand, mash potato flesh with butter and sour cream. Add hot sauce and season to taste. Add remaining ingredients except paprika, mixing gently.

3. Spoon potato mixture into empty shells and sprinkle with paprika. Bake for about 10–15 minutes, or until cheese is melted and potatoes are heated.

NUTRITIONAL INFORMATION PER SERVING
Calories 334 | Calories from fat 17% | Fat 6 g
Saturated Fat 4 g | Cholesterol 98 mg | Sodium 206 mg
Carbohydrate 48 g | Dietary Fiber 4 g | Sugars 4 g | Protein 21 g

DIABETIC EXCHANGES
3 starch | 2 lean meat

TERRIFIC TIDBIT

Louisiana crawfish tails are found in bags fresh or frozen. Depending on the size of the potato, halves may be filled instead of whole potatoes.

trim&TERRIFIC™ GULF COAST FAVORITES

ROASTED GARLIC MASHED POTATOES

MAKES 4–6 SERVINGS

Basic mashed potatoes infused with a subtle garlic essence perfectly accentuate any meal.

2 pounds baking potatoes, peeled and cubed

Water (enough to cover potatoes)

2 tablespoons butter

3/4 cup buttermilk

1 bulb Roasted Garlic (recipe to the right), or 2 tablespoons roasted garlic from jar

Salt and pepper to taste

1. Place potatoes in a pot and add water. Bring to a boil, reduce heat, cover, and cook about 15–20 minutes, or until potatoes are tender.

2. Drain and return potatoes to pan. Add remaining ingredients and mash to desired consistency.

NUTRITIONAL INFORMATION PER SERVING
Calories 173 | Calories from fat 21% | Fat 4 g
Saturated Fat 3 g | Cholesterol 11 mg | Sodium 67 mg
Carbohydrate 30 g | Dietary Fiber 2 g | Sugars 2 g | Protein 5 g

DIABETIC EXCHANGES
2 starch | 1/2 fat

TERRIFIC TIDBIT

Use a potato masher to mash by hand or an electric mixer to whip quickly. A food processor will over mix the potatoes and can make them gummy. The key is to not over mix.

ROASTED GARLIC

MAKES ABOUT 2 TABLESPOONS

When I roast garlic, I usually do several heads at a time. Freshly roasted garlic is also superb served on hot bread instead of butter.

1 large head garlic

Olive oil

Salt and pepper

1. Preheat oven to 400°F. Remove white, papery outer layer from garlic, leaving head intact. (Do not peel or separate cloves).

2. Cut off top 1/4 inch of cloves, brush with olive oil and season to taste. Wrap in foil and bake for 40 minutes or until soft.

3. When cool, squeeze soft garlic pulp from cloves by pushing hard on the garlic head.

MICROWAVE GARLIC

For the no-time-to-wait version, try microwaving the oil-coated garlic cloves, unpeeled, on high for 1 minute or until you begin to smell them. This isn't as good as oven-roasted garlic, but it softens the flavor as roasting does, when you need it quickly!

BOURBON MASHED SWEET POTATOES

MAKES 10 (1/2-CUP) SERVINGS

Sweet potatoes with brown sugar and Creole seasoning give this dish a sweet-salty taste and a touch of bourbon finishes it off. The Praline Topping adds an unforgettable final touch.

4 cups mashed cooked sweet potatoes (yams), about 3 1/2 pounds sweet potatoes, or 2 (29-ounce) cans sweet potatoes, drained and mashed

1/3 cup light brown sugar

1 teaspoon Creole seasoning

1 teaspoon ground cinnamon

1/4 cup skim milk

2 tablespoons butter, melted

1/4 cup bourbon (may be omitted)

Praline Topping (recipe to the right), optional

1. Place all ingredients in a bowl and blend until creamy. If not using topping, transfer to serving dish.

2. If using Praline Topping, transfer to a baking dish and follow recipe directions.

NUTRITIONAL INFORMATION PER SERVING
(NOT INCLUDING TOPPING)
Calories 167 | Calories from fat 13% | Fat 2 g
Saturated Fat 1 g | Cholesterol 6 mg | Sodium 89 mg
Carbohydrate 31 g | Dietary Fiber 3 g | Sugars 15 g | Protein 2 g

DIABETIC EXCHANGES
2 starch

PRALINE TOPPING

It's so hard to resist this topping!

2/3 cup all-purpose flour

2/3 cup light brown sugar

1/4 cup butter

1 teaspoon vanilla extract

1/3 cup chopped pecans

1. Preheat oven to 350°F.

2. In a bowl, combine all ingredients except pecans with a fork until crumbly. Add pecans and stir.

3. Sprinkle over sweet potatoes and bake for about 40 minutes or until topping is lightly browned.

NUTRITIONAL INFORMATION PER SERVING
Calories 154 | Calories from fat 43% | Fat 7 g
Saturated Fat 3 g | Cholesterol 12 mg | Sodium 38 mg
Carbohydrate 21 g | Dietary Fiber 1 g | Sugars 14 g | Protein 1 g

DIABETIC EXCHANGES
1 1/2 carbohydrate | 1/2 fat

TERRIFIC TIDBIT
Sweet potatoes from Louisiana are referred to as "yams" as they are the sweetest and moistest of sweet potatoes because of the climate and soil in Louisiana. Look for Louisiana yams in the supermarkets.

LEMON SWEET POTATO CASSEROLE

MAKES 10–12 SERVINGS

Make this lemon-lover's easy sweet potato casserole by simply tossing the ingredients together into one dish. Use a food processor for a quick method to shred sweet potatoes.

6 cups shredded peeled sweet potatoes (yams) (about 3 medium)

2 tablespoons butter, melted

1/2 cup sugar

1 cup skim milk

2 eggs

1/2 teaspoon ground cinnamon

1 (4-serving) box instant lemon pudding and pie filling

1. Preheat oven to 325°F.

2. Combine all ingredients in a 2-quart oblong casserole dish.

3. Cover tightly with foil and bake for 1 hour. Remove foil and continue cooking 20–30 minutes or until top is golden brown.

NUTRITIONAL INFORMATION PER SERVING
Calories 157 | Calories from fat 15% | Fat 3 g
Saturated Fat 1 g | Cholesterol 41 mg | Sodium 180 mg
Carbohydrate 31 g | Dietary Fiber 2 g | Sugars 12 g | Protein 3 g

DIABETIC EXCHANGES
2 starch

TWO POTATO ROAST

MAKES 6–8 SERVINGS

I turn to this simple-to-prepare side for a guaranteed hit. Any variety of potatoes may be used.

1 pound sweet potatoes (yams), peeled and cut into small chunks

1 pound red potatoes, unpeeled and cut into small chunks

1 tablespoon minced garlic

1/4 cup chopped green onions

2 tablespoons olive oil

Salt and pepper to taste

1. Preheat oven to 450°F. Coat a baking sheet with nonstick cooking spray, or line with foil.

2. In a large bowl, combine all ingredients and transfer to prepared pan.

3. Bake about 40–50 minutes or until potatoes are browned, stirring every 15–20 minutes.

NUTRITIONAL INFORMATION PER SERVING
Calories 136 | Calories from fat 22% | Fat 3 g
Saturated Fat 0 g | Cholesterol 0 mg | Sodium 36 mg
Carbohydrate 22 g | Dietary Fiber 3 g | Sugars 3 g | Protein 2 g

DIABETIC EXCHANGES
1 1/2 starch | 1/2 fat

TERRIFIC TIDBIT
Sweet potatoes are packed with beta-carotene, vitamin B6, iron, potassium, and fiber. They have virtually no fat or sodium, and are low in calories.

VEGETABLES & SIDES

Red Beans and Rice pg. 103

RED BEANS AND RICE
MAKES 10 (1/2-CUP) SERVINGS

This Deep South favorite is served at most restaurants on Mondays in Louisiana. Try my easy home version using canned beans. Serve over rice with hot cornbread.

8 ounces reduced-fat sausage, sliced into 1/2-inch thick rounds

1 onion, chopped

1/3 cup chopped celery

1 teaspoon minced garlic

3 (16-ounce) cans red kidney beans, rinsed and drained

1/2 cup tomato sauce

1 1/2 cups fat-free chicken broth

Salt and pepper to taste

1/3 cup chopped parsley

1/2 cup chopped green onions

1. In a large nonstick skillet coated with nonstick cooking spray, cook sausage over medium heat, stirring, until crispy brown. Set aside.

2. In a large nonstick pot coated with nonstick cooking spray, sauté onion, celery, and garlic until tender, about 5–7 minutes.

3. Add beans, tomato sauce, broth, and sausage. Season to taste. Bring to a boil, reduce heat, and cover. Simmer for about 8–10 minutes, or until thickened, mashing some of the beans with a fork.

4. Add parsley and green onions, and continue cooking several more minutes.

NUTRITIONAL INFORMATION PER SERVING
Calories 178 | Calories from fat 8% | Fat 2 g
Saturated Fat 0 g | Cholesterol 8 mg | Sodium 601 mg
Carbohydrate 27 g | Dietary Fiber 8 g | Sugars 5 g | Protein 12 g

DIABETIC EXCHANGES
2 starch | 1 very lean meat

VEGETABLES & SIDES

STIR FRIED VEGETABLE RICE

MAKES 4–6 SERVINGS

My standard fried rice recipe always hits the spot. Try adding cooked shrimp or chicken!

2 egg whites, lightly beaten

2 tablespoons sesame oil, divided

1/2 cup chopped onion

1 teaspoon minced garlic

2 tablespoons low-sodium soy sauce

3 cups cooked brown rice

1 cup chopped green onions

1 (5-ounce) can sliced water chestnuts, drained

1/2 cup shelled edamame, cooked according to package directions

1. In a small nonstick skillet coated with nonstick cooking spray, cook egg whites without stirring (as you would with an omelet) until almost dry. Remove from pan, cut into thin strips, and set aside.

2. In a large nonstick skillet, heat 1 tablespoon oil and sauté onion and garlic until tender, about 5–7 minutes. Stir in soy sauce and rice.

3. Cook for about 3 minutes, stirring frequently. Add remaining ingredients, remaining oil, and egg strips. Stir-fry for 1 minute to heat through.

NUTRITIONAL INFORMATION PER SERVING
Calories 198 | Calories from fat 28% | Fat 6 g
Saturated Fat 1 g | Cholesterol 0 mg | Sodium 236 g
Carbohydrate 30 g | Dietary Fiber 5 g | Sugars 3 g | Protein 6 g

DIABETIC EXCHANGES
1 1/2 starch | 1 vegetable | 1 fat

CREAMY GARLIC HERB SPINACH

MAKES 10 (1/2-CUP) SERVINGS

A creamy, garlic spinach side that's as good as any you order at a steak restaurant.

3 (10-ounce) packages frozen chopped spinach, reserve 1/2 cup spinach liquid from cooking

1 onion, chopped

1 teaspoon minced garlic

3 tablespoons all-purpose flour

1 1/2 cups evaporated skim milk

3/4 cup light garlic and herb spreadable cheese

Salt and pepper to taste

1. Cook spinach according to package directions. Drain well, reserving 1/2 cup spinach liquid. Set aside.

2. In a medium nonstick pot coated with nonstick cooking spray, sauté onion and garlic until tender. Add flour and stir. Gradually add milk and spinach liquid to make sauce. Cook over medium heat, stirring, until mixture is bubbly and thickened.

3. Add cheese, stirring until melted. Add cooked spinach and mix well. Season to taste.

NUTRITIONAL INFORMATION PER SERVING
Calories 110 | Calories from fat 30% | Fat 4 g
Saturated Fat 2 g | Cholesterol 14 mg | Sodium 156 mg
Carbohydrate 13 g | Dietary Fiber 3 g | Sugars 8 g | Protein 8 g

DIABETIC EXCHANGES
1 carbohydrate | 1 lean meat

SPINACH GRATIN

MAKES 14 (1/2-CUP) SERVINGS

Spinach cooked in a wonderful white sauce with a crunchy baked topping makes this side stupendous. The recipe may be made ahead of time and baked when ready.

1 tablespoon butter

1 1/2 cups chopped onion

1/4 cup all-purpose flour

1/4 teaspoon ground nutmeg

2 cups skim milk

1 1/2 cups fat-free half-and-half

5 (10-ounce) packages frozen chopped spinach, thawed and squeezed dry

1 cup shredded light Swiss or Jarlsberg cheese

2/3 cup grated Parmesan cheese, divided

Salt and pepper to taste

1. Preheat oven to 425°F. Coat a 2-quart baking dish with nonstick cooking spray.

2. In a large nonstick pot, melt butter and sauté onion until very tender, about 7-10 minutes. Add flour and nutmeg, stirring for 30 seconds. Gradually add milk and half-and-half, cooking over medium heat until bubbly and thickened.

3. Add spinach, Swiss cheese, and 1/3 cup Parmesan cheese. Season to taste.

4. Transfer to prepared dish and sprinkle with remaining Parmesan cheese. Bake for 20 minutes or until hot and bubbly.

NUTRITIONAL INFORMATION PER SERVING
Calories 125 | Calories from fat 27% | Fat 4 g
Saturated Fat 2 g | Cholesterol 10 mg | Sodium 192 mg
Carbohydrate 14 g | Dietary Fiber 4 g | Sugars 5 g | Protein 12 g

DIABETIC EXCHANGES
1 vegetable | 1/2 fat-free milk | 1/2 lean meat

TERRIFIC TIDBIT

To remove all the liquid from frozen spinach, wrap thawed spinach in a dish towel or cheese-cloth and squeeze until dry.

VEGETABLES & SIDES

SPINACH PROSCIUTTO RAVIOLI

MAKES 10–12 SERVINGS

A spinach, ricotta, and prosciutto filling served in an oregano cream sauce creates an exceptional light entree or side. Easy-to-use won ton wrappers keep this recipe from being time consuming.

1 (10-ounce) package frozen chopped spinach, thawed and squeezed dry

1 (15-ounce) container part-skim ricotta cheese

4 ounces thinly sliced prosciutto, chopped

1 egg white

Salt and pepper to taste

48 won ton wrappers

1 tablespoon butter

1/2 cup chopped tomatoes

1/2 cup chopped onion

1 cup fat-free half-and-half

1 teaspoon dried oregano leaves

1. In a medium bowl, combine spinach, ricotta, prosciutto, egg white, salt, and pepper.

2. Place 1 heaping teaspoon of spinach mixture in the center of a won ton wrapper. Brush edge of wrapper lightly with water. Fold wrapper in half, enclosing filling completely and forming a triangle. Pinch edges to seal. Transfer to a baking sheet. Repeat with remaining filling and wrappers.

3. Bring a large pot of water to boil. Add ravioli in batches and cook until tender, about 4 minutes. Ravioli will float to top when done. Transfer with a slotted spoon to a plate.

4. In a large nonstick skillet, melt butter and sauté tomatoes and onion until tender, about 5 minutes. Add half-and-half and cook over medium heat, stirring, for about 5–7 minutes. Add oregano. Toss ravioli in cream sauce and serve.

NUTRITIONAL INFORMATION PER SERVING
Calories 191 | Calories from fat 25% | Fat 6 g
Saturated Fat 3 g | Cholesterol 28 mg | Sodium 287 mg
Carbohydrate 25 g | Dietary Fiber 2 g | Sugars 4 g | Protein 12 g

DIABETIC EXCHANGES
1 1/2 starch | 1 medium-fat meat

TERRIFIC TIDBIT

Fill the won ton wrappers ahead of time, refrigerate, and boil when ready to serve. Omit the proscuitto for a vegetarian version.

WILD RICE AND OYSTER DISH

MAKES 8–10 SERVINGS

This dish will steal the show! Crispy oysters top this deliciously creamy wild rice, creating just the right blend of flavors.

2 tablespoons olive oil

1/2 cup chopped onion

1/2 pound sliced mushrooms (I prefer portabella mushrooms)

3 tablespoons all-purpose flour

1 1/4 cups skim milk

3 tablespoons sherry (optional)

Salt and pepper to taste

6 cups cooked wild rice

1 pint small oysters, well drained

2 tablespoons butter, melted

1/2 cup plain breadcrumbs

2 tablespoons chopped parsley

2 tablespoons chopped green onion stems

1. Preheat broiler. Coat a 3-quart baking dish with nonstick cooking spray

2. In a large nonstick skillet, heat oil and sauté onions and mushrooms until tender, about 5 minutes. Add flour and stir for 1 minute. Gradually stir in milk, cooking until mixture comes to a boil and thickens. Add sherry and season to taste.

3. Remove from heat and combine with wild rice in prepared baking dish, mixing well. Roll oysters in butter, and coat with breadcrumbs. Arrange on top of rice.

4. Place baking dish under broiler on middle rack and broil for 10 minutes, or until oyster edges begin to curl and are browned and crispy. Sprinkle with parsley and green onions. Serve immediately.

NUTRITIONAL INFORMATION PER SERVING
Calories 229 | Calories from fat 26% | Fat 7 g
Saturated Fat 3 g | Cholesterol 40 mg | Sodium 202 mg
Carbohydrate 32 g | Dietary Fiber 3 g | Sugars 3 g | Protein 11 g

DIABETIC EXCHANGES
2 starch | 1 very lean meat | 1 fat

TERRIFIC TIDBIT

The rice may be made ahead of time, but the oyster topping needs to be assembled fresh when serving.

Veggie Paella pg. 109

VEGGIE PAELLA

MAKES 8 SERVINGS

Deceptively easy, this colorful recipe boasts a balance of flavor and nutrition.

1 tablespoon olive oil

1 cup chopped onion

1 red bell pepper, cored and chopped

1 cup sliced mushrooms

1 teaspoon minced garlic

2 (5-ounce) packages yellow rice

Water (according to rice package directions)

1 cup chopped tomatoes

1 (15-ounce) can black beans, rinsed and drained

1 (10-ounce) package frozen peas, thawed

1/2 teaspoon paprika

1 teaspoon dried basil leaves

1. In a large nonstick pot, heat oil and sauté onion, pepper, mushrooms, and garlic about 5–7 minutes.

2. Add rice and water and bring to a boil. Reduce heat, cover, and cook for 20–25 minutes or until rice is done.

3. Stir in remaining ingredients and cook until heated through.

NUTRITIONAL INFORMATION PER SERVING
Calories 227 | Calories from fat 9% | Fat 2 g
Saturated Fat 0 g | Cholesterol 0 mg | Sodium 668 mg
Carbohydrate 43 g | Dietary Fiber 6 g | Sugars 5 g | Protein 9 g

DIABETIC EXCHANGES
2 1/2 starch | 1 vegetable

ZUCCHINI AU GRATIN

MAKES 8 (3/4-CUP) SERVINGS

Garden fresh sautéed zucchini and tomatoes cooked in a white sauce are divine.

1 tablespoon butter

1 onion, chopped

2 pounds zucchini, sliced 1/4-inch thick (about 6 cups)

1 1/2 cups chopped tomatoes

1/4 teaspoon ground nutmeg

Salt and pepper to taste

2 tablespoons all-purpose flour

3/4 cup skim milk

1 cup shredded, reduced-fat, Jarlsberg or Swiss cheese

1. Preheat oven to 350°F. Coat a large nonstick skillet with nonstick cooking spray.

2. Melt butter and sauté onion over medium heat for 5 minutes, stirring continuously. Add zucchini and cook, covered, for 10 minutes, stirring occasionally. Add tomatoes and cook another 5 minutes.

3. Add nutmeg and season to taste. Stir in flour and gradually add milk. Cook over medium heat, stirring continuously, until thickened and bubbly.

4. Pour into an 11 × 7 × 2-inch baking dish. Top with cheese and bake for 12–15 minutes, or until bubbly and cheese is melted.

NUTRITIONAL INFORMATION PER SERVING
Calories 98 | Calories from fat 37% | Fat 4 g
Saturated Fat 2 g | Cholesterol 11 mg | Sodium 54 mg
Carbohydrate 10 g | Dietary Fiber 2 g | Sugars 5 g | Protein 8 g

DIABETIC EXCHANGES
2 vegetable | 1 lean meat

VEGETABLES & SIDES

Spicy Fish with Shrimp Corn Sauté pg. 115

SEAFOOD

BAKED PARMESAN TROUT

MAKES 6–8 SERVINGS

A quick, easy, and exceptionally good way to dress up any mild fish. This recipe tastes just as good the next day.

2 pounds trout fillets (or any mild fish)
Salt and pepper to taste
3/4 cup nonfat sour cream
2 tablespoons finely chopped onion
1/2 teaspoon minced garlic
2 tablespoons lemon juice
1/2 teaspoon hot sauce
1/3 cup grated Parmesan cheese
Paprika to sprinkle

1. Preheat oven to 350°F. Coat a baking pan with nonstick cooking spray.

2. Season fish to taste and place in a single layer in prepared pan. In a small bowl, combine remaining ingredients, except paprika. Spread over fish and let sit for 10 minutes. Sprinkle with paprika.

3. Bake for 25 minutes or until fish flakes easily with fork. Serve immediately.

NUTRITIONAL INFORMATION PER SERVING
Calories 174 | Calories from fat 25% | Fat 5 g
Saturated Fat 1 g | Cholesterol 74 mg | Sodium 107 mg
Carbohydrate 5 g | Dietary Fiber 0 g | Sugars 2 g | Protein 26 g

DIABETIC EXCHANGES
3 lean meat

PECAN-CRUSTED TROUT

MAKES 6–8 SERVINGS

Give this fantastic crunchy pecan-crusted fish a try! This recipe works equally as good with catfish.

1/3 cup chopped pecans
2/3 cup Italian breadcrumbs
1 egg white
1/3 cup skim milk
2 pounds trout fillets (or any mild fish)
Salt and pepper to taste
1/3 cup all-purpose flour

1. In a food processor, process pecans until finely ground. Combine ground pecans with breadcrumbs on plate.

2. In a small shallow bowl, whisk together egg white and milk. Set aside.

3. Season fish to taste, dust with flour, and dip in egg mixture. Press fish into bread-crumb mixture, coat thoroughly.

4. Heat a large nonstick skillet coated with nonstick cooking spray and cook fish about 5 minutes on each side, or until fish flakes easily with fork.

NUTRITIONAL INFORMATION PER SERVING
Calories 231 g | Calories from fat 30% | Fat 8 g
Saturated Fat 1 g | Cholesterol 67 mg | Sodium 190 mg
Carbohydrate 12 g | Dietary Fiber 1 g | Sugars 1 g | Protein 26 g

DIABETIC EXCHANGES
1 starch | 3 lean meat

TROUT WITH SPICY PECANS

MAKES 6 SERVINGS

Seasoned fish topped with spicy pecans turns an ordinary dish into a meal with sass. This crispy fish will entice those who miss fried foods. The pecans may be omitted for simple pan-fried fish.

6 (4–6 ounce) trout fillets (about 1 1/2 pounds)

Salt and pepper to taste

1 1/2 cups all-purpose flour

1/2 cup skim milk

1 egg white, beaten

3 tablespoons canola oil

Spicy Pecans (recipe to the right)

Green onions, chopped

1. Season fish to taste. In a bowl, season flour to taste.

2. In a shallow bowl, combine milk and egg white. Coat fish with seasoned flour, dip in milk mixture, and coat again with flour.

3. In a large nonstick skillet coated with nonstick cooking spray, heat oil and cook fish, over medium heat, until flaky and golden brown on each side.

4. Top with Spicy Pecans and sprinkle with green onions.

NUTRITIONAL INFORMATION PER SERVING
(NOT INCLUDING PECANS)
Calories 320 | Calories from fat 33% | Fat 11 g
Saturated Fat 1 g | Cholesterol 67 g | Sodium 54 g
Carbohydrate 25 g | Dietary Fiber 1 g | Sugars 1 g | Protein 28 g

DIABETIC EXCHANGES
1 1/2 starch | 3 lean meat

SPICY PECANS

These pecans will jazz up any recipe.

1 tablespoon canola oil

1 teaspoon minced garlic

1/3 cup pecan halves

Salt to taste

1 tablespoon Worcestershire sauce

Dash hot sauce

1 tablespoon lemon juice

1. In a nonstick skillet, heat oil and sauté garlic and pecans until pecans are light brown.

2. Add remaining ingredients and heat thoroughly.

NUTRITIONAL INFORMATION PER SERVING
(PECANS ONLY)
Calories 65 | Calories from fat 86% | Fat 7 g
Saturated Fat 1 g | Cholesterol 0 mg | Sodium 28 mg
Carbohydrate 2 g | Dietary Fiber 1 g | Sugars 1 g | Protein 1 g

DIABETIC EXCHANGES
1 1/2 fat

TERRIFIC TIDBIT

Other Gulf Coast fish include: amberjack, flounder, grouper, speckled trout, mahi mahi, and catfish.

SEAFOOD

DIJON FISH WITH SPINACH AND TOMATOES

MAKES 4–6 SERVINGS

Dijon-Italian dressing spruces up quickly broiled fish and adds a jolt of flavor to this simple six-ingredient recipe.

1/4 cup Dijon mustard

1/4 cup reduced-fat Italian dressing

1 1/2 pounds fish fillets

1/2 cup chopped onion

1 (10-ounce) bag fresh baby spinach

1 cup chopped tomatoes

1. Preheat broiler. Coat a baking pan with nonstick cooking spray or line with foil.

2. In a small bowl, combine mustard and Italian dressing. Arrange fish on prepared pan and brush half the mixture over fish.

3. Broil fish for 8–10 minutes or until topping is golden and fish flakes easily. Watch carefully that it doesn't burn.

4. In a large nonstick skillet, sauté onion in remaining mixture for 3–5 minutes or until tender. Add spinach and tomatoes, and continue sautéing until spinach is wilted and tomatoes are tender. Serve fish over spinach mixture.

NUTRITIONAL INFORMATION PER SERVING
Calories 134 | Calories from fat 19% | Fat 3 g
Saturated Fat 0 g | Cholesterol 43 mg | Sodium 393 mg
Carbohydrate 7 g | Dietary Fiber 2 g | Sugars 3 g | Protein 21 g

DIABETIC EXCHANGES
1/2 carbohydrate | 3 very lean meat

FISH WITH HORSERADISH DILL CAPER SAUCE

MAKES 6–8 SERVINGS

A simple, flavorful horseradish, mustard, and dill sauce perks up baked fish. Any type of fish may be used, so pick your favorite, and prepare for a enjoyable dinner.

2 pounds fish fillets (trout, red fish, orange roughy, tilapia, or your favorite)

Salt and pepper to taste

1/2 cup plain nonfat yogurt

1 teaspoon cornstarch

1 tablespoon prepared horseradish

2 teaspoons dry mustard

1/4 cup grated Parmesan cheese

2 tablespoons lemon juice

1 teaspoon dried dill weed leaves

1 tablespoon capers, drained

1. Preheat oven to 375°F. Line a baking sheet with foil and coat with nonstick cooking spray.

2. Season fish to taste. In a small bowl, combine remaining ingredients. Dip each fish fillet into the mixture and lay on prepared pan.

3. Bake for 20–25 minutes or until fish flakes easily with a fork.

NUTRITIONAL INFORMATION PER SERVING
Calories 162 | Calories from fat 27% | Fat 5 g
Saturated Fat 1 g | Cholesterol 69 mg | Sodium 123 mg
Carbohydrate 2 g | Dietary Fiber 0 g | Sugars 1 g | Protein 25 g

DIABETIC EXCHANGES
3 lean meat

SPICY FISH WITH SHRIMP CORN SAUTÉ

MAKES 6–8 SERVINGS

This well-seasoned fish is flawlessly complemented by sweet mild corn, making this the perfect pairing for a flavor-packed meal.

2 tablespoons paprika

2 tablespoons ground cumin

Salt and pepper to taste

2 pounds trout fillets (or fish of choice)

2 tablespoons canola oil

1 small red onion, chopped

1 green bell pepper, cored and chopped

1 teaspoon minced garlic

1/2 pound small peeled shrimp

1 jalapeño, cored and finely chopped

1 cup frozen corn, thawed

Dash sugar

2 tablespoons lime juice

1. In a small bowl, combine paprika, cumin, salt, and pepper. Sprinkle on both sides of fish.

2. In a large nonstick skillet, heat oil and sauté fish on each side, about 3 minutes or until it is opaque and flakes easily with fork. Remove fish from pan and set aside.

3. In the same pan, sauté onion and green pepper for several minutes. Add garlic, shrimp, and jalapeño, cooking over medium heat until shrimp are done, about 5 minutes.

4. Add remaining ingredients and cook for 2 minutes. Season to taste and serve with fish.

NUTRITIONAL INFORMATION PER SERVING
Calories 227 | Calories from fat 32% | Fat 8 g
Saturated Fat 1 g | Cholesterol 109 mg | Sodium 89 mg
Carbohydrate 9 g | Dietary Fiber 2 g | Sugars 3 g | Protein 29 g

DIABETIC EXCHANGES
1/2 starch | 4 lean meat

TERRIFIC TIDBIT

Try this recipe with flounder, redfish, or catfish.

SEAFOOD

Simply Sensational Fish Carlysle pg. 117; Sweet Potato Fries pg. 97

SIMPLY SENSATIONAL FISH CARLYSLE

MAKES 4–6 SERVINGS

My buddy, Don, keeps me spoiled with his fresh fish, and my photographer, David, gave me the scoop on his divine Carlysle Sauce. The fish is also tasty served alone without the sauce. Adjust the seafood to preference and availability.

1 1/2 pounds fish fillets

Salt and pepper to taste

Dash cayenne

1 tablespoon butter, melted

1 tablespoon olive oil

1 teaspoon minced garlic

1 tablespoon Worcestershire sauce

2 tablespoons lemon juice

2 tablespoons chopped parsley

Carlysle Sauce (recipe to the right), optional

1. Preheat oven to 400°F. Season fish with salt, pepper, and cayenne.

2. In a bowl, combine butter, oil, garlic, and Worcestershire sauce. Coat both sides of fish with mixture and place in a baking dish.

3. Bake for about 15–20 minutes, depending on the thickness of the fillets, or until fish flakes easily with fork. Remove from oven, drizzle with lemon juice, and sprinkle with parsley. Serve topped with Carlysle Sauce, if desired.

NUTRITIONAL INFORMATION PER SERVING
Calories 176 | Calories from fat 40% | Fat 8 g
Saturated Fat 2 g | Cholesterol 72 mg | Sodium 77 mg
Carbohydrate 1 g | Dietary Fiber 0 g | Sugars 0 g | Protein 23 g

DIABETIC EXCHANGES
3 lean meat

CARLYSLE SAUCE

MAKES 6 (1/2-CUP) SERVINGS

Top rated seafood makes this sauce special. Any seafood combination may be used.

1 red bell pepper, cored and thinly sliced into two-inch pieces

1/2 teaspoon minced garlic

1/2 cup chopped tomatoes

1/4 cup white wine or cooking wine

1 bunch green onions, chopped

1/2 cup medium peeled shrimp, cooked

1/2 cup crawfish tails, rinsed and drained

1/2 cup lump or white crabmeat, picked through for shells

Salt and pepper to taste

1. In a nonstick skillet coated with non-stick cooking spray, sauté red pepper for several minutes. Add garlic and tomatoes and cook for another 2 minutes.

2. Add wine and reduce the liquid by half. Add remaining ingredients and cook until well heated. Season to taste.

NUTRITIONAL INFORMATION PER SERVING
Calories 60 | Calories from fat 8% | Fat 1 g
Saturated Fat 0 g | Cholesterol 48 mg | Sodium 91 mg
Carbohydrate 5 g | Dietary Fiber 2 g | Sugars 3 g | Protein 8 g

DIABETIC EXCHANGES
1 vegetable | 1 very lean meat

FISH CAKES

MAKES 8 FISH CAKES

This is a fisherman's answer to the crab cake and it rates at the top of my list. Pop a fish cake in a bun for unique and tasty "burger."

1 1/2 pounds fish fillets (red snapper, trout or your choice)
1/2 cup chopped onion
1/2 cup chopped green bell pepper
1/2 cup chopped red bell pepper
1/2 teaspoon minced garlic
2 egg whites
Salt and pepper to taste
Dash hot sauce
3/4 cup Ritz cracker crumbs
1/2 cup chopped green onions

1. Preheat oven to 375°F. Coat a small nonstick skillet and a baking sheet with nonstick cooking spray.

2. Chop fish into small pieces with a knife or food processor. Transfer to a large bowl, and set aside.

3. In prepared skillet, sauté onion, green and red peppers, and garlic until tender, about 5 minutes. Add to fish along with egg whites, salt, pepper, and hot sauce and mix well. Stir in cracker crumbs and green onions.

4. Form into 8 round portions and place on prepared pan. Bake for 30 minutes or until fish flakes easily with fork.

NUTRITIONAL INFORMATION PER SERVING
Calories 136 | Calories from fat 19% | Fat 3 g
Saturated Fat 1 g | Cholesterol 30 mg | Sodium 116 mg
Carbohydrate 8 g | Dietary Fiber 1 g | Sugars 2 g | Protein 19 g

DIABETIC EXCHANGES
1/2 starch | 2 1/2 very lean meat

TERRIFIC TIDBIT

Wrap the uncooked fish cakes individually and place in freezer bags, making them easy to pull out for dinner.

FISH SOFT TACOS

MAKES 8 SERVINGS

Taco-seasoned fish contrasts with tomatoes and mild, creamy coleslaw, all wrapped up in a corn tortilla. The best flavors of the southwest and seafood come together in one especially appealing recipe. Serve with diced avocados, if desired.

1 1/2 pounds fish fillets

1 (1.25-ounce) package low-sodium taco seasoning mix

2 tablespoons lime juice

2 cups cole slaw (shredded cabbage)

1/3 cup nonfat sour cream

1 tablespoon light mayonnaise

1 bunch green onions, chopped

3 tablespoons chopped green chilies

Salt and pepper to taste

8 (6-inch) corn or flour tortillas

1 cup chopped tomatoes

1. Coat fish with taco seasoning and lime juice. In a large nonstick skillet coated with nonstick cooking spray, sauté fish over medium heat for 5–7 minutes, or until done and fish flakes easily with fork.

2. In a bowl, combine cole slaw, sour cream, mayonnaise, green onions, and green chilies. Season to taste and set aside.

3. Warm tortillas according to package directions or heat in microwave for 30 seconds. Fill each tortilla with fish, cole slaw mixture, and tomatoes. Fold in half and serve. Repeat with remaining tortillas.

NUTRITIONAL INFORMATION PER SERVING
Calories 144 | Calories from fat 9% | Fat 2 g
Saturated Fat 0 g | Cholesterol 35 mg | Sodium 344 mg
Carbohydrate 15 g | Dietary Fiber 3 g | Sugars 3 g | Protein 15 g

DIABETIC EXCHANGES
1 carbohydrate | 2 1/2 very lean meat

TERRIFIC TIDBIT

Check the produce area in the grocery for a bag of shredded cabbage or cole slaw to use in this recipe.

SEAFOOD

FISH VERACRUZ

MAKES 4–6 SERVINGS

This combination yields a fantastic bold-flavored sauce with any fish.

1 tablespoon olive oil

1 cup chopped onion

1 teaspoon minced garlic

3 cups cherry tomato halves

3 tablespoons sliced green olives

2 tablespoons capers, drained

2 tablespoons jalapeño slices (found in jar)

Salt and pepper to taste

1 1/2 pounds red fish fillets (or fish of choice)

2 tablespoons lemon juice

1. Preheat oven to 450°F.

2. In a large nonstick skillet coated with non-stick cooking spray, heat oil and sauté onion and garlic over medium heat for 5 minutes.

3. Add tomatoes, olives, capers, and jalapeños. Lower heat and cook for about 10 minutes, stirring occasionally. Season to taste.

4. Lay fish in a baking dish, drizzle with lemon juice, and sprinkle with pepper. Spoon sauce over fish and cover lightly with foil. Bake for 10 to 12 minutes or until fish is almost done. Uncover and bake for an additional 5 minutes.

NUTRITIONAL INFORMATION PER SERVING
Calories 161 | Calories from fat 21% | Fat 4 g
Saturated Fat 1 g | Cholesterol 40 mg | Sodium 200 mg
Carbohydrate 8 g | Dietary Fiber 2 g | Sugars 4 g | Protein 24 g

DIABETIC EXCHANGES
2 vegetable | 3 very lean meat

GLAZED MUSTARD SALMON

MAKES 6 SERVINGS

With its distinctive sauce, this recipe is one of those last minute simple-to-prepare dinners with gourmet appeal.

3 tablespoons light brown sugar

1 tablespoon honey

1/4 cup Dijon mustard

2 tablespoons low-sodium soy sauce

1/2 teaspoon ground ginger

6 (6-ounce) salmon fillets

1 tablespoon olive oil

1. In a microwave-safe dish, heat brown sugar, honey, mustard, and soy sauce until melted together, about 30 seconds. Add ginger.

2. Coat salmon with oil and place skin side down in a heated nonstick skillet coated with nonstick cooking spray. Cover salmon with glaze and cook for 5 minutes or until golden brown and crispy.

3. Turn salmon over and cover opposite side with glaze. Continue cooking for 3–5 minutes longer or until salmon is cooked to desired doneness. Add remaining glaze to pan, heat well for 1 minute, and serve with salmon.

NUTRITIONAL INFORMATION PER SERVING
Calories 271 | Calories from fat 29% | Fat 9 g
Saturated Fat 1 g | Cholesterol 88 mg | Sodium 523 mg
Carbohydrate 12 g | Dietary Fiber 0 g | Sugars 10 g | Protein 35 g

DIABETIC EXCHANGES
1 carbohydrate | 5 lean meat

BLACKENED SALMON

MAKES 4 SERVINGS

No fuss and lots of flavor is the motto of this dish. Sweet and spicy collide for a taste you will not soon forget. If desired, other fish may be used, such as grouper, halibut, tilapia, or catfish.

2 tablespoons paprika

1 tablespoon chili powder

2 teaspoons light brown sugar

1 teaspoon pepper

1/2 teaspoon salt

4 (6-ounce) salmon fillets

1. In a small bowl, combine all ingredients, except salmon. Rub mixture on both sides of salmon.

2. In a large nonstick skillet, cook salmon over medium heat for about 4–5 minutes on each side or until desired doneness.

NUTRITIONAL INFORMATION PER SERVING
Calories 223 g | Calories from fat 26% | Fat 7 g
Saturated Fat 1 g | Cholesterol 88 mg | Sodium 427 mg
Carbohydrate 5 g | Dietary Fiber 2 g | Sugars 3 g | Protein 35 g

DIABETIC EXCHANGES
5 lean meat

TERRIFIC TIDBIT

Don't overcook salmon as it is best served golden brown on the outside with a warm rare interior.

BARBECUED SALMON

MAKES 4 SERVINGS

No grill needed here! Baked in a bold, rich sauce, this salmon is prepared in the convenience of your own kitchen.

4 (6-ounce) salmon fillets

Salt and pepper to taste

1/2 teaspoon garlic powder

2 strips center-cut bacon, cut in pieces

1 red onion half, thinly sliced

1/4 cup barbecue sauce

2 tablespoons honey

1. Preheat oven to 400°F. Coat a 9 × 9 × 2-inch baking dish with nonstick cooking spray.

2. Lay salmon in dish and season to taste. Sprinkle with garlic powder. Top with bacon pieces and onion slices.

3. In a small bowl, combine barbecue sauce and honey. Spread over salmon. Bake for 20–25 minutes or until salmon flakes easily with fork.

NUTRITIONAL INFORMATION PER SERVING
Calories 281 | Calories from fat 22% | Fat 7 g
Saturated Fat 1 g | Cholesterol 91 mg | Sodium 284 mg
Carbohydrate 17 g | Dietary Fiber 0 g | Sugars 16 g | Protein 35 g

DIABETIC EXCHANGES
1 carbohydrate | 5 lean meat

SEAFOOD

ONE DISH SALMON SURPRISES

MAKES 4 SERVINGS

A simple, yet sophisticated one-dish dinner.

2 cups cooked couscous

1/3 cup coarsely chopped cashews

1/2 cup chopped green onions

4 cups fresh baby spinach, divided

4 (6-ounce) salmon fillets, skin removed

Salt and pepper to taste

1/4 cup sherry or cooking sherry

2 tablespoons low-sodium soy sauce

1 teaspoon sesame oil

1 tablespoon grated fresh ginger or
   1 teaspoon ground ginger

1. Preheat oven to 375°F. Tear off four sheets of heavy foil.

2. In a bowl, combine couscous, cashews, and green onions. Divide couscous mixture onto of each foil square. Top each with 1 cup of spinach and a salmon fillet. Season to taste.

3. In a small bowl, whisk together remaining ingredients. Pour evenly over salmon.

4. Roll up edges of the foil to seal and place on baking sheet. Bake for 25 minutes or until salmon flakes easily with a fork.

NUTRITIONAL INFORMATION PER SERVING
Calories 389 | Calories from fat 29% | Fat 13 g
Saturated Fat 2 g | Cholesterol 88 mg | Sodium 452 mg
Carbohydrate 25 g | Dietary Fiber 3 g | Sugars 1 g | Protein 40 g

DIABETIC EXCHANGES
1 1/2 starch | 5 lean meat

BARBECUE SHRIMP

MAKES 4–6 SERVINGS

Spicy, big shrimp in an amazing, rich sauce. Serve with French bread and angel hair pasta.

1/4 cup olive oil

1/4 cup fat-free Italian or reduced-fat
   Caesar dressing

1 tablespoon minced garlic

1 teaspoon onion powder

1/4 teaspoon cayenne

1/4 cup Worcestershire sauce

1 tablespoon paprika

2 teaspoons dried oregano leaves

2 teaspoons dried thyme leaves

Salt and pepper to taste

2 pounds large shrimp (unpeeled)

1/3 cup light beer, room temperature

1/2 cup clam juice or fat-free chicken broth

1. In a large nonstick skillet, combine all ingredients, except shrimp, beer, and broth. Cook over medium heat until sauce begins to boil.

2. Add shrimp and cook about 5 minutes. Add beer and broth and cook until shrimp are done, about 5–7 minutes.

NUTRITIONAL INFORMATION PER SERVING
Calories 207 | Calories from fat 44% | Fat 10 g
Saturated Fat 2 g | Cholesterol 196 mg | Sodium 614 mg
Carbohydrate 6 g | Dietary Fiber 1 g | Sugars 2 g | Protein 22 g

DIABETIC EXCHANGES
1/2 carbohydrate | 3 lean meat

SHRIMP BOAT

MAKES 10–12 SERVINGS

A crisp crusty French bread loaf loaded with shrimp (great for leftover shrimp) and melted cheese makes an awesome sandwich. Cut into large slices for lunch or thinner slices for a quick snack or party pick up.

1 (16-ounce) loaf French bread

3/4 pound peeled shrimp, grilled or cooked

1/2 cup shredded, reduced-fat Monterey Jack or mozzarella cheese

1 large tomato, thinly sliced

1. Preheat oven to 350°F.

2. Slice French bread loaf in half lengthwise and scoop out one side. Fill with shrimp and sprinkle with cheese. Arrange tomato slices over top and replace the top half of bread.

3. Wrap in foil and bake until cheese is melted, about 15–20 minutes. Remove from oven and slice.

NUTRITIONAL INFORMATION PER SERVING
Calories 126 | Calories from fat 11% | Fat 2 g
Saturated Fat 1 g | Cholesterol 58 mg | Sodium 278 mg
Carbohydrate 17 g | Dietary Fiber 1 g | Sugars 1 g | Protein 11 g

DIABETIC EXCHANGES
1 starch | 1 very lean meat

TERRIFIC TIDBIT

Have fun and be creative by adding whatever condiments or veggies you have hanging around.

BLACKENED SHRIMP

MAKES 4 SERVINGS

Simple roasted shrimp with a slightly sweet but very spicy seasoning delivers instant flavor with little effort. Also works well in a salad, sandwich, or tossed with pasta. Or, add Blackened Shrimp to the Shrimp Boat recipe on the left for instant pizzazz.

3 tablespoons chili powder

1 tablespoon light brown sugar

1/4 teaspoon ground cinnamon

1/4 teaspoon ground cumin

Salt and freshly ground pepper to taste

24 large peeled shrimp

2 tablespoons olive oil

1. Preheat oven to 400°F.

2. In a resealable plastic bag or bowl, combine all seasonings. Add shrimp and shake to coat evenly.

3. Place shrimp on a baking sheet and drizzle with oil. Roast for 5–7 minutes or until cooked thoroughly.

NUTRITIONAL INFORMATION PER SERVING
Calories 177 | Calories from fat 43% | Fat 9 g
Saturated Fat 1 g | Cholesterol 168 mg | Sodium 254 mg
Carbohydrate 7 g | Dietary Fiber 2 g | Sugars 4 g | Protein 19 g

DIABETIC EXCHANGES
1/2 carbohydrate | 3 lean meat

SEAFOOD

Coconut Shrimp with Pineapple Salsa pg. 125

COCONUT SHRIMP WITH PINEAPPLE SALSA

MAKES 4–6 SERVINGS

Coconut shrimp is one of my personal favorites, and this easy oven baked version will win you over! Fragrant Pineapple Salsa complements the shrimp nicely, but the shrimp may also be served alone or on a salad.

1/3 cup cornstarch

1/2 teaspoon cayenne or to taste

Salt to taste

3 egg whites

1 1/4 cups flaked coconut

1 1/2 pounds medium peeled shrimp

Pineapple Salsa (recipe to the right)

1. Preheat oven to 400°F. Coat a baking sheet with nonstick cooking spray

2. In a shallow bowl, combine cornstarch, cayenne, and salt. In another bowl, beat egg whites until frothy, about 2 minutes. Place coconut on a plate.

3. Coat shrimp with cornstarch mixture, dip into egg whites, and roll in coconut. Place shrimp on prepared pan.

4. Bake for 15 minutes, turn shrimp, and continue baking another 5–10 minutes or until shrimp are done. Serve with Pineapple Salsa.

NUTRITIONAL INFORMATION PER SERVING
(NOT INCLUDING SALSA)
Calories 192 | Calories from fat 25% | Fat 5 g
Saturated Fat 4 g | Cholesterol 168 mg | Sodium 265 mg
Carbohydrate 15 g | Dietary Fiber 2 g | Sugars 6 g | Protein 20 g

DIABETIC EXCHANGES
1 carbohydrate | 3 lean meat

PINEAPPLE SALSA

MAKES 2 CUPS

A sweet spicy chutney style sauce. For a time saver, buy pre-cut fresh pineapple.

1 1/2 cups finely chopped fresh pineapple

1/3 cup chopped red onion

2 tablespoons finely chopped fresh cilantro

1/3 cup pineapple preserves

1 tablespoon finely chopped fresh jalapeño

1 tablespoon lime juice

1. In a bowl, combine all ingredients.

NUTRITIONAL INFORMATION PER SERVING
Calories 69 | Calories from fat 0% | Fat 0 g
Saturated Fat 0 g | Cholesterol 0 mg | Sodium 1 mg
Carbohydrate 18 g | Dietary Fiber 1 g | Sugars 15 g | Protein 0 g

DIABETIC EXCHANGES
1 fruit

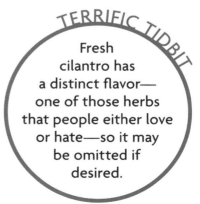

TERRIFIC TIDBIT

Fresh cilantro has a distinct flavor—one of those herbs that people either love or hate—so it may be omitted if desired.

SEAFOOD

SHRIMP CREOLE

MAKES 6–8 SERVINGS

This southern family favorite with a typical creole sauce of tomatoes, onions, and green peppers is usually served over rice. However, try serving it with Cheese Grits (pg. 44) for a perfect balance of flavors.

1 onion, chopped

1/2 teaspoon minced garlic

1 small green bell pepper, cored and chopped

1/4 cup all-purpose flour

1 (28-ounce) can chopped tomatoes with juice

1 cup evaporated skim milk

2 pounds medium peeled shrimp

1 bay leaf

1 tablespoon Worcestershire sauce

1/4 teaspoon cayenne or to taste

Salt and pepper to taste

1 bunch green onions, chopped

1. In a large nonstick skillet coated with nonstick cooking spray, sauté onion, garlic, and green pepper over medium heat until tender, about 7 minutes. Add flour and stir for 30 seconds.

2. Gradually add chopped tomatoes with juice. Stir in milk, shrimp, bay leaf, Worcestershire sauce, and cayenne. Bring to a boil, reduce heat, and continue cooking for 5–7 minutes longer or until mixture thickens slightly and shrimp are done.

3. Season to taste. Remove bay leaf and sprinkle with green onions before serving.

NUTRITIONAL INFORMATION PER SERVING
Calories 150 | Calories from fat 6% | Fat 1 g
Saturated Fat 0 g | Cholesterol 169 mg | Sodium 522 mg
Carbohydrate 13 g | Dietary Fiber 1 g | Sugars 8 g | Protein 22 g

DIABETIC EXCHANGES
1 carbohydrate | 3 very lean meat

TERRIFIC TIDBIT

Purchase good quality canned tomatoes. It definitely makes a difference!

SHRIMP PARMESAN

MAKES 4–6 SERVINGS

Easy and terrific, Italian seasoned shrimp baked with marinara sauce and melted cheese instantly won over our entire house.

1 1/2 pounds medium peeled shrimp

1/3 cup all-purpose flour

2 egg whites, beaten

1 1/2 cups Italian breadcrumbs

1 1/2 tablespoons olive oil

1 1/2 cups marinara sauce

1 cup shredded, part-skim, mozzarella cheese

1. Preheat broiler. Coat a baking sheet with nonstick cooking spray

2. Coat shrimp with flour, dip into egg whites, and coat with breadcrumbs. Place on prepared pan. Drizzle with oil.

3. Broil for 4–5 minutes on one side, turn, and broil 2–3 minutes or until shrimp are golden brown. Watch carefully.

4. Reduce oven to 350°F. Line a shallow 2-quart baking dish with a very thin layer of marinara sauce. Arrange shrimp in a single layer on top.

5. Spoon remaining marinara sauce over shrimp and sprinkle with mozzarella cheese. Bake for 10 minutes or until cheese is melted. Serve with angel hair pasta.

NUTRITIONAL INFORMATION PER SERVING
Calories 314 | Calories from fat 26% | Fat 9 g
Saturated Fat 3 g | Cholesterol 180 mg | Sodium 939 mg
Carbohydrate 27 g | Dietary Fiber 2 g | Sugars 1 g | Protein 28 g

DIABETIC EXCHANGES
2 starch | 3 lean meat

SPECIAL SHRIMP SCAMPI

MAKES 4 SERVINGS

Classic shrimp scampi in a light lemon sauce gets dressed up with avocado and cheese for a burst of flavor.

2 tablespoons olive oil

1 teaspoon minced garlic

2 tablespoons chopped red onion

1 tablespoon finely chopped parsley

Dash Worcestershire sauce

2 tablespoons lemon juice

Salt and pepper to taste

1 pound medium peeled shrimp

3 tablespoons white wine or cooking wine

1/3 cup coarsely chopped avocado

1/4 cup grated Parmesan cheese

1. In a large nonstick skillet, heat oil over medium heat. Sauté garlic, onion, parsley, Worcestershire sauce, and lemon juice for 1 minute. Season to taste.

2. Add shrimp and continue cooking for 2 minutes, stirring continuously. Add wine, salt, and pepper and continue cooking until shrimp are done, about 3-4 minutes.

3. Remove from heat. Stir in avocado and cheese. Serve immediately.

NUTRITIONAL INFORMATION PER SERVING
Calories 205 | Calories from fat 52% | Fat 12 g
Saturated Fat 3 g | Cholesterol 174 mg | Sodium 263 mg
Carbohydrate 3 g | Dietary Fiber 1 g | Sugars 1 g | Protein 20 g

DIABETIC EXCHANGES
3 very lean meat | 2 fat

SEAFOOD

GREEK SHRIMP SCAMPI

MAKES 4 SERVINGS

A quick stir-fry combines classic Mediterranean ingredients into one fabulous dish. Serve with angel hair pasta.

1 tablespoon olive oil

1 tablespoon minced garlic

1/3 cup chopped parsley

2 teaspoons dried oregano leaves

2 cups grape tomatoes, halved or 1 (28-ounce) can diced tomatoes, drained

1 cup fat-free chicken broth

1 1/4 pounds medium peeled shrimp

4 cups fresh baby spinach

1 tablespoon pine nuts, toasted

1/4 cup crumbled reduced fat feta cheese

1. In a large nonstick skillet, heat oil. Sauté garlic for 30 seconds. Add parsley, oregano, tomatoes, and broth.

2. Bring to a boil, reduce heat, and simmer for 10–12 minutes. Add shrimp and cook for several minutes, or until shrimp start to turn pink.

3. Stir in spinach and continue cooking until spinach is wilted and shrimp are done, just a few minutes. Toss with pine nuts and sprinkle with feta cheese.

NUTRITIONAL INFORMATION PER SERVING
Calories 206 | Calories from fat 30% | Fat 7 g
Saturated Fat 2 g | Cholesterol 213 mg | Sodium 499 mg
Carbohydrate 9 g | Dietary Fiber 3 g | Sugars 4 g | Protein 27 g

DIABETIC EXCHANGES
2 vegetable | 4 lean meat

KUNG PAO SHRIMP

MAKES 4 SERVINGS

This easy Asian inspired shrimp dish comes together fast and furious with a bang. Serve with rice or pasta, or as an easy appetizer.

2 tablespoons hoisin sauce

1 tablespoon sherry

1/2 to 1 teaspoon chili garlic sauce or oil

1 tablespoon cornstarch

1 egg white

1 pound medium peeled shrimp

2 tablespoons canola oil

1/2 teaspoon fresh grated ginger or 1/4 teaspoon ground ginger

1/2 teaspoon minced garlic

2 tablespoons dry-roasted peanuts

1. In a small bowl, combine hoisin sauce, sherry, and chili garlic sauce, and set aside.

2. In a medium bowl, whisk cornstarch into egg white. Add shrimp and coat well.

3. In a large nonstick skillet or wok, heat oil. Add shrimp, ginger, and garlic. Cook over medium heat for 2–3 minutes, or until shrimp are almost done, stirring.

4. Add hoisin sauce mixture and cook for 1–2 minutes or until shrimp are coated, stirring. Sprinkle with peanuts and serve.

NUTRITIONAL INFORMATION PER SERVING
Calories 197 | Calories from fat 45% | Fat 10 g
Saturated Fat 1 g | Cholesterol 168 mg | Sodium 257 mg
Carbohydrate 6 g | Dietary Fiber 0 g | Sugars 2 g | Protein 20 g

DIABETIC EXCHANGES
1/2 carbohydrate | 3 lean meat

QUICK LEMON BASIL SHRIMP

MAKES 4 SERVINGS

Need a quick, easy mouth-watering dish? Pop this in the oven and serve alone, or with rice or pasta, for a light tasty dinner.

2 tablespoons olive oil

2 teaspoons minced garlic

1 1/2 pounds medium to large peeled shrimp

2 tablespoons fresh chopped basil leaves or 2 teaspoons dried basil leaves

2 tablespoons chopped parsley (fresh is preferred)

2 tablespoons lemon juice

Salt and pepper to taste

1. Preheat oven to 400°F.

2. In an oblong, shallow baking dish, combine oil and garlic. Heat in oven 2–3 minutes, watching carefully that garlic does not brown.

3. Add shrimp to oil mixture and return to oven. Bake for 4 minutes, stir shrimp, and continue cooking 4–6 minutes until shrimp are done.

4. Remove from oven and sprinkle with basil, parsley, and lemon juice. Season to taste.

NUTRITIONAL INFORMATION PER SERVING
Calories 193 | Calories from fat 37% | Fat 8 g
Saturated Fat 1 g | Cholesterol 252 mg | Sodium 291 mg
Carbohydrate 1 g | Dietary Fiber 0 g | Sugars 0 g | Protein 27 g

DIABETIC EXCHANGES
4 lean meat

SKILLET SHRIMP WITH TOMATOES AND FETA

MAKES ABOUT 4 (1-CUP) SERVINGS

This one-skillet dish, featuring bold flavors and a simple elegance, can be prepared in mere minutes. Serve with pasta.

1 tablespoon olive oil

1 onion, chopped

1 teaspoon minced garlic

4 cups cherry tomatoes, halved if large

1 pound medium peeled shrimp

1 teaspoon dried oregano leaves

1/2 cup white wine or fat-free chicken broth

2 tablespoons chopped parsley

Salt and pepper to taste

2 tablespoons crumbled, reduced-fat feta cheese

1. In a large nonstick skillet coated with nonstick cooking spray, heat oil and sauté onion for about 3 minutes.

2. Stir in garlic and tomatoes, and cook for 3 minutes. Add shrimp and oregano, and continue cooking for about 3 minutes longer, stirring often.

3. Add wine and parsley. Season to taste. Continue cooking until shrimp are done and sauce slightly thickens. Sprinkle with feta and serve.

NUTRITIONAL INFORMATION PER SERVING
Calories 196 | Calories from fat 25% | Fat 6 g
Saturated Fat 1 g | Cholesterol 170 mg | Sodium 279 mg
Carbohydrate 14 g | Dietary Fiber 3 g | Sugars 9 g | Protein 21 g

DIABETIC EXCHANGES
3 vegetable | 3 lean meat

SEAFOOD

SHRIMP DELUXE PIZZA

MAKES 6–8 SLICES

No need to order out for pizza when you can easily have hot-out-of-the-oven pizza in the comfort of your own home. Shrimp and a great assortment of my favorite fresh ingredients make this an amazing pizza. For a vegetarian pizza, simply omit the shrimp.

1 (12-inch) thin pizza crust

1 tablespoon olive oil

1 tablespoon minced garlic

1 tablespoon dried basil leaves

1/4 pound sliced mushrooms

2 cups fresh baby spinach

1/2 pound medium peeled shrimp, seasoned and cooked

1/2 cup chopped tomatoes

1/4 cup chopped red onion

1/4 pound fresh mozzarella cheese, sliced or
    1 cup shredded, part-skim, mozzarella cheese

1. Preheat oven to 400°F. Coat crust with oil and garlic. Sprinkle with basil.

2. In a small nonstick skillet coated with nonstick cooking spray, sauté mushrooms for about 5 minutes or until tender. Add spinach, stirring until wilted.

3. Evenly spoon spinach mixture over crust and top with remaining ingredients. Bake for 8–10 minutes, or until cheese is melted and crust is browned.

NUTRITIONAL INFORMATION PER SERVING
Calories 189 | Calories from fat 35% | Fat 8 g
Saturated Fat 3 g | Cholesterol 65 mg | Sodium 265 mg
Carbohydrate 17 g | Dietary Fiber 1 g | Sugars 2 g | Protein 13 g

DIABETIC EXCHANGES
1 starch | 1 1/2 medium-fat meat

TERRIFIC TIDBIT

Fresh mozzarella cheese has a different texture and taste than packaged mozzarella cheese. It is slightly higher in fat but I think it is worth the flavor.

SHRIMP ENCHILADAS

MAKES 8–10 ENCHILADAS

Don't fret about the ingredient list, as this is just an assembly-job recipe that can easily be prepared ahead of time, refrigerated, and pulled out when ready to cook. Serve with salsa, chopped avocado, or guacamole, if desired.

1/2 cup chopped red onion

1 green bell pepper, cored and chopped

1 fresh jalapeño pepper, cored and minced (or to taste)

1/2 teaspoon minced garlic

3 tablespoons all-purpose flour

1 cup skim milk

1/2 teaspoon dried oregano leaves

1/2 teaspoon chili powder

1/2 teaspoon ground cumin

1 pound medium peeled shrimp

1 1/4 cups shredded, reduced-fat Mexican-blend cheese, divided

1/3 cup nonfat sour cream

3/4 cup chopped green onions, divided

1 cup chopped tomatoes, divided

Salt and pepper to taste

8–10 (8-inch) flour or wheat tortillas

1. Preheat oven to 350°F. Coat a large nonstick skillet and a 3-quart oblong baking dish with nonstick cooking spray.

2. In prepared skillet, sauté onion, green pepper, jalapeño, and garlic until tender, about 5–7 minutes. Stir in flour and gradually add milk, mixing until well blended. Reduce heat and continue stirring until slightly thickened.

3. Add oregano, chili powder, cumin and shrimp. Cook over medium heat until shrimp are done, about 5 minutes. Stir in 1 cup cheese. Remove from heat and stir in sour cream, 1/2 cup green onions, and 1/2 cup tomatoes. Season to taste.

4. Spoon mixture onto the center of a tortilla and roll tightly. Place tortilla seam side down in prepared dish. Repeat with remaining tortillas.

5. Cover with foil and bake for 15–20 minutes or until well heated. Remove foil and sprinkle with remaining cheese, green onions, and tomatoes. Cook for an additional 5–10 minutes, or until cheese is melted.

NUTRITIONAL INFORMATION PER SERVING
Calories 233 | Calories from fat 13% | Fat 4 g
Saturated Fat 2 g | Cholesterol 77 mg | Sodium 529 mg
Carbohydrate 31 g | Dietary Fiber 3 g | Sugars 4 g | Protein 17 g

DIABETIC EXCHANGES
2 starch | 2 very lean meat

TERRIFIC TIDBIT

Crawfish tails or crab-meat may be used instead of shrimp.

CRAWFISH ENCHILADAS

MAKES 16 ENCHILADAS (16 SERVINGS)

Crawfish with a cheesy creamy filling and southwestern seasonings turn enchiladas into a seafood fiesta.

1 onion, chopped

1 teaspoon minced garlic

1/2 cup chopped green bell pepper

1 (10-ounce) can diced tomatoes and green chilies, drained

2 tablespoons all-purpose flour

1 cup fat-free half-and-half

1 pound crawfish tails, rinsed and drained

1 teaspoon chili powder

4 ounces light processed cheese spread

Salt and pepper to taste

16 (6-inch) flour tortillas

1 cup canned enchilada sauce

1/2 cup shredded, reduced-fat Cheddar cheese

1. Preheat oven to 350°F. Coat a large nonstick skillet and a 3-quart oblong baking dish with nonstick cooking spray.

2. Sauté onion, garlic, and green pepper until tender, about 5 minutes. Add tomatoes and green chilies. Stir in flour and gradually add half-and-half. Add crawfish and chili powder and cook until bubbly and thickened.

3. Reduce heat, stir in processed cheese until melted, and season to taste. Spoon crawfish mixture (about 1/4 cup) onto a tortilla, roll and lay seam side down in prepared dish. Repeat for remaining tortillas.

4. Top with enchilada sauce and sprinkle with Cheddar cheese. Bake for 10 minutes or until heated and cheese is melted.

NUTRITIONAL INFORMATION PER SERVING
Calories 172 | Calories from fat 20% | Fat 4 g
Saturated Fat 2 g | Cholesterol 44 mg | Sodium 492 mg
Carbohydrate 23 g | Dietary Fiber 2 g | Sugars 3 g | Protein 11 g

DIABETIC EXCHANGES
11/2 starch | 1 lean meat

TERRIFIC TIDBIT

Keep a jar of minced garlic in the refrigerator for convenience. 1 medium clove fresh garlic = 1/2 teaspoon jar minced garlic

trim&TERRIFIC™ GULF COAST FAVORITES

CRAWFISH ETOUFFEE

MAKES 4 (1-CUP) SERVINGS

Tender crawfish is simmered with onion, green pepper, and garlic in a light roux. This easy to follow recipe for a popular Louisiana staple will quickly become part of your Cajun recipe repertoire. Serve over rice.

2 tablespoons olive oil

3 tablespoons all-purpose flour

1 onion, chopped

1/2 cup chopped green bell pepper

1 teaspoon minced garlic

1 cup fat-free chicken broth

1 tablespoon paprika

1 pound crawfish tails, rinsed and drained

Salt and pepper to taste

1 bunch green onions, stems only, finely chopped

1. In large nonstick skillet coated with nonstick cooking spray, heat oil and stir in flour. Cook over medium heat until light brown, about 6–8 minutes, stirring constantly. Add onion, green pepper, and garlic. Sauté until tender, about 5 minutes.

2. Gradually add broth and stir until thickened. Add paprika and crawfish. Bring to a boil, reduce heat, cover, and cook for about 15 minutes, stirring occasionally. Season to taste.

3. Stir in green onions and cook for another few minutes before serving.

NUTRITIONAL INFORMATION PER SERVING
Calories 220 | Calories from fat 36% | Fat 9 g
Saturated Fat 1 g | Cholesterol 155 mg | Sodium 217 mg
Carbohydrate 13 g | Dietary Fiber 4 g | Sugars 4 g | Protein 22 g

DIABETIC EXCHANGES
1 carbohydrate | 3 lean meat

TERRIFIC TIDBIT

The browned flour and oil/butter creates a roux that gives the etouffee a deep rich flavor.

SEAFOOD

CRAWFISH ELEGANTE
MAKES 6–8 SERVINGS

Crawfish in a divine sherry white sauce may be served in patty shells or over rice for a main course, or serve it in a chafing dish with Melba Rounds as a dip. This recipe will leave a lasting impression!

3 tablespoons butter

1 cup finely chopped onion

1 bunch green onions, chopped

1/2 cup chopped fresh parsley

3 tablespoons all-purpose flour

1 cup skim milk

3 tablespoons sherry or cooking sherry

1 pound crawfish tails, rinsed and drained

1 teaspoon onion powder

1 teaspoon garlic powder

Dash cayenne

Salt and pepper to taste

1. In medium nonstick skillet, melt butter and sauté onion, green onion, and parsley until tender, about 7 minutes.

2. Sprinkle with flour and stir for 1 minute. Gradually add milk, stirring to mix.

3. Add sherry, followed by remaining ingredients. Season to taste.

4. Bring mixture to a boil, reduce heat, and cook for an additional 3–5 minutes, stirring continuously.

NUTRITIONAL INFORMATION PER SERVING
Calories 133 | Calories from fat 33% | Fat 5 g
Saturated Fat 3 g | Cholesterol 90 mg | Sodium 107 mg
Carbohydrate 8 g | Dietary Fiber 2 g | Sugars 4 g | Protein 12 g

DIABETIC EXCHANGES
1/2 carbohydrate | 2 lean meat

TERRIFIC TIDBIT

Crawfish tails are available peeled in bags, fresh or frozen. Always buy Louisiana crawfish tails for the best quality.

CRAWFISH AND EGGPLANT RED CURRY

MAKES 5 (1-CUP) SERVINGS

Louisiana crawfish goes Thai in this fantastic yet unassuming stir-fry. I think fresh basil adds a subtle hint of sweetness, however, if you don't have it just leave it out. Serve over rice.

4 cups peeled and chopped eggplant (about 1 1/4 pounds)

1 cup chopped onion

1 teaspoon minced garlic

1 (13.5-ounce) can light coconut milk

1 tablespoon light brown sugar

1–2 tablespoons red curry paste (to taste)

3/4 cup water

1 pound crawfish tails

Salt to taste

1/4 cup loosely packed, torn, fresh basil leaves (optional)

1. In a nonstick skillet coated with nonstick cooking spray, cook eggplant and onion over medium heat until almost tender, about 10–12 minutes.

2. Add garlic, coconut milk, brown sugar, red curry paste, and water. Stir well. Bring to a boil, reduce heat, and cook for about 10–12 minutes or until eggplant is tender.

3. Add crawfish and season to taste. If desired, add fresh basil, and stir until wilted.

NUTRITIONAL INFORMATION PER SERVING
Calories 167 | Calories from fat 27% | Fat 5 g
Saturated Fat 3 g | Cholesterol 124 mg | Sodium 175 mg
Carbohydrate 13 g | Dietary Fiber 3 g | Sugars 7 g | Protein 17 g

DIABETIC EXCHANGES
1 carbohydrate | 2 1/2 lean meat

TERRIFIC TIDBIT

Red curry paste adds heat to the recipe so add gradually depending on your preference, and tolerance, for spiciness. It is found in the Asian foods section of supermarkets.

CRAWFISH CAKES WITH HORSERADISH SAUCE

MAKES 8 CRAWFISH CAKES

Move over crab cakes—crawfish adds a new slant to an old classic. Outrageously delicious!

1 cup saltine cracker crumbs

1 tablespoon Dijon mustard

2 tablespoons light mayonnaise

1 teaspoon hot sauce

1 bunch green onions, chopped

1/3 cup chopped fresh parsley

1/3 cup shredded, reduced-fat sharp
    Cheddar cheese

1 pound crawfish tails, rinsed and drained

Salt and pepper to taste

1 tablespoon olive oil

Flour

Horseradish Sauce (recipe to the right)

1. In a medium bowl, carefully combine all ingredients except oil and flour.

2. Cover and chill for 30 minutes, if time permits. Shape into 8 patties.

3. In a large nonstick skillet, heat oil. Lightly dust patties with flour, and cook over medium heat for 3–5 minutes on each side, or until browned.

4. Serve with Horseradish Sauce.

NUTRITIONAL INFORMATION PER SERVING
Calories 149 | Calories from fat 35% | Fat 6 g
Saturated Fat 1 g | Cholesterol 81 mg | Sodium 278 mg
Carbohydrate 10 g | Dietary Fiber 1 g | Sugars 1 g | Protein 12 g

DIABETIC EXCHANGES
1/2 starch | 2 lean meat

HORSERADISH SAUCE

Quick and easy, this sauce has bite.

1/4 cup nonfat sour cream

2 tablespoons light mayonnaise

1 tablespoon lemon juice

2 tablespoons prepared horseradish

Pinch sugar

1. In a bowl, combine all ingredients. Mix well.

NUTRITIONAL INFORMATION PER SERVING
Calories 22 | Calories from fat 50% | Fat 1 g
Saturated Fat 0 g | Cholesterol 0 mg | Sodium 48 mg
Carbohydrate 2 g | Dietary Fiber 0 g | Sugars 1 g | Protein 1 g

DIABETIC EXCHANGES
Free

TERRIFIC TIDBIT

To make ahead of time, mold into patties, and refrigerate, covered, until ready to cook. Shrimp may be substituted if you prefer. For cracker crumbs, place crackers in a food processor or blender. If freezing, freeze uncooked.

Crawfish Cakes with Horseradish Sauce pg. 136

CRABMEAT AU GRATIN

MAKES ABOUT 5 (3/4-CUP) SERVINGS

This mouth-watering, popular creation works equally well as an entrée or as a dip served with crackers.

1 tablespoon butter

1 onion, chopped

1/3 cup chopped celery

1/2 cup chopped green bell pepper

1 teaspoon minced garlic

1/4 cup all-purpose flour

2 cups skim milk

1 egg yolk

1/4 cup breadcrumbs

1 bunch green onions, chopped

1/4 teaspoon cayenne

Salt and pepper to taste

1 pound lump or white crabmeat, picked through for shells

1 cup shredded, reduced-fat sharp Cheddar cheese

1. Preheat oven to 375°F. Coat a nonstick pot and a 9 × 9 × 2-inch baking dish with nonstick cooking spray. An au gratin dish or ramekin(s) may also be used.

2. In prepared pot, melt butter. Sauté onion, celery, green pepper, and garlic until tender, about 5 minutes. Stir in flour and continue cooking for 1 minute, stirring continuously. Gradually add milk and stir over low heat until mixture is bubbly and thickens.

3. Place egg yolk in a small bowl and gradually stir in a small amount of hot mixture. Return mixture with yolk to the pot and stir until well heated. Stir in breadcrumbs, green onions, and cayenne. Season to taste.

4. Gently fold in crabmeat. Transfer to prepared baking dish and sprinkle with cheese. Bake for 10–15 minutes or until cheese is melted and mixture is well heated.

NUTRITIONAL INFORMATION PER SERVING
Calories 302 | Calories from fat 25% | Fat 9 g
Saturated Fat 5 g | Cholesterol 130 mg | Sodium 601 mg
Carbohydrate 21 g | Dietary Fiber 3 g | Sugars 9 g | Protein 32 g

DIABETIC EXCHANGES
1 starch | 1 vegetable | 4 lean meat

TERRIFIC TIDBIT

Crabmeat:
Lump—large nuggets of white crabmeat; rich, delicious, and pricey
White—small pieces of white crabmeat
Claw—distinctive sweetness; partially brown color; used in stuffings, gumbos, and stews

BAKED ITALIAN OYSTERS

MAKES 10–12 SERVINGS

Reminiscent of a dish from a great New Orleans restaurant, oysters baked in a dynamic Italian breadcrumb mixture offer a rich distinctive taste.

2 pints oysters, drained

1/3 cup olive oil

1 teaspoon minced garlic

1/3 cup chopped parsley

1 bunch green onions, chopped

2 cups Italian breadcrumbs

1/3 cup grated Parmesan cheese

Crushed red pepper flakes

1/4 cup lemon juice

1. Preheat oven to 400°F.

2. Place drained oysters in a shallow oblong 2-quart baking dish.

3. In a bowl, combine remaining ingredients and spread evenly over oysters. Bake for 25–30 minutes or until oysters are done and topping is browned.

NUTRITIONAL INFORMATION PER SERVING
Calories 209 | Calories from fat 40% | Fat 9 g
Saturated Fat 2 g | Cholesterol 52 mg | Sodium 524 mg
Carbohydrate 20 g | Dietary Fiber 2 g | Sugars 1 g | Protein 10 g

DIABETIC EXCHANGES
1 1/2 starch | 1 lean meat | 1 fat

SEARED SCALLOPS WITH PESTO VERDE

MAKES 4 SERVINGS, 1/2 CUP PESTO VERDE

Sweet buttery scallops come alive with pesto for a simple, yet chic dish.

2 cups loosely packed flat-leaf (Italian) parsley leaves

3 cloves garlic

1 tablespoon capers, drained

1 tablespoon Dijon mustard

1 tablespoon white wine vinegar

Salt and pepper to taste

3 tablespoons olive oil

2 tablespoons water

12 large scallops, patted dry with paper towels

1. In a food processor, process parsley, garlic, capers, mustard, vinegar, salt, and pepper until combined.

2. With processor still running, add olive oil in a thin stream and continue processing until smooth and creamy. Add water to loosen mixture slightly.

3. In a large nonstick skillet coated with nonstick cooking spray, sear scallops over medium heat until crispy brown on both sides, about 3 minutes on each side.

4. Pour sauce over scallops and serve.

NUTRITIONAL INFORMATION PER SERVING
Calories 180 | Calories from fat 55% | Fat 11 g
Saturated Fat 1 g | Cholesterol 33 mg | Sodium 313 mg
Carbohydrate 6 g | Dietary Fiber 1 g | Sugars 1 g | Protein 15 g

DIABETIC EXCHANGES
1/2 carbohydrate | 2 very lean meat | 2 fat

Mole Duck Enchiladas pg. 162

POULTRY & GAME BIRD

The Gulf of Mexico is an integral part of our nation's economic and ecological vitality. This region helps fuel and feed the nation by providing the largest domestic market for shrimp, oysters and many species of fishes for the nation.

Gulf of Mexico Alliance

WETLANDS FACT

BLACKENED CHICKEN TENDERS

MAKES 4 SERVINGS

Quick, spicy, and always a hit—a full-bodied sauce provides the perfect harmony to well-seasoned chicken tenders. Serve over pasta or rice for an entrée, or serve the tenders alone as an appetizer with the sauce on the side.

2 tablespoons paprika

1 tablespoon chili powder

1 teaspoon light brown sugar

1 teaspoon pepper

1/2 teaspoon salt

1 1/2 pounds boneless, skinless chicken breasts, cut into strips

1 tablespoon olive oil

1 green bell pepper, cored and chopped

1 red bell pepper, cored and chopped

1 cup chopped red onion

1 (5-ounce) can evaporated skim milk

1/4 cup chopped green onions

1 In a large resealable plastic bag, combine paprika, chili powder, brown sugar, pepper, and salt. Add chicken and shake to coat.

2. In a large nonstick skillet coated with nonstick cooking spray, heat oil over medium heat and sauté chicken until browned and done, about 5–7 minutes. Remove chicken and set aside.

3. To the same skillet add green pepper, red pepper, and onion. Cook over medium heat for 5 minutes or until tender, scraping bits from bottom of pan.

4. Add milk, stirring for one minute or until heated and bubbly. Serve chicken with sauce and sprinkle with green onions, if desired.

NUTRITIONAL INFORMATION PER SERVING
Calories 299 | Calories from fat 19% | Fat 6 g
Saturated Fat 1 g | Cholesterol 100 mg | Sodium 472 mg
Carbohydrate 16 g | Dietary Fiber 4 g | Sugars 10 g | Protein 44 g

DIABETIC EXCHANGES
1 carbohydrate | 6 very lean meat

TERRIFIC TIDBIT

Blackening refers to a cooking method originating in New Orleans. Fish, chicken, or beef is cooked in a hot skillet to produce a slightly burnt-looking, dark-brown exterior and moist interior.

Blackened Chicken Tenders pg. 142

CHICKEN AND SAUSAGE JAMBALAYA

MAKES 8 (1-CUP) SERVINGS

This crowd-pleasing jambalaya is a bountiful, true Louisiana meal with hearty chicken, sausage, and rice all in one dish. For a short-cut, use rotisserie chicken.

7 ounces reduced-fat smoked sausage, thinly sliced

1 onion, chopped

1 green bell pepper, cored and chopped

2 teaspoons minced garlic

3 cups fat-free beef broth

1 1/2 cups rice

2 cups cooked, diced, boneless, skinless chicken breasts

1 teaspoon hot sauce

1 bunch green onions, chopped

Salt and pepper to taste

1. Coat a large nonstick pot with nonstick cooking spray and cook sausage over medium heat, turning constantly, until browned.

2. Add onion, pepper, and garlic. Cook until tender, about 5–7 minutes, stirring continuously. Scrape brown bits from bottom of pan. (This adds color to the jambalaya.)

3. Add broth, rice, and chicken. Bring to a boil, reduce heat, cover, and simmer until liquid is absorbed and rice is tender, about 25–30 minutes.

4. Remove lid, stir in hot sauce and green onions. Season to taste. Cover and cook 5 minutes more before serving.

NUTRITIONAL INFORMATION PER SERVING
Calories 212 | Calories from fat 6% | Fat 1 g
Saturated Fat 0 g | Cholesterol 28 mg | Sodium 659 mg
Carbohydrate 33 g | Dietary Fiber 2 g | Sugars 3 g | Protein 16 g

DIABETIC EXCHANGES
2 starch | 2 very lean meat

TERRIFIC TIDBIT

Look for turkey sausage or leaner cuts.

CHICKEN MARABELLA

MAKES 8 SERVINGS

Unique layers of sweet, tart, and savory flavors enliven this simple chicken dish. My version of this delectable recipe will guarantee requests for seconds. I like to use this dish on a buffet as it is also good served at room temperature.

4 pounds boneless, skinless chicken breasts or chicken thighs

1 tablespoon minced garlic

2 tablespoons dried oregano leaves

Salt and pepper to taste

1/4 cup red wine vinegar

3 tablespoons olive oil

1/2 cup dried pitted plums

1/4 cup pitted Spanish green olives

1/4 cup capers, drained

3 bay leaves

1/3 cup light brown sugar

1/2 cup white wine or cooking wine

1. Preheat oven to 350°F.

2. In large glass bowl or resealable plastic bag, combine all ingredients except brown sugar and wine. Cover and let marinate in refrigerator (overnight, if time permits).

3. Arrange chicken in a single layer in a large shallow baking pan. Cover with marinade, sprinkle with brown sugar, and top with wine.

4. Bake 50 minutes to 1 hour or until chicken is very tender, basting frequently with pan juices. Serve immediately or at room temperature.

NUTRITIONAL INFORMATION PER SERVING
Calories 362 | Calories from fat 20% | Fat 8 g
Saturated Fat 2 g | Cholesterol 132 mg | Sodium 365 mg
Carbohydrate 15 g | Dietary Fiber 1 g | Sugars 11 g | Protein 53 g

DIABETIC EXCHANGES
1 carbohydrate | 7 very lean meat

TERRIFIC TIDBIT

Keep a jar of minced garlic in the refrigerator to always have garlic on hand.

CHICKEN PARMESAN
MAKES 8 SERVINGS

Italian-crusted chicken in a rich tomato sauce transforms your kitchen into a fancy Italian restaurant! Serve over angel hair pasta to complete the meal. A jar of marinara sauce may be substituted for the Quick Marinara Sauce.

8 boneless, skinless thin chicken breasts (about 2 pounds), flattened

1 cup Italian breadcrumbs

1 tablespoon dried oregano leaves

1 teaspoon dried thyme leaves

2 egg whites or 1/4 cup egg beaters

2 tablespoons skim milk

1/2 cup all-purpose flour

Quick Marinara Sauce (recipe below)

1 cup shredded, part-skim mozzarella cheese

1/4 cup grated Parmesan cheese

1. Preheat oven to 350°F. Coat a large non-stick skillet with nonstick cooking spray.

2. To flatten chicken breasts, place between two pieces of plastic wrap and pound to about 1/3-inch thick.

3. In a bowl, combine breadcrumbs, oregano, and thyme. In another bowl, whisk together egg whites and milk.

4. Coat each chicken breast in flour and shake off excess. Dip chicken into egg mixture and coat with seasoned breadcrumb mixture.

5. Heat prepared skillet and cook chicken breasts until done and lightly browned, about 5–7 minutes on each side.

6. Place half of the Quick Marinara Sauce in the bottom of a 3-quart oblong baking dish and top with chicken. Cover with remaining marinara and bake for about 20–25 minutes or until bubbly. Sprinkle with cheeses and bake for 5 minutes or until cheese is melted.

QUICK MARINARA SAUCE

2 tablespoons olive oil

1 small onion, chopped

1 teaspoon minced garlic

2 (28-ounce) cans chopped tomatoes with juice

1 teaspoon dried oregano leaves

1 teaspoon dried basil leaves

Salt and pepper to taste

1. In a large nonstick skillet, heat oil over medium heat and sauté onion and garlic until tender, about 5 minutes. Add tomatoes and bring to a boil. Add oregano and basil.

2. Lower heat, cover, and cook for 10-15 minutes. Season to taste.

NUTRITIONAL INFORMATION PER SERVING
Calories 339 | Calories from fat 21% | Fat 8 g
Saturated Fat 3 g | Cholesterol 77 mg | Sodium 682 mg
Carbohydrate 29 g | Dietary Fiber 5 g | Sugars 8 g | Protein 36 g

DIABETIC EXCHANGES
1 starch | 2 vegetable | 4 lean meat

CHICKEN IN PARMESAN PINE-NUT CRUST WITH PESTO SAUCE

MAKES 8 SERVINGS

You will experience many sensational flavors in one bite with this trendy dish of chicken coated in a crust of Parmesan cheese, pine nuts, and breadcrumbs and topped with pesto.

2 pounds boneless, skinless chicken breasts (about 8), flattened

Salt and pepper to taste

1/4 cup all-purpose flour

2 egg whites, lightly beaten

1 cup Italian breadcrumbs

1/4 cup grated Parmesan cheese

Hearty dash red pepper flakes

1/2 teaspoon minced garlic

1/4 cup pine nuts

2 tablespoons olive oil

Pesto Sauce (recipe to the right)

1. Season chicken breasts to taste and lightly coat with flour. Place egg whites in a shallow dish.

2. In a food processor, process remaining ingredients, except oil, to fine crumbs. Transfer mixture to a plate.

3. Dip flour coated chicken breasts in egg and coat with breadcrumb mixture.

4. In a large nonstick skillet, heat oil over medium heat and cook breaded chicken breasts until golden brown and done, about 5–7 minutes on each side.

5. Serve with Pesto Sauce.

PESTO SAUCE

You can find pre-made pesto in the grocery store but this easy recipe requires little more than tossing a handful of ingredients into a food processor. You must use fresh basil and fresh parsley.

1 cup loosely packed fresh basil leaves

2/3 cup loosely packed fresh parsley leaves

3 tablespoons lemon juice

1 large Roma tomato, chopped

Salt and freshly ground black pepper, to taste

1. In a food processor, process basil and parsley until minced. Stir in lemon juice and tomato. Season to taste.

NUTRITIONAL INFORMATION PER SERVING
Calories 265 | Calories from fat 26% | Fat 8 g
Saturated Fat 2 g | Cholesterol 68 mg | Sodium 344 mg
Carbohydrate 16 g | Dietary Fiber 1 g | Sugars 1 g | Protein 32 g

DIABETIC EXCHANGES
1 starch | 3 1/2 lean meat

CHICKEN STIR-FRY WITH SPICY PEANUT SAUCE

MAKES 6 SERVINGS

An easy and exceptional homemade peanut sauce is the secret to this recipe's tremendous flavor. The stir-fry cooking method is the secret to its speed. Serve with rice.

1 3/4 pounds boneless, skinless chicken breasts, cut into strips

1 tablespoon minced garlic

Salt and pepper to taste

1 onion, halved and thinly sliced

1 red bell pepper, cored and thinly sliced

1 cup shredded carrots

1/3 pound fresh snow peas, ends snapped if needed (can use frozen)

Spicy Peanut Sauce (recipe to the right)

1 bunch green onions, chopped

Chopped peanuts (optional)

1. Season chicken strips with garlic, salt, and pepper.

2. In a large nonstick skillet coated with nonstick cooking spray, stir-fry chicken and onion over medium heat for several minutes. Add red pepper, carrots, and snow peas, cooking for 3–5 minutes until chicken is tender.

3. Add Spicy Peanut Sauce to pan and continue cooking until chicken is done.

4. Add green onions, heat for an additional minute. Serve sprinkled with chopped peanuts, if desired.

SPICY PEANUT SAUCE

This can also be used as a dipping sauce.

4 tablespoons peanut butter

3 tablespoons Tamari or low-sodium soy sauce

2 tablespoons honey

1 tablespoon fresh grated ginger or 1/2 teaspoon ground ginger

1/2 to 1 teaspoon crushed red pepper flakes (depending on taste)

1/2 teaspoon minced garlic

1. In a microwave-safe dish, combine all ingredients. Heat for 30 seconds and stir to combine.

NUTRITIONAL INFORMATION PER SERVING
Calories 286 | Calories from fat 18% | Fat 6 g
Saturated Fat 1 g | Cholesterol 77 mg | Sodium 496 mg
Carbohydrate 22 g | Dietary Fiber 4 g | Sugars 13 g | Protein 35 g

DIABETIC EXCHANGES
2 vegetable | 1 carbohydrate | 4 1/2 lean meat

TERRIFIC TIDBIT

Buy pre-shredded carrots and frozen snow peas for speedy preparation.

CHICKEN SCALOPPINI

MAKES 4–6 SERVINGS

Lightly-crusted chicken cooked in a simple lemon and wine sauce delivers a luxurious finish.

1/3 cup all-purpose flour

1/4 cup grated Parmesan cheese

Salt and pepper to taste

4–6 boneless, skinless thin chicken breasts, flattened

2 tablespoons olive oil

3 garlic cloves

3/4 cup fat-free chicken broth

1 tablespoon lemon juice

1/3 cup white wine or cooking wine

1 tablespoon chopped parsley

1. In a bowl, combine flour, Parmesan cheese, salt, and pepper. Coat chicken with mixture.

2. In a large nonstick skillet coated with nonstick cooking spray, heat oil. Add garlic and chicken breasts, and cook until lightly brown, about 3–4 minutes each side.

3. Add broth, lemon juice, and wine. Bring to a boil, reduce heat, cover, and simmer until chicken is tender, about 15–20 minutes. Remove garlic cloves and sprinkle with parsley before serving.

NUTRITIONAL INFORMATION PER SERVING
Calories 214 | Calories from fat 28% | Fat 7 g
Saturated Fat 2 g | Cholesterol 69 mg | Sodium 174 mg
Carbohydrate 6 g | Dietary Fiber 0 g | Sugars 0 g | Protein 29 g

DIABETIC EXCHANGES
1/2 starch | 3 lean meat

SOUTHWESTERN ROASTED CHICKEN

MAKES 6–8 SERVINGS

This quick-to-fix, flavorful chicken pops in and out of the oven with ease.

1 tablespoon olive oil

1 tablespoon chili powder

1 tablespoon ground cumin

1 teaspoon minced garlic

Dash cayenne

Salt and pepper to taste

2 pounds boneless, skinless chicken breasts

1 green bell pepper, cored and cut into strips

1/3 cup chopped red onion

1 tomato, thinly sliced

2/3 cup shredded, reduced-fat Mexican-blend cheese (optional)

1. Preheat oven to 400°F. Line a baking sheet with foil.

2. In a resealable plastic bag, combine oil, chili powder, cumin, garlic, cayenne, salt, and pepper. Add chicken and coat well. Transfer chicken to baking sheet.

3. Top each chicken piece with green pepper, onion, and tomato. Bake for 25–30 minutes or until chicken is tender. If desired, sprinkle with cheese and serve.

NUTRITIONAL INFORMATION PER SERVING
Calories 155 | Calories from fat 20% | Fat 3 g
Saturated Fat 1 g | Cholesterol 66 mg | Sodium 87 mg
Carbohydrate 3 g | Dietary Fiber 1 g | Sugars 1 g | Protein 27 g

DIABETIC EXCHANGES
3 very lean meat

POULTRY & GAME BIRD

Marinated Chicken with Roasted Tomato Topping and Mozzarella Cheese pg. 151

MARINATED CHICKEN WITH ROASTED TOMATO TOPPING AND MOZZARELLA CHEESE

MAKES 6 SERVINGS

Broiled, marinated chicken topped with mild green chilies, fresh tomatoes, spinach, and mozzarella cheese makes a quick and dynamic dinner.

3 tablespoons lemon juice

3 tablespoons white balsamic vinegar

1 teaspoon dried oregano leaves

1 teaspoon paprika

6 (4-ounce) boneless, skinless chicken breasts

3/4 cup chopped onion

1/2 teaspoon minced garlic

3 tablespoons chopped green chilies, drained

1 cup grape or cherry tomato halves

1 cup fresh baby spinach leaves

Salt and pepper to taste

1/3 cup shredded, part-skim mozzarella cheese

1. In a resealable plastic bag, combine lemon juice, vinegar, oregano, and paprika. Add chicken and coat well. Refrigerate for 1 hour or until ready to cook.

2. Preheat broiler. Line a baking pan with foil. Place chicken breasts on pan and discard extra marinade. Broil chicken for 7–9 minutes on each side.

3. In a nonstick skillet coated with nonstick cooking spray, sauté onion and garlic until tender, about 5 minutes. Add green chilies and tomatoes, and sauté a few minutes longer. Add spinach, cooking only until leaves are wilted. Season to taste.

4. Divide mixture on top of each chicken breast and sprinkle with mozzarella cheese. Return to broiler and broil only until cheese is melted. Watch carefully.

NUTRITIONAL INFORMATION PER SERVING
Calories 159 | Calories from fat 14% | Fat 3 g
Saturated Fat 1 g | Cholesterol 70 mg | Sodium 148 mg
Carbohydrate 4 g | Dietary Fiber 1 g | Sugars 2 g | Protein 28 g

DIABETIC EXCHANGES
3 1/2 very lean meat

TERRIFIC TIDBIT

Instead of white balsamic, try different flavored rice vinegars, such as pesto or red pepper, for a lively flavor.

SLOW-COOKED GREEK CHICKEN

MAKES 6–8 SERVINGS

Start this recipe in the morning and come home to Grecian aromas and a complete meal of chicken, carrots, and potatoes.

2 tablespoons lemon juice

1 teaspoon minced garlic

1 onion, chopped

1 (28-ounce) can chopped tomatoes, with juice

1 bay leaf

1/8 teaspoon pepper

1 teaspoon dried oregano leaves

2 pounds boneless, skinless chicken breast halves

1 cup baby carrots

1 pound peeled red potatoes, cut in fourths

2 tablespoons all-purpose flour

3 tablespoons warm water

1/4 cup crumbled reduced-fat feta cheese

1. Combine lemon juice, garlic, onion, tomatoes, bay leaf, pepper, and oregano in a crock pot. If desired, brown chicken on both sides in skillet coated with nonstick cooking spray over medium heat or just add chicken directly to cooker.

2. Cover and cook on low heat for 8–10 hours. Add carrots and potatoes within the last few hours of cooking.

3. Before serving, remove chicken breasts and vegetables, and pour sauce from cooker into a saucepan. In a small bowl, combine flour and water to form a paste and add to sauce. Stir sauce over medium heat until bubbly and thickened.

4. To serve, pour sauce over chicken and vegetables, and sprinkle with feta cheese.

NUTRITIONAL INFORMATION PER SERVING
Calories 216 | Calories from fat 8% | Fat 2 g
Saturated Fat 1 g | Cholesterol 67 mg | Sodium 416 g
Carbohydrate 20 g | Dietary Fiber 2 g | Sugars 5 g | Protein 30 g

DIABETIC EXCHANGES
1 starch | 1 vegetable | 3 very lean meat

TERRIFIC TIDBIT

This recipe may also be prepared in a large skillet. Cook chicken until almost tender. Add tomatoes and vegetables and cook about 40–50 minutes over low heat until chicken is done and vegetables are tender.

EASY CHICKEN ENCHILADAS
MAKES 12 ENCHILADAS

Whip up these "wow"-inducing enchiladas in no time using rotisserie or leftover chicken. Toss in a can of black beans, drained and rinsed, for added flavor and nutrition.

2 cups nonfat sour cream

2 (10 3/4-ounce) cans fat-free cream of chicken soup

1 onion, chopped

1 (4-ounce) can chopped green chilies

3 cups cooked, diced skinless chicken breasts

1 1/2 cups shredded, reduced-fat Mexican-blend cheese, divided

1 cup frozen corn (optional)

12 flour tortillas

1 (10-ounce) can enchilada sauce

1/4 cup chopped green onions

1. Preheat oven to 350°F. Coat a 13 × 9 × 2-inch baking dish with nonstick cooking spray.

2. In a large bowl, combine sour cream, soup, onion, and green chilies. Mix well. In another bowl, combine chicken, 1 cup cheese, and corn. Add about one-third of the sour cream mixture and mix well.

3. Spoon chicken mixture onto a tortilla, roll and place seam-side down in prepared pan. Repeat with remaining tortillas. Spoon remaining sour cream mixture evenly on top of filled tortillas. Sprinkle with remaining cheese and top with enchilada sauce.

4. Cover with foil and bake for 20 minutes or until well heated. Remove foil and sprinkle with the green onions. Cook for 5 more minutes before serving,

---

NUTRITIONAL INFORMATION PER SERVING
Calories 283 | Calories from fat 25% | Fat 8 g
Saturated Fat 3 g | Cholesterol 49 mg | Sodium 670 mg
Carbohydrate 31 g | Dietary Fiber 2 g | Sugars 5 g | Protein 20 g

DIABETIC EXCHANGES
2 starch | 2 lean meat

TERRIFIC TIDBIT

Add a can of black beans, rinsed and drained, to the filling for added flavor and nutrition.

CHICKEN AND DUMPLINGS

MAKES 16 (1-CUP) SERVINGS

When I think of comfort food, chicken and dumplings, our family favorite, tops my list. This trouble-free recipe is made with drop dumplings. Using pre-cooked rotisserie chicken really speeds up the process.

2 pounds boneless, skinless chicken breasts, cut into 1-inch pieces

1 cup chopped onion

1 cup chopped celery

1/4 cup plus 3 cups all-purpose flour, divided

10 cups fat-free chicken broth

2 cups sliced carrots

1 teaspoon dried thyme leaves

1 tablespoon plus 1 teaspoon baking powder

1 1/2 cups buttermilk

Salt and pepper to taste

1. In a large nonstick pot coated with nonstick cooking spray, cook chicken with onion and celery over medium heat until chicken is browned, about 7–10 minutes.

2. Sprinkle with 1/4 cup flour and gradually stir in broth, carrots, and thyme. Bring to a boil, reduce heat, and cover. Cook until chicken is tender, stirring occasionally, about 10–15 minutes.

3. In a bowl, combine baking powder and remaining 3 cups flour. Stir in buttermilk. Drop dough by tablespoonfuls into chicken soup.

4. Bring to a boil and reduce heat. Cook, covered, over medium heat 15 minutes or until dumplings are done. Season to taste.

NUTRITIONAL INFORMATION PER SERVING
Calories 186 | Calories from fat 6% | Fat 1 g
Saturated Fat 0 g | Cholesterol 34 mg | Sodium 418 mg
Carbohydrate 24 g | Dietary Fiber 2 g | Sugars 2 g | Protein 18 g

DIABETIC EXCHANGES
1 1/2 starch | 2 very lean meat

TERRIFIC TIDBIT

Another easy dumpling recipe: Combine 1 2/3 cups all-purpose baking mix with 2/3 cup milk. Drop by tablespoonfuls into the broth.

trim&TERRIFIC™ GULF COAST FAVORITES

CHICKEN AND WILD RICE CASSEROLE

MAKES 8 SERVINGS

Chicken and wild rice take on a fancy flair with mushrooms, artichokes, and sherry.

2 (6-ounce) packages long grain and wild rice mix

2 pounds boneless, skinless chicken breasts

1 teaspoon paprika

1/4 teaspoon pepper

1 (14-ounce) can artichoke hearts, drained and halved

1/2 pound sliced mushrooms

4 tablespoons all-purpose flour

1/2 teaspoon dried thyme leaves

2 cups fat-free chicken broth

1/2 cup sherry or cooking sherry (optional)

1. Preheat oven to 375°F. Coat a large nonstick skillet with nonstick cooking spray

2. Cook rice according to package directions, omitting any salt and oil. Spoon cooked wild rice into a 2-quart oblong baking dish and set aside

3. Sprinkle chicken with paprika and pepper. In prepared skillet, brown chicken over medium heat, about 5 minutes. Arrange chicken on top of rice and top with artichoke hearts.

4. In the same skillet, sauté mushrooms over medium heat until tender, about 5 minutes. In a small bowl, combine flour with thyme and gradually add broth and sherry. Add to skillet and cook until thickened and bubbly, stirring constantly.

5. Spoon sauce over chicken in baking dish. Bake, covered, for 45–60 minutes or until chicken is done.

NUTRITIONAL INFORMATION PER SERVING
Calories 304 | Calories from fat 5% | Fat 2 g
Saturated Fat 0 g | Cholesterol 66 mg | Sodium 830 mg
Carbohydrate 37 g | Dietary Fiber 2 g | Sugars 2 g | Protein 33 g

DIABETIC EXCHANGES
2 1/2 starch | 3 very lean meat

TERRIFIC TIDBIT

Pick up a fresh mushroom variety pack for a more earthy flavor and some pizzaz.

BARBECUE CHICKEN BAKE WITH CORNBREAD CRUST

MAKES 4 (3/4-CUP) SERVINGS

A cornbread crust dresses up leftover chicken cooked in a spunky barbecue sauce. Reminiscent of chicken pot pie, this recipe is one of those easy, family-pleasing meals that you will prepare time and time again.

1 cup chopped onion

1/2 cup chopped green bell pepper

1/4 cup finely chopped carrots

1/2 teaspoon minced garlic

1/2 teaspoon ground cumin

2 tablespoons cider vinegar

1 cup fat-free chicken broth

1/2 cup chili sauce

1 tablespoon light brown sugar

1 teaspoon cocoa

2 cups shredded or coarsely chopped cooked chicken

1/2 (11.5-ounce) can refrigerated cornbread twists, pie pastry or biscuits

1. Preheat oven to 375°F. Coat a nonstick skillet and a 9 × 9 × 2-inch baking dish with nonstick cooking spray

2. In prepared skillet, sauté onion, green pepper, carrots and garlic until tender, about 5–7 minutes. Add cumin and continue stirring. Stir in vinegar and scrape the pan.

3. Add broth, chili sauce, brown sugar, and cocoa. Mix well and continue cooking for about 10 minutes, until bubbly and heated. Stir in chicken.

4. Transfer chicken mixture into prepared baking dish. Separate corn bread twists and arrange on top in a lattice pattern.

5. Bake for 25 minutes or until cornbread is done and golden brown. Let stand for 10 minutes before serving.

NUTRITIONAL INFORMATION PER SERVING
Calories 329 | Calories from fat 24% | Fat 9 g
Saturated Fat 2 g | Cholesterol 59 mg | Sodium 934 mg
Carbohydrate 35 g | Dietary Fiber 2 g | Sugars 16 g | Protein 26 g

DIABETIC EXCHANGES
2 starch | 1 vegetable | 3 lean meat

TERRIFIC TIDBIT

For a time saver, use leftover or rotessire chicken and a 1 (10-ounce) package frozen mixed vege-tables, thawed. Another crust option is 1 (8-ounce) can refrigerated reduced-fat crescent rolls, use only 6 triangles.

Barbecue Chicken Bake with Cornbread Crust pg. 156

CHICKEN CAESAR SANDWICH

MAKES 6 SANDWICHES

Turn leftover chicken into a super sandwich. The loaf of bread is easier to hollow out if you cut it into six servings first.

1 (16-ounce) loaf French bread (whole wheat may also be used)

1 large head romaine lettuce, torn into pieces

1/4 cup grated Parmesan cheese

2 cups chopped grilled or leftover cooked chicken breasts

2 tablespoons nonfat sour cream

2 tablespoons light mayonnaise

1 teaspoon minced garlic

2 tablespoons lemon juice

1 tablespoon vinegar

1 teaspoon Worcestershire sauce

1/2 teaspoon dry mustard

1. Hollow out inside of French bread. Discard extra bread and set aside.

2. In a bowl, combine lettuce, cheese, and chicken.

3. In a small bowl, whisk together remaining ingredients. Toss mixtures together and stuff into each hollow bread section.

NUTRITIONAL INFORMATION PER SERVING
Calories 304 | Calories from fat 18% | Fat 6 g
Saturated Fat 2 g | Cholesterol 45 mg | Sodium 518 mg
Carbohydrate 38 g | Dietary Fiber 4 g | Sugars 4 g | Protein 24 g

DIABETIC EXCHANGES
2 1/2 starch | 2 lean meat

GRILLED DOVE BREASTS

MAKES 15 APPETIZER SERVINGS

Beautifully grilled bacon-wrapped dove breasts have a surprise filling of jalapeños and cream cheese.

2 cups reduced-fat Italian dressing

2 tablespoons Worcestershire sauce

30 dove breasts

2 fresh jalapeños, cored and sliced lengthwise

1 (8-ounce) package reduced-fat cream cheese

7 1/2 strips center-cut bacon, cut in half

1. In a shallow bowl, combine dressing and Worcestershire sauce. Add dove breasts and marinate in refrigerator overnight or for at least 8 hours. Discard marinade.

2. Place a jalapeño slice and about 1 table-spoon cream cheese on a dove breast and cover with another dove breast. Wrap together with half of a bacon slice and secure with a toothpick. Repeat with remaining dove breasts.

3. Grill over medium heat. (Watch carefully as bacon may cause flames to flare.)

NUTRITIONAL INFORMATION PER SERVING
Calories 135 | Calories from fat 35% | Fat 5 g
Saturated Fat 3 g | Cholesterol 67 mg | Sodium 330 mg
Carbohydrate 1 g | Dietary Fiber 0 g | Sugars 1 g | Protein 16 g

DIABETIC EXCHANGES
2 lean meat

WILD DOVE IN WINE SAUCE

MAKES 4 SERVINGS

Doves smothered in a wonderful wine sauce look and taste like a dish straight from a five-star restaurant. This recipe works great with quail also.

8 doves, cleaned and dressed

Salt and pepper to taste

1/4 cup plus 2 tablespoons all-purpose flour, divided

1 tablespoon butter

2 tablespoons olive oil

1 onion, chopped

1/2 cup chopped green bell pepper

1 teaspoon minced garlic

1/2 pound sliced mushrooms

1 1/2 cups Madeira wine or Madeira cooking wine

1–2 cups fat-free chicken broth

1. Season doves to taste and dust with 1/4 cup flour.

2. In a large heavy pot, melt butter and oil and brown doves on all sides. Remove and set aside. In the same pot, sauté onion, green pepper, garlic, and mushrooms until tender, about 5 minutes. Add remaining 2 tablespoons flour, stir for 1 minute.

3. Gradually add wine and broth, cook for two minutes. Return doves to the pot. Bring to a boil, reduce heat, cover, and simmer for 1 hour, or until doves are very tender. Remove skin before eating.

NUTRITIONAL INFORMATION PER SERVING
Calories 419 | Calories from fat 28% | Fat 12 g
Saturated Fat 3 g | Cholesterol 114 mg | Sodium 200 mg
Carbohydrate 23 g | Dietary Fiber 2 g | Sugars 8 g | Protein 30 g

DIABETIC EXCHANGES
1 starch | 1 vegetable | 3 lean meat | 1/2 fat

TERRIFIC TIDBIT

Keep Madiera cooking wine and cooking sherry in your pantry to have available whenever needed.

POULTRY & GAME BIRD

BAKED QUAIL IN SHERRY SAUCE

MAKES 6 SERVINGS

The tender quail baked in this delicious sauce is best when served with a starch like rice or potatoes.

6 quail breasts

Salt and pepper to taste

1/3 cup plus 1 tablespoon all-purpose flour, divided

1 tablespoon butter

1 tablespoon olive oil

1/2 pound sliced mushrooms

1 bunch green onions, chopped

2 tablespoons chopped parsley

1/2 cup sherry or cooking sherry

2 cups fat-free chicken broth

1. Preheat oven to 350°F.

2. Season quail to taste and coat with 1/3 cup flour. In a large nonstick skillet, heat butter and oil, add quail and brown on both sides. Remove quail and set in a baking dish.

3. In the same skillet, add mushrooms, green onions, parsley, and remaining 1 table-spoon flour. Gradually stir in sherry and broth. Bring to a boil, stirring continuously, until slightly thickened.

4. Pour sauce over quail and bake, covered, for 1 hour. Remove skin before eating.

NUTRITIONAL INFORMATION PER SERVING
Calories 206 | Calories from fat 37% | Fat 9 g
Saturated Fat 3 g | Cholesterol 69 mg | Sodium 193 mg
Carbohydrate 7 g | Dietary Fiber 1 g | Sugars 1 g | Protein 23 g

DIABETIC EXCHANGES
1/2 starch | 3 lean meat

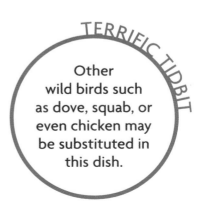

TERRIFIC TIDBIT

Other wild birds such as dove, squab, or even chicken may be substituted in this dish.

CROCK POT TEAL

MAKES 3–4 SERVINGS

For a savory meal, prepare the duck, put it in a crock pot, and forget about it. Serve over rice.

3 teal ducks, cleaned and dried

Salt and pepper to taste

1 onion, quartered

1 red apple, peeled, cored and quartered

1 stalk celery, chopped

1 (10-ounce) can fat-free cream of mushroom soup

1/2 cup water

1. Season ducks to taste inside and out. Stuff cavities with onion, apple, and celery.

2. Place ducks, breast side down, in a crock pot. Add soup and water, and cook on low for 5 hours or until meat is tender and falls off the bone. Remove skin before eating.

NUTRITIONAL INFORMATION PER SERVING
Calories 271 | Calories from fat 35% | Fat 11 g
Saturated Fat 4 g | Cholesterol 120 mg | Sodium 645 mg
Carbohydrate 13 g | Dietary Fiber 2 g | Sugars 7 g | Protein 29 g

DIABETIC EXCHANGES
1 carbohydrate | 4 lean meat

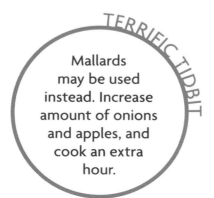

TERRIFIC TIDBIT

Mallards may be used instead. Increase amount of onions and apples, and cook an extra hour.

POT ROASTED DUCK

MAKES 8 SERVINGS

My friend, Dana Bernhard, told me her husband Jim had a reputation for his pot roasted duck and I was thrilled he shared this recipe. Blackened duck served over hot fluffy rice, this recipe is a true hunter's dream.

4 whole skin-on ducks, cleaned and plucked

1/4 cup plus 4 teaspoons Creole seasoning, divided

4 onions, chopped

4 tablespoons garlic, chopped

5 1/2 cups water, divided

1. Coat outside skin of ducks heavily with 1/4 cup Creole seasoning.

2. In a large ungreased cast iron pot, blacken ducks over medium heat for approximately 1 hour, turning frequently. Add onion and garlic, and sauté until tender, about 5–7 minutes.

3. Add 4 cups water and remaining Creole seasoning to the pot. Cook over low heat, covered, for 1 1/2 hours. Add remaining water and continue cooking, covered, 1 1/2 hours longer or until ducks are tender. Remove skin before eating.

NUTRITIONAL INFORMATION PER SERVING
Calories 229 | Calories from fat 35% | Fat 9 g
Saturated Fat 4 g | Cholesterol 117 mg | Sodium 355 mg
Carbohydrate 7 g | Dietary Fiber 2 g | Sugars 5 g | Protein 28 g

DIABETIC EXCHANGES
1 vegetable | 4 lean meat

MOLE DUCK ENCHILADAS

MAKES 22 ENCHILADAS

Hank Gray shared his infamous duck enchilada recipe with me. I trimmed it down, but kept it terrific. Southwestern condiments and a hit of lime juice compliment the boldly flavored yet light mole sauce. This recipe is a little fussy, but well worth the effort!

3 tablespoons canola oil, divided

6 boneless, skinless duck breasts, trimmed of excess fat

5 cups water

Salt and pepper to taste

1 teaspoon minced garlic

1 onion, chopped

2 dried ancho chilies stemmed, cored, torn into large pieces, and placed in boiling water for 5 minutes to soften

2 dried pasilla chilies, cored, torn into large pieces, and placed in boiling water for 5 minutes to soften

1/4 cup slivered almonds, coarsely chopped

1/4 cup coarsely chopped pecans

24 (6-inch) white corn tortillas, divided

1/4 cup raisins

1/4 teaspoon dried oregano leaves

1/4 teaspoon ground allspice

1 tomato, cored and quartered

2 cups fat-free chicken broth

1 teaspoon cocoa

2 cups shredded, reduced-fat, Mexican-blend cheese

1/2 cup finely crumbled cotija cheese (optional)

Diced avocado, chopped red onion, chopped cilantro, sour cream, lime (optional)

1. In a large nonstick pot, heat 2 tablespoons oil over medium heat and brown duck breasts. Add water and season to taste. Bring to a boil, reduce heat, cover, and cook for about 15 minutes. Transfer ducks to a plate and reserve 2 cups broth.

2. In another nonstick pot, heat remaining 1 tablespoon oil and sauté garlic and onion over medium heat until golden brown, about 5–7 minutes. Add chilies and nuts, and cook for 2–3 minutes. Cut 2 tortillas into quarters and add with raisins, oregano, allspice, and tomato. Cook until softened, about 2–3 minutes.

3. Add reserved duck broth and chicken broth. Bring to a boil, reduce heat, cover, and cook until slightly thickened, about 30 minutes. Cool and transfer to a blender to purée, or use a hand held blender in the pot. Add cocoa, stirring. Set aside.

4. Return duck to the pot with sauce and season to taste. Reduce heat and simmer about 40–50 minutes, or until tender. Remove duck from pot and shred tender duck breasts with a fork, discarding any tough pieces. Toss duck with enough sauce (about 1–1 1/2 cups) to make a moist paste. Reserve remaining sauce.

Continued on next page

Continued from previous page

5. Preheat oven to 350°.

6. Heat tortillas covered with a damp paper towel in the microwave to soften. Spread about 1 teaspoon reserved sauce on a tortilla, top with 1 heaping tablespoon duck mixture, and about 1 tablespoon Mexican-blend cheese. Roll tortilla and place seam side down in an oblong baking dish. Repeat with remaining tortillas.

7. Cover filled tortillas with remaining sauce. Sprinkle with remaining cheese. Bake, loosely covered with foil, until bubbly, about 25–30 minutes. If desired, sprinkle with Cotija cheese and choice of condiments.

NUTRITIONAL INFORMATION PER SERVING
Calories 170 | Calories from fat 41% | Fat 8 g
Saturated Fat 2 g | Cholesterol 40 mg | Sodium 152 mg
Carbohydrate 11 g | Dietary Fiber 2 g | Sugars 2 g | Protein 14 g

DIABETIC EXCHANGES
1/2 starch | 2 lean meat

TERRIFIC TIDBIT

Cotija, the most popular cheese in Mexico, is robust in flavor and is used to top enchiladas or salads.

BACON WRAPPED DUCK BREASTS

MAKES 6 SERVINGS

Crisp, flavorful bacon keeps the duck moist, while jalapeño adds a blast of heat. The wrapped ducks may also be grilled.

6 boneless skinless duck breasts

6–12 thin fresh jalapeño strips

6–12 thin onion strips

Dash cayenne

Salt and pepper to taste

6 strips center-cut bacon

1/3 cup barbecue sauce

1. Preheat oven to 375°F. Line a baking sheet with foil.

2. Cut one to two slits in each side of duck breasts. Place a jalapeño and an onion strip into each breast cavity, depending on taste. Sprinkle with cayenne and season to taste.

3. Wrap each breast with a strip of bacon, securing it with a toothpick.

4. Place breasts onto prepared baking sheet and top with barbecue sauce. Cook for about 45 minutes, or until bacon is crisp and duck is done.

NUTRITIONAL INFORMATION PER SERVING
Calories 261 | Calories from fat 32% | Fat 9 g
Saturated Fat 3 g | Cholesterol 134 mg | Sodium 315 mg
Carbohydrate 6 g | Dietary Fiber 0 g | Sugars 6 g | Protein 35 g

DIABETIC EXCHANGES
1/2 carbohydrate | 7 lean meat

Steak Tacos with Cucumber Avocado Salsa pg. 175

BEEF, PORK, VEAL & VENISON

Between 1990 and 2000, Louisiana's wetland loss was approximately 24 square miles per year—that is the equivalent of approximately one football field lost every 38 minutes.

Louisiana Department of Natural Resources

WETLANDS FACT

DIRTY RICE

MAKES 8 (1-CUP) SERVINGS

Turn leftover rice into a hearty meal with meat, seasonings, and eggplant for a Louisiana specialty.

2 medium eggplants, peeled and cubed

2 celery stalks, chopped

1 green bell pepper, cored and chopped

1 tablespoon minced garlic

1 pound ground sirloin

1/4 cup chopped parsley

1 bunch green onions, chopped

Dash cayenne

Salt and pepper to taste

2 1/2 cups cooked white or brown rice

1. In a large nonstick pot coated with nonstick cooking spray, cook eggplant, celery, green pepper, garlic, and meat over medium heat, covered, until meat is done and vegetables are tender, about 20–25 minutes.

2. Add parsley, green onions, and cayenne. Season to taste.

3. Add rice and mix well, continuing to cook for a few minutes or until well heated.

NUTRITIONAL INFORMATION PER SERVING
Calories 183 | Calories from fat 15% | Fat 3 g
Saturated Fat 1 g | Cholesterol 31 mg | Sodium 60 mg
Carbohydrate 24 g | Dietary Fiber 6 g | Sugars 4 g | Protein 15 g

DIABETIC EXCHANGES
1 starch | 2 vegetable | 2 very lean meat

EGGPLANT BEEF BAKE

MAKES 8 SERVINGS

Plentiful amounts of eggplant, beef, marinara, and cheese give you an instant, one-dish casserole great for everyday meals.

6 cups peeled, chopped, eggplant

1 onion, chopped

1 teaspoon minced garlic

1/2 pound ground sirloin

1 teaspoon dried oregano leaves

1/2 teaspoon dried basil leaves

3 cups cooked rice (brown preferred)

Salt and pepper to taste

2 cups marinara sauce

1 cup shredded, part-skim, mozzarella cheese

1. Preheat oven to 350°F.

2. In a large nonstick skillet coated with nonstick cooking spray, sauté eggplant, onion, garlic, and meat until meat is done and eggplant is tender, about 20 minutes. Add oregano, basil, and rice. Season to taste and mix well.

3. Transfer to a 2-quart casserole dish. Cover with marinara sauce and sprinkle with cheese. Bake for 20–30 minutes or until thoroughly heated.

NUTRITIONAL INFORMATION PER SERVING
Calories 212 | Calories from fat 24% | Fat 6 g
Saturated Fat 2 g | Cholesterol 25 mg | Sodium 372 mg
Carbohydrate 28 g | Dietary Fiber 5 g | Sugars 3 g | Protein 13 g

DIABETIC EXCHANGES
1 1/2 starch | 1 vegetable | 1 1/2 lean meat

MEDITERRANEAN MEATLOAF

MAKES 8 SERVINGS

This dish packs an explosion of flavors in a surprise center of roasted red peppers, feta, and spinach, with a perfect blend of Mediterranean spices on the outside. If freezing for later, freeze unbaked.

1 1/2 pounds ground sirloin

1/2 cup chopped onion

1/2 cup chopped green bell pepper

1 teaspoon minced garlic

1 teaspoon dried basil leaves

1 1/2 teaspoons dried oregano leaves

Salt and pepper to taste

2 egg whites

1/2 cup Italian breadcrumbs

1/2 cup coarsely chopped roasted red peppers, drained (found in jar)

1/4 cup reduced-fat crumbled feta cheese

1 cup coarsely chopped fresh baby spinach leaves

1. Preheat oven to 350°F.

2. In a large bowl, combine all ingredients, except roasted red peppers, feta, and spinach. Mix well. Transfer half into a nonstick 9 × 5 × 3-inch loaf pan.

3. Arrange a layer of roasted red peppers, feta, and spinach. Cover with remaining meat mixture.

4. Bake for 45–50 minutes or until meat is done.

NUTRITIONAL INFORMATION PER SERVING
Calories 161 | Calories from fat 27% | Fat 5 g
Saturated Fat 2 g | Cholesterol 49 mg | Sodium 259 mg
Carbohydrate 8 g | Dietary Fiber 1 g | Sugars 1 g | Protein 21 g

DIABETIC EXCHANGES
1/2 starch | 3 lean meat

TERRIFIC TIDBIT

To reduce the fat further, or if you're not a fan, leave the feta out. You'll still be amazed by this meatloaf's fabulous flavor.

ULTIMATE ITALIAN MEATLOAF

MAKES 6–8 SERVINGS

One of my favorite local Italian restaurants makes an incredible Italian meatloaf. Here's my "trim and terrific," yet still authentic, version which is unbelievably good too!

1 onion, finely chopped

1/3 cup finely chopped celery

1/4 cup finely chopped red bell pepper

1 tablespoon minced garlic

1 1/2 pounds ground sirloin

1/2 pound ground Italian sausage

1/3 cup chopped green onions

1/3 cup chopped Italian (flat-leaf) parsley

2 egg whites

1/3 cup fat-free half-and-half

1/4 cup ketchup

1 tablespoon Worcestershire sauce

1 1/2 teaspoons dried basil leaves

1 1/2 teaspoons dried oregano leaves

3/4 cup Italian breadcrumbs

Salt and pepper to taste

1/3 cup marinara sauce

1. Preheat oven to 350°F. Coat a large nonstick skillet with nonstick cooking spray

2. In prepared pan, sauté onion, celery, red pepper, and garlic over medium heat for about 5–7 minutes, or until tender. Remove from heat.

3. In a large bowl, combine all remaining ingredients, except marinara sauce. Add sautéed vegetables and mix well.

4. Transfer to a 9 × 5 × 3-inch nonstick loaf pan and top with marinara sauce. Bake meatloaf for 1 hour or until meat is done. Let sit for 5 minutes before cutting.

NUTRITIONAL INFORMATION PER SERVING
Calories 234 | Calories from fat 27% | Fat 7 g
Saturated Fat 3 g | Cholesterol 55 mg | Sodium 566 mg
Carbohydrate 16 g | Dietary Fiber 2 g | Sugars 5 g | Protein 27 g

DIABETIC EXCHANGES
1 starch | 3 lean meat

TERRIFIC TIDBIT
Fresh Italian sausage may be found in groceries in casings or ground. If found in casings, remove and crumble. There are a variety of Italian sausages (chicken and vegetable combinations) and they may be used to reduce the fat content further.

FIESTA BEEF ENCHILADAS

MAKES 12–14 ENCHILADAS

Enchiladas filled with meat, corn, spinach, and tomatoes and baked in a Mexican white sauce offer the ultimate Southwestern enchilada.

1 1/2 pounds ground sirloin

1 onion, chopped

1 teaspoon minced garlic

1 (4-ounce) can chopped green chilies, drained

1 (11-ounce) can Mexi-corn, drained (any corn may be used)

1 cup packed fresh baby spinach

1 cup chopped tomatoes

2 teaspoons chili powder

Salt and pepper to taste

12–14 (6–8-inch) flour tortillas

2 cups shredded, reduced-fat Mexican-blend cheese, divided

Enchilada Sauce (recipe below)

1 bunch green onions, chopped

1. Preheat oven to 350°F. Coat a 13 × 9 × 2-inch baking dish with nonstick cooking spray

2. In a large nonstick skillet, cook meat, onion, and garlic over medium heat for about 6–8 minutes or until meat is done. Drain any excess fat.

3. Add green chilies, corn, spinach, tomatoes, and chili powder. Season to taste and continue cooking for about 5 minutes. Remove from heat and set aside.

4. Heat tortillas in microwave between damp paper towels for about 30 seconds. Spoon meat mixture and about 1 tablespoon cheese onto a tortilla. Roll and place seam side down in prepared baking dish. Repeat for remaining tortillas.

5. Pour Enchilada Sauce evenly over filled tortillas and sprinkle with remaining cheese and green onions.

6. Bake, covered with foil, for about 20 minutes or until thoroughly heated.

ENCHILADA SAUCE

You can substitute canned enchilada sauce in a pinch, but this homemade sauce is easy to make and definitely enhances the recipe.

1/4 cup all-purpose flour

1 1/2 cups skim milk

1 cup fat-free chicken broth

2 teaspoons chili powder

1. In a nonstick pot, whisk together flour and milk. Bring to a boil, whisking constantly.

2. Add broth and chili powder. Return to a boil, and cook for several minutes or until thickened.

NUTRITIONAL INFORMATION PER SERVING
Calories 255 | Calories from fat 26% | Fat 7 g
Saturated Fat 4 g | Cholesterol 36 mg | Sodium 517 mg
Carbohydrate 27 g | Dietary Fiber 3 g | Sugars 4 g | Protein 19 g

DIABETIC EXCHANGES
1 1/2 starch | 1 vegetable | 2 lean meat

BEEF, PORK, VEAL & VENISON

BARBECUED POT ROAST

MAKES 8–10 SERVINGS

A barbecue twist to the classic pot roast earns this recipe high marks! The leftovers make tasty sandwiches. This recipe works great in a crock pot.

4 pounds sirloin tip roast, trimmed of excess fat

Garlic powder

Salt and pepper to taste

1 large onion, cut into rings

1 red bell pepper, cored and sliced into rings

1 1/4 cups barbecue sauce

1/4 cup molasses

1 tablespoon chili powder

1 tablespoon dry mustard

1 pound bag baby carrots

1. Preheat oven to 325°F. Coat a roaster with nonstick cooking spray

2. Sprinkle meat with garlic powder and season to taste. In prepared roaster, brown meat on both sides over medium heat on stove top. Remove meat and set aside.

3. Add remaining ingredients, except carrots, to the roaster. Scrape bottom of the pan. Bring to a boil, return meat to pan, and place in oven.

4. Cook for 1 1/2 hours. Add carrots and continue cooking for another 1 1/2 hours or until meat is tender.

NUTRITIONAL INFORMATION PER SERVING
Calories 352 | Calories from fat 20% | Fat 8 g
Saturated Fat 3 g | Cholesterol 74 mg | Sodium 319 mg
Carbohydrate 26 g | Dietary Fiber 2 g | Sugars 21 g | Protein 40 g

DIABETIC EXCHANGES
1 1/2 carbohydrate | 1 vegetable | 5 1/2 lean meat

TERRIFIC TIDBIT

In a rush?
Skip browning
the meat. Simply mix
the sauce ingredients,
and pop the roast and
sauce in the oven
to bake.

Barbecued Pot Roast pg. 170

PULLED POT ROAST
MAKES 10 SERVINGS

Just a few ingredients effortlessly create a tender pulled beef roast in a fantastic flavorful sauce that quickly won over my family. Pork roast may also be used. This recipe works great in a crock pot.

1 (4-pound) tip sirloin roast

1 (1.25-ounce) package fajita seasoning

2 (14 1/2-ounce) cans stewed tomatoes with Mexican seasoning

2 cups water

1. Coat a roaster with nonstick cooking spray.

2. Rub roast evenly with fajita seasoning. In prepared roaster, brown roast on all sides over medium heat on stove top.

3. Add tomatoes and water. Bring to a boil, reduce heat, cover, and simmer for 5 hours or until the roast is tender.

4. Remove roast and pull apart with a fork. Return pulled roast to sauce and serve.

———————

NUTRITIONAL INFORMATION PER SERVING
Calories 280 | Calories from fat 32% | Fat 10 g
Saturated Fat 3 g | Cholesterol 78 mg | Sodium 887 mg
Carbohydrate 6 g | Dietary Fiber 1 g | Sugars 5 g | Protein 39 g

DIABETIC EXCHANGES
1 vegetable | 5 1/2 lean meat

TERRIFIC TIDBIT

If you can't find Mexican stewed tomatoes, substitute with different tomatoes.

BEEF BRISKET
MAKES 12–14 SERVINGS

With simple preparation—season the brisket, refrigerate overnight, and pop in the oven—the delightful smell of tender brisket in a spicy-sweet sauce will fill your kitchen hours before it's done.

1 cup finely chopped onions

1 teaspoon minced garlic

2 tablespoons Dijon mustard

1/4 cup light brown sugar

1/4 cup Worcestershire sauce

1/4 cup molasses

1 teaspoon chili powder

1/4 cup low-sodium soy sauce

1/4 cup red wine or cooking wine

1 (4–5) pound beef brisket, trimmed of excess fat

1. In a rectangular glass baking dish, combine all ingredients, except brisket.

2. Add brisket to marinade. Cover and refrigerate overnight.

3. When ready to cook, preheat oven to 325°F.

4. Place brisket and marinade in oven in a heavy pot. Bake, covered, for about 4–5 hours, or until brisket is tender.

———————

NUTRITIONAL INFORMATION PER SERVING
Calories 253 | Calories from fat 25% | Fat 7 g
Saturated Fat 3 g | Cholesterol 69 mg | Sodium 324 mg
Carbohydrate 11 g | Dietary Fiber 0 g | Sugars 8 g | Protein 34 g

DIABETIC EXCHANGES
1 carbohydrate | 5 lean meat

BEEF LETTUCE WRAPS

MAKES 8 (1/2-CUP) SERVINGS

These easy yet exotic wraps embrace ground meat, Asian sauces, cucumber, and carrot. Serve with additional hoisin or peanut sauce, if desired.

1 pound ground sirloin

1/3 cup hoisin sauce

1/4 cup peanut sauce

Salt and pepper to taste

1/2 cup shredded carrot

1 cucumber, peeled, seeded and chopped

1 (8-ounce) can water chestnuts, drained and finely chopped

2 tablespoons torn fresh mint leaves (optional)

Boston lettuce leaves or red tip lettuce

1. In a large nonstick skillet coated with nonstick cooking spray, cook meat over medium heat for about 7 minutes, or until done. Drain any excess fat.

2. Stir in hoisin and peanut sauces and heat thoroughly. Season to taste.

3. Just before serving, add carrot, cucumber, water chestnuts, and mint, if desired.

4. Spoon mixture onto a lettuce leaf and wrap. Repeat with remaining leaves

---

NUTRITIONAL INFORMATION PER SERVING
Calories 126 | Calories from fat 34% | Fat 5 g
Saturated Fat 2 g | Cholesterol 31 mg | Sodium 122 mg
Carbohydrate 8 g | Dietary Fiber 1 g | Sugars 4 g | Protein 13 g

DIABETIC EXCHANGES
1/2 carbohydrate | 2 lean meat

QUICK BEEF THAI STIR-FRY

MAKES 4 SERVINGS

A touch of Thai gives dramatic flair to an easy stir-fry. Serve over Coconut Rice (pg. 174).

1 pound round steak, trimmed of excess fat and cut into strips

1 bunch green onions, chopped

2 cups broccoli florets

2 cups asparagus stems, trimmed and cut into 2-inch pieces

3/4 cup low-sodium, fat-free beef broth

2 teaspoons cornstarch

1/3 cup Thai peanut sauce

2 tablespoons dry roasted chopped peanuts (optional)

1. In a large nonstick skillet coated with nonstick cooking spray, cook meat until amost done, about 5–7 minutes.

2. Add green onions, broccoli, and asparagus. Sauté for 4 minutes or until vegetables are crisp tender. In a small bowl, combine broth and cornstarch. Add to vegetables. Add Thai peanut sauce.

3. Bring to a boil, reduce heat, and cook until thickened and beef is tender. Serve over rice and sprinkle with peanuts, if desired.

NUTRITIONAL INFORMATION PER SERVING
Calories 258 | Calories from fat 31% | Fat 9 g
Saturated Fat 2 g | Cholesterol 64 mg | Sodium 186 mg
Carbohydrate 12 g | Dietary Fiber 5 g | Sugars 3 g | Protein 31 g

DIABETIC EXCHANGES
2 vegetable | 3 1/2 lean meat

INDONESIAN BEEF SAUTÉ WITH COCONUT RICE

MAKES 4–6 SERVINGS

An Indonesian recipe with powerful flavors is simplified and adapted for the home cook. The heat of peppers, fresh ginger, and garlic complement the mild coconut rice.

1 1/2 pounds lean top round, trimmed and cut into thin strips

1/2 cup chopped green onions

2 tablespoons peeled, minced fresh ginger or 2 teaspoons ground ginger

6 garlic cloves, chopped

2 Serrano chilies, cored and finely chopped

1 teaspoon ground cumin

1/2 teaspoon ground cloves

1 1/2 cups fat-free beef broth

Salt and pepper

1 tablespoon lime juice

Coconut Rice (recipe below)

1. In a large nonstick skillet coated with nonstick cooking spray, cook meat until browned, about 5 minutes.

2. Add green onions, ginger, garlic, chilies, cumin, cloves, and broth. Bring to a boil, reduce heat, cover, and simmer for about 30 minutes or until beef is tender.

3. Season to taste and stir in lime juice. Serve over Coconut Rice.

NUTRITIONAL INFORMATION PER SERVING
(NOT INCLUDING RICE)
Calories 156 | Calories from fat 21% | Fat 4 g
Saturated Fat 1 g | Cholesterol 64 mg | Sodium 137 mg
Carbohydrate 3 g | Dietary Fiber 1 g | Sugars 1 g | Protein 27 g

DIABETIC EXCHANGES
3 lean meat

COCONUT RICE

If you don't have basmati rice, any rice will work fine.

1 1/4 cups water

1 cup light canned coconut milk

1 cup basmati rice

1. In a nonstick pot, bring water and coconut milk to a boil. Add rice.

2. Reduce heat, cover, and cook until liquid is absorbed and rice is tender, about 15–20 minutes. Fluff with fork and serve.

NUTRITIONAL INFORMATION PER SERVING
Calories 124 | Calories from fat 16% | Fat 2 g
Saturated Fat 1 g | Cholesterol 0 mg | Sodium 16 mg
Carbohydrate 23 g | Dietary Fiber 1 g | Sugars 1 g | Protein 2 g

DIABETIC EXCHANGES
1 1/2 starch

STEAK TACOS WITH CUCUMBER AVOCADO SALSA

MAKES 4–6 SERVINGS

A juicy, spice-rubbed steak with a cool, refreshing salsa is sure to be a family favorite.

1 tablespoon chili powder

1/4 teaspoon ground cinnamon

Pinch cayenne

Salt to taste

1/2 teaspoon minced garlic

1 1/4 pounds top sirloin steak, (1-inch thick), trimmed of excess fat

4–6 small flour tortillas

Cucumber Avocado Salsa (recipe to the right)

1. In a small bowl, combine chili powder, cinnamon, cayenne, salt, and garlic. Rub mixture on both sides of steak.

2. Grill or pan-fry steak in a nonstick skillet for 5–6 minutes on each side, or until done, according to preference. Cut into thin slices.

3. Heat tortillas in microwave between damp paper towels for about 30 seconds.

4. Fill tortillas with steak and serve topped with Cucumber Avocado Salsa.

NUTRITIONAL INFORMATION PER SERVING
(NOT INCLUDING SALSA)
Calories 220 | Calories from fat 24% | Fat 6 g
Saturated Fat 2 g | Cholesterol 38 mg | Sodium 194 mg
Carbohydrate 17 g | Dietary Fiber 1 g | Sugars 0 g | Protein 23 g

DIABETIC EXCHANGES
1 starch | 3 lean meat

CUCUMBER AVOCADO SALSA

MAKES 2 CUPS

Mild avocados, cool cumbers, tomatoes, and spicy peppers tossed in lime juice flawlessly balance the fiery steak.

2 cups finely chopped, peeled seeded cucumber

1/2 cup diced avocado

1/2 cup cherry tomatoes, cut into fourths

1/3 cup chopped red onion

3 tablespoons chopped jalapenos (found in jar)

2 tablespoons lime juice

Salt and pepper to taste

1. In a bowl, combine all ingredients.

NUTRITIONAL INFORMATION PER SERVING
Calories 37 | Calories from fat 48% | Fat 2 g
Saturated Fat 0 g | Cholesterol 0 mg | Sodium 104 mg
Carbohydrate 5 g | Dietary Fiber 2 g | Sugars 2 g | Protein 1 g

DIABETIC EXCHANGES
1 vegetable | 1/2 fat

FLANK STEAK AND SAUTÉED ONION WRAP

MAKES 8 WRAPS

Flank steak marinated in bold flavors, topped with crispy, sautéed onions and Boursin cheese, makes for an exceptional wrap.

1/4 cup low-sodium soy sauce

1 tablespoon Worcestershire sauce

1 teaspoon minced garlic

1 tablespoon light brown sugar

1 teaspoon ground ginger

2 tablespoons olive oil, divided

1 1/2 pounds lean flank steak, trimmed of excess fat

2 onions, thinly sliced

1 (4.4-ounce) container light Boursin cheese (about 1/2 cup)

1/4 cup nonfat sour cream

8 flour tortillas or wraps

8 romaine lettuce leaves

1. In a resealable plastic bag, combine soy sauce, Worcestershire sauce, garlic, brown sugar, ginger, and 1 tablespoon oil. Add meat to the bag, seal, and refrigerate for a minimum of 2 hours, time permitting.

2. Sear meat in a nonstick skillet or grill, just until rare, about 10-12 minutes. Remove from heat and cut into thin slices at an angle across the grain.

3. In a nonstick skillet coated with nonstick cooking spray, heat remaining 1 tablespoon oil and sauté onions over medium heat. Cook until light brown and crispy, about 15 minutes.

4. In a small bowl, combine Boursin cheese and sour cream. Spread a heaping table-spoon on each tortilla or wrap. Top with a lettuce leaf, add onions and several slices of flank steak.

5. Roll tightly to enclose filling. Cut in half at an angle and serve.

NUTRITIONAL INFORMATION PER SERVING
Calories 295 | Calories from fat 36% | Fat 12 g
Saturated Fat 5 g | Cholesterol 40 mg | Sodium 503 mg
Carbohydrate 22 g | Dietary Fiber 2 g | Sugars 4 g | Protein 24 g

DIABETIC EXCHANGES
1 starch | 1 vegetable | 3 lean meat | 1/2 fat

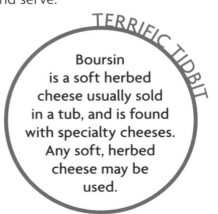

TERRIFIC TIDBIT

Boursin is a soft herbed cheese usually sold in a tub, and is found with specialty cheeses. Any soft, herbed cheese may be used.

OVEN-STYLE BABY BACK BARBECUE RIBS

MAKES 6 SERVINGS

Craving ribs but don't feel like barbecuing? Whip up this quick barbecue sauce and cook the ribs slowly in an oven for a just-off-the-grill taste.

1 (12-ounce) bottle chili sauce

1/4 cup dark brown sugar

1/4 cup Worcestershire sauce

1/2 cup finely chopped onion

1/4 cup cider vinegar

3/4 cup apple juice

2 teaspoons paprika

1 tablespoon garlic powder

2 slabs baby back ribs (about 4 pounds)

1. Preheat oven to 275°F.

2. In a bowl, combine all ingredients except ribs. Reserving about 1 1/4 cup sauce, pour the rest over ribs. If time permits, marinate in refrigerator for 2 hours or overnight.

3. Place ribs in heavy pot or roaster, cover, and cook for 2 hours. Remove from oven, baste with sauce, return to oven, and cook for 1 hour. Repeat basting, and cook for another 2 hours, or until meat is tender and pulls easily off the bone.

NUTRITIONAL INFORMATION PER SERVING
Calories 633 | Calories from fat 58% | Fat 41 g
Saturated Fat 15 g | Cholesterol 163 mg | Sodium 1024 mg
Carbohydrate 31 g | Dietary Fiber 1 g | Sugars 24 g | Protein 34 g

DIABETIC EXCHANGES
2 carbohydrate | 5 high-fat meat

BOURBON GLAZED PORK TENDERLOIN

MAKES 12–16 SERVINGS

A sweet and savory, bourbon-based marinade for the pork tenderloins will satisfy even the most insatiable appetite.

1/2 cup bourbon

1/3 cup light brown sugar

2/3 cup low-sodium soy sauce

1/4 cup lemon juice

1 tablespoon Worcestershire sauce

1 teaspoon dried thyme leaves

2 (2-pound) pork tenderloins, trimmed of excess fat

1. Preheat oven to 350°F.

2. In a bowl, combine all ingredients except tenderloins. Place meat in a dish or large resealable plastic bag and pour marinade over meat. If time permits, refrigerate overnight, turning meat several times.

3. Roast in oven for 40 minutes or until a meat thermometer inserted into the thickest portion registers 160°F.

NUTRITIONAL INFORMATION PER SERVING
Calories 142 | Calories from fat 24% | Fat 4 g
Saturated Fat 1 g | Cholesterol 63 mg | Sodium 355 mg
Carbohydrate 1 g | Dietary Fiber 0 g | Sugars 1 g | Protein 23 g

DIABETIC EXCHANGES
3 very lean meat

TERRIFIC TIDBIT

Ribs are high in fat—beef ribs are a bit lower.

HERB ROASTED TENDERLOIN

MAKES 4 SERVINGS

Dried herbs give the tenderloin tremendous flavor without marinating. If desired, serve with a delightful Sherry Sauce.

1 (1-pound) pork tenderloin trimmed of excess fat

1 tablespoon Dijon mustard

1 teaspoon dried rosemary leaves

1 teaspoon dried oregano leaves

1 teaspoon dried thyme leaves

1/2 teaspoon coarsely ground pepper

Sherry Sauce (recipe to the right), if desired

1. Preheat oven to 450°F.

2. Brush tenderloin with mustard. In a small bowl, combine rosemary, oregano, and thyme, and pat evenly onto tenderloin. Sprinkle with pepper.

3. Place tenderloin on rack in a roasting pan. Place in oven and immediately reduce temperature to 350°F.

4. Roast until meat thermometer inserted in thickest part of tenderloin registers 160°F, about 30-35 minutes.

5. Slice and serve with Sherry Sauce, if desired.

NUTRITIONAL INFORMATION PER SERVING
(NOT INCLUDING SAUCE)
Calories 140 | Calories from fat 27% | Fat 4 g
Saturated Fat 1 g | Cholesterol 63 mg | Sodium 122 mg
Carbohydrate 1 g | Dietary Fiber 1 g | Sugars 0 g | Protein 23 g

DIABETIC EXCHANGES
3 very lean meat

SHERRY SAUCE

Flavorful and light, this sauce goes with any meat.

1 (14-ounce) can fat free beef broth with onions

1/4 cup sherry or cooking sherry

1 1/2 teaspoons cornstarch

1. In a nonstick pot, whisk together all ingredients, mixing well, over medium heat.

2. Bring to a boil, reduce heat, and simmer for 5 minutes or until thickened.

3. Serve sauce over sliced tenderloin.

NUTRITIONAL INFORMATION PER SERVING
Calories 24 | Calories from fat 0% | Fat 0 g
Saturated Fat 0 g | Cholesterol 0 mg | Sodium 417 mg
Carbohydrate 2 g | Dietary Fiber 0 g | Sugars 1 g | Protein 1 g

DIABETIC EXCHANGES
Free

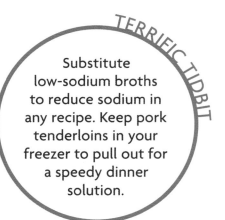

TERRIFIC TIDBIT

Substitute low-sodium broths to reduce sodium in any recipe. Keep pork tenderloins in your freezer to pull out for a speedy dinner solution.

SOUTHWESTERN PORK CHOPS

MAKES 4 SERVINGS

Looking for a quick dinner? A pack of pork chops and a few seasonings become a great tasting meal bursting with flavor in less than 20 minutes.

2 tablespoons light brown sugar

1 teaspoon ground cumin

1 teaspoon chili powder

Salt and pepper to taste

4 center-cut pork chops, trimmed of excess fat

1. In a small bowl, combine brown sugar, cumin, and chili powder.

2. Season pork chops to taste and sprinkle each side with brown sugar mixture.

3. Heat a nonstick skillet or grill pan coated with nonstick cooking spray, and cook pork chops for 5–7 minutes on each side, until browned and done.

NUTRITIONAL INFORMATION PER SERVING
Calories 179 | Calories from fat 31% | Fat 6 g
Saturated Fat 2 g | Cholesterol 61 mg | Sodium 54 mg
Carbohydrate 7 g | Dietary Fiber 0 g | Sugars 7 g | Protein 23 g

DIABETIC EXCHANGES
1/2 carbohydrate | 3 lean meat

TERRIFIC TIDBIT

Try different flavors of seasoned vinegar to enhance the marinade.

MARINATED HOISIN PORK CHOPS

MAKES 6–8 SERVINGS

This Asian-inspired, sweet, spicy, and salty, marinade hits every taste bud and works great on everything from pork to tuna. Hoisin sauce is a sweet, spicy sauce sold in the Asian food section of groceries.

1/3 cup hoisin sauce

2 tablespoons seasoned rice vinegar

2 tablespoons bourbon

2 tablespoons pure maple syrup

1 teaspoon grated fresh ginger or 1/4 teaspoon ground ginger

1/2 teaspoon chili paste

1 teaspoon minced garlic

6–8 pork center loin pork chops, trimmed

1. In a shallow dish, combine all ingredients, except pork chops. Add pork chops and marinate, refrigerated, until ready to cook.

2. Heat a nonstick skillet or grill pan coated with nonstick cooking spray, and cook pork chops until browned and done, about 5 minutes on each side.

NUTRITIONAL INFORMATION PER SERVING
Calories 165 | Calories from fat 32% | Fat 6 g
Saturated Fat 2 g | Cholesterol 61 mg | Sodium 85 mg
Carbohydrate 3 g | Dietary Fiber 0 g | Sugars 3 g | Protein 22 g

DIABETIC EXCHANGES
3 lean meat

VERY GOOD VEAL
MAKES 6 SERVINGS

Tender veal strips cooked with mushrooms and tomatoes produce a scrumptious dish that goes great with angel hair pasta.

1 pound veal scaloppini, cut into 1-inch strips

4 tablespoons all-purpose flour

Salt and pepper to taste

1 onion, chopped

1/2 pound sliced baby portabellas or mushrooms

1/2 cup white wine or chicken broth

1/2 cup fat-free chicken broth

1/2 teaspoon minced garlic

1 teaspoon dried oregano leaves

1 cup cherry or grape tomatoes, halved

1. Coat veal with flour and season to taste.

2. In a large nonstick skillet coated with nonstick cooking spray, cook veal over medium heat until brown on both sides, stirring constantly. Add onion and mushrooms, and cook until vegetables are tender.

3. Add remaining ingredients, scraping bottom of the pan. Bring to a boil, reduce heat, cover, and simmer for 5–7 minutes or until veal is tender

---

NUTRITIONAL INFORMATION PER SERVING
Calories 132 | Calories from fat 16% | Fat 2 g
Saturated Fat 1 g | Cholesterol 63 mg | Sodium 104 mg
Carbohydrate 8 g | Dietary Fiber 2 g | Sugars 3 g | Protein 18 g

DIABETIC EXCHANGES
1 vegetable | 2 very lean meat

TERRIFIC TIDBIT

If you've never tried the versatile and tasty meaty portabella mushroom, look for the baby pre-sliced variety in the grocery. A large portabella, thinly sliced, may also be used.

VENISON TENDERLOIN

MAKES 2 SERVINGS

My friend, Dr. Randy Brown, is a hunter, and his wife, Debbie, is famous for her venison tenderloin. This recipe was so good, I just had to include it in my book!

8-ounce venison backstrap tenderloin, well trimmed

1 teaspoon olive oil

2 tablespoons coarsely ground black pepper

2 tablespoons dried thyme leaves

1 teaspoon dried oregano leaves

1/4 teaspoon salt

1/4 teaspoon cayenne

1 teaspoon white pepper

1 teaspoon garlic powder

1. Rub venison tenderloin with oil. In a small bowl, combine remaining ingredients and rub over tenderloin. Cover with plastic wrap and refrigerate for 8 hours or overnight.

2. When ready to cook, preheat oven to 500°F.

3. Place tenderloin on rack in a baking pan and cook for 5 minutes. Reduce temperature to 350°F and continue cooking for 15–20 minutes. Slice and serve with pan juices.

NUTRITIONAL INFORMATION PER SERVING
Calories 193 | Calories from fat 24% | Fat 5 g
Saturated Fat 1 g | Cholesterol 96 mg | Sodium 353 mg
Carbohydrate 9 g | Dietary Fiber 4 g | Sugars 0 g | Protein 27 g

DIABETIC EXCHANGES
1/2 carbohydrate | 3 lean meat

TERRIFIC TIDBIT
Venison may be eaten as steaks, roasts, sausages, or ground. It has a similar flavor to beef, but it is usually leaner and lower in calories, cholesterol, and fat than most cuts of beef or pork—give it a try!

VENISON SCALOPPINI

MAKES 4–6 SERVINGS

I consulted my friend Debbie, the resident venison expert, for this recipe which high-lights the venison in a rich delicious sauce. Serve with angel hair pasta.

1 1/2 pounds venison round steak, trimmed and thinly sliced

1/3 cup all-purpose flour

1/4 cup olive oil

1 onion, chopped

1/2 green bell pepper, cored and chopped

Pinch dried rosemary leaves

Pinch dried thyme leaves

Pinch dried oregano leaves

Salt to taste

1 (10-ounce) can tomato soup

1/2 cup water

1/2 cup port wine

1 (4-ounce) can mushrooms, drained

1/2 cup shredded, reduced-fat Cheddar cheese, optional

1. Coat venison with flour.

2. In a large nonstick skillet, heat oil and sauté onion and green pepper until tender. Remove vegetables from pan and set aside.

3. In the same pan, add meat and brown on both sides. Add remaining ingredients, except mushrooms and cheese.

4. Return onions and peppers to pan and add mushrooms. Cover, reduce heat, and simmer for about 35–45 minutes, or until meat is tender. Sprinkle with cheese, if desired.

NUTRITIONAL INFORMATION PER SERVING
Calories 306 | Calories from fat 36% | Fat 12 g
Saturated Fat 2 g | Cholesterol 96 mg | Sodium 416 mg
Carbohydrate 18 g | Dietary Fiber 2 g | Sugars 8 g | Protein 28 g

DIABETIC EXCHANGES
1 starch | 3 1/2 lean meat

TERRIFIC TIDBIT

Green peppers are rich sources of fiber, vitamins C and A, folate, and other nutrients. Unwashed bell peppers may be stored in the vegetable compartment of the refrigerator for up to one week.

VENISON ROAST

MAKES 10 SERVINGS

The longer this roast cooks, the better it gets. My good friend Marty, who shared this favorite recipe of hers with me, said it works great in a crock pot. If you have an open bottle of red wine, toss some in.

1 (4-pound) venison hindquarter roast, stripped of membranes
Creole seasoning
Salt and pepper to taste
1/4 cup all-purpose flour
5 strips center-cut bacon, cut in half
1 onion, chopped
1 green bell pepper, cored and chopped
2 teaspoons minced garlic
1 (14 1/2-ounce) can fat-free beef broth
1 (10.5-ounce) can Golden Mushroom Soup
1 beef bouillon cube
1 (10-ounce) can diced green tomatoes and green chilies

1. Preheat oven 325°F.

2. Sprinkle roast with Creole seasoning, season to taste, and dust with flour.

2. Lay bacon strips in bottom of a roaster and place roast on top. Add remaining ingredients, cover, and cook for 5–8 hours or until tender.

NUTRITIONAL INFORMATION PER SERVING
Calories 281 | Calories from fat 21% | Fat 7 g
Saturated Fat 2 g | Cholesterol 159 mg | Sodium 765 mg
Carbohydrate 8 g | Dietary Fiber 1 g | Sugars 2 g | Protein 45 g

DIABETIC EXCHANGES
1/2 starch | 6 very lean meat

VENISON POT ROAST

MAKES 12 SERVINGS

For a tender roast cooked in delicious onion gravy, my friend Debbie simply throws this all together in one pot. Thicken, if needed, and serve over rice with carrots and potatoes.

3 pound venison roast, trimmed
4 garlic cloves, peeled and sliced
2 tablespoons Creole seasoning
Flour to coat
1/4 cup canola oil
2 (10.5-ounce) cans French Onion soup, plus 2 cans of water
2 baking potatoes, cut into chunks
1 cup baby carrots

1. Preheat oven to 350°F.

2. Make slits in roast with a knife and insert garlic cloves. Rub roast with Creole seasoning and dust with flour.

3. In a large roasting pot, heat oil and brown roast on all sides. Remove roast, discard excess oil, and return roast to pot. Add soup and water.

4. Bake, covered, for 3 hours or until tender. Add potatoes and carrots, and continue baking for an additional hour.

NUTRITIONAL INFORMATION PER SERVING
Calories 224 | Calories from fat 32% | Fat 8 g
Saturated Fat 2 g | Cholesterol 98 mg | Sodium 598 mg
Carbohydrate 9 g | Dietary Fiber 1 g | Sugars 2 g | Protein 28 g

DIABETIC EXCHANGES
1/2 starch | 3 lean meat

Garden Fresh Penne pg. 196

PASTA

WETLANDS FACT

Louisiana coastal wetlands provide storm protection for ports that carry 487 million tons of waterborne commerce annually. That accounts for 19% of all waterborne commerce in the United States each year.

Louisiana Department of Natural Resources

SHRIMP AND ITALIAN SAUSAGE FETTUCCINE

MAKES 6–8 SERVINGS

This exceptionally flavorful dish combines lightly cola sweetened Italian sausage with fettuccine, creating a dramatic pasta finale that will tantalize your taste buds.

1 (12-ounce) package fettuccine

8 ounces Italian sausage, crumbled

1 cup diet cola

1 pound medium peeled shrimp

1 (10-ounce) can diced tomatoes and green chilies

1 tablespoon minced garlic

1/2 cup white wine or cooking wine

1 cup chopped fresh flat-leaf Italian parsley

1 bunch green onions, chopped

1/4 pound fresh mozzarella, cut into small pieces (optional)

1. Cook pasta according to package directions, omitting any salt or oil. Drain and set aside.

2. In a nonstick skillet, cook sausage over medium heat until browned. Remove from heat and gradually add cola, stirring. Return to heat and cook until cola is reduced to about 1/4 cup, about 10 minutes. Set aside.

3. In another large nonstick skillet coated with nonstick cooking spray, sauté shrimp for about a minute. Add tomatoes and green chilies and garlic, cooking for 3 minutes. Add wine, cooking and stirring until shrimp are done. Stir in parsley and green onions, cooking for one minute.

4. Toss pasta and Italian sausage with shrimp mixture. If desired, top with fresh mozzarella, and serve.

NUTRITIONAL INFORMATION PER SERVING
Calories 272 | Calories from fat 12% | Fat 4 g
Saturated Fat 1 g | Cholesterol 93 mg | Sodium 414 mg
Carbohydrate 37 g | Dietary Fiber 3 g | Sugars 3 g | Protein 20 g

DIABETIC EXCHANGES
2 starch | 1 vegetable | 2 very lean meat

TERRIFIC TIDBIT

Look for fresh homemade Italian sausage and other varieties of sausage blends in many groceries.

MARINATED ITALIAN SHRIMP PARMESAN PASTA

MAKES 4–6 SERVINGS

Shrimp marinated with Italian seasoning and broiled quickly with a light crispy topping make this pasta dish hard to miss!

2 tablespoons olive oil

1/2 cup white wine or cooking wine

1 tablespoon minced garlic

2 tablespoons chopped parsley

1 tablespoon lemon juice

1 teaspoon dried oregano leaves

1 teaspoon dried basil leaves

Salt and pepper to taste

1 1/2 pounds medium peeled shrimp

2/3 cup breadcrumbs (fresh preferred)

1/3 cup grated Parmesan cheese

1 (8-ounce) package angel hair pasta

1. In a shallow dish or resealable plastic bag, combine oil, wine, garlic, parsley, lemon juice, oregano, basil, salt, and pepper. Add shrimp to mixture, cover, and refrigerate up to 4 hours, or as time permits.

2. Preheat oven to 500°F. Line a baking sheet with foil.

3. Arrange shrimp, covered with marinade, in prepared baking sheet. Bake for 12–15 minutes or until shrimp are almost done.

4. Sprinkle with breadcrumbs and Parmesan cheese. Continue baking for 3–5 minutes or until cheese is melted and breadcrumbs are light brown.

5. Cook pasta according to package directions, omitting any salt or oil. Drain and toss with shrimp, or serve pasta topped with shrimp and sauce.

NUTRITIONAL INFORMATION PER SERVING
Calories 309 | Calories from fat 22% | Fat 8 g
Saturated Fat 2 g | Cholesterol 172 mg | Sodium 299 mg
Carbohydrate 32 g | Dietary Fiber 1 g | Sugars 2 g | Protein 25 g

DIABETIC EXCHANGES
2 starch | 3 lean meat

TERRIFIC TIDBIT

To make fresh breadcrumbs, place slices of bread in the food processor and process until fine crumbs. Whole-wheat bread may be used.

SHRIMP AND CRABMEAT FETTUCCINE

MAKES 6–8 SERVINGS

Every seafood lover's dream, succulent shrimp and tender crabmeat fuse perfectly with a touch of white wine to create a sublimely flavored white sauce for fettuccine. Any pasta may be used.

1 (16-ounce) package fettuccini

1 onion, chopped

1 green bell pepper, cored and chopped

2 tablespoons all-purpose flour

2 cups fat-free chicken broth

1/2 cup white wine or cooking wine

1 1/2 cups fat-free half-and-half

1/2 cup grated Parmesan cheese

1 tablespoon Creole or grainy mustard

1 pound peeled shrimp, seasoned and cooked

1 pound lump or white crabmeat, picked through for shells

1/2 cup chopped green onions

Dash cayenne

Salt and pepper to taste

1. Cook fettuccine according to package directions, omitting any oil or salt. Drain and set aside.

2. In a large nonstick pot coated with nonstick cooking spray, sauté onion and green pepper until tender, about 5–7 minutes. Stir in flour and gradually add broth and wine. Cook over low heat for 10 minutes or until bubbly, stirring constantly.

3. Add half-and-half, cheese, and mustard. Continue cooking until cheese is melted and mixture is well heated. Gently fold in remaining ingredients, except pasta.

4. Serve over fettuccine.

NUTRITIONAL INFORMATION PER SERVING
Calories 408 | Calories from fat 8% | Fat 4 g
Saturated Fat 1 g | Cholesterol 158 mg | Sodium 631 mg
Carbohydrate 54 g | Dietary Fiber 3 g | Sugars 7 g | Protein 38 g

DIABETIC EXCHANGES
3 1/2 starch | 4 very lean meat

TERRIFIC TIDBIT

Keep bottles of red and white cooking wine in your pantry for consistency in flavor as cooking wine is made especially for cooking.

188

CRAWFISH FETTUCCINE

MAKES 4–6 SERVINGS

When I want to showcase crawfish and need to prepare enough to feed a crowd—whether it is the volleyball team, my daughter's college friends, or a casual gathering—I often double this make-ahead recipe and it always comes to my rescue.

1 (8-ounce) package fettuccine

1 tablespoon butter

1 onion, chopped

1 green bell pepper, cored and chopped

1 teaspoon minced garlic

2 tablespoons all-purpose flour

1 (12-ounce) can evaporated skim milk

4 ounces reduced-fat pasteurized cheese spread

1/2 cup shredded, part-skim, mozzarella cheese

1 pound crawfish tails, rinsed and drained

2 tablespoons chopped parsley

1 tablespoon Worcestershire sauce

1 teaspoon hot sauce

1 bunch green onion, chopped

1. Cook fettuccine according to directions on package. Drain and set aside.

2. In a large nonstick pot, melt butter and sauté onion, green pepper, and garlic until tender. Add flour and stir until combined.

3. Gradually stir in milk until mixture is smooth and bubbly. Add cheese spread and mozzarella, stirring until melted. Add the remaining ingredients, except green onions, and cook for 2 minutes or until heated.

4. Toss with pasta and green onions and serve.

NUTRITIONAL INFORMATION PER SERVING
Calories 376 | Calories from fat 18% | Fat 7 g
Saturated Fat 4 g | Cholesterol 125 mg | Sodium 563 mg
Carbohydrate 46 g | Dietary Fiber 3 g | Sugars 14 g | Protein 30 g

DIABETIC EXCHANGES
2 starch | 1/2 fat-free milk | 1 vegetable | 3 lean meat

TERRIFIC TIDBIT

Try using whole wheat or multi-grain blend pastas

PASTA

CRABMEAT ANGEL HAIR PASTA

MAKES 6–8 SERVINGS

Easy and impressive, an extraordinary crabmeat sauce laced with mushrooms and spinach boasts grand flavors.

1 (8-ounce) package angel hair pasta

1 tablespoon butter

1 tablespoon olive oil

1/2 pound sliced mushrooms

1/2 cup chopped green onions

1/3 cup chopped fresh parsley

1 teaspoon minced garlic

1 tablespoon cornstarch

1 (12-ounce) can evaporated skim milk, divided

1/3 cup white wine or cooking wine

1 cup packed fresh baby spinach leaves

1 pound lump or white crabmeat, picked through for shells

Salt and pepper to taste

1/3 cup grated Parmesan cheese (optional)

1. Cook pasta according to package directions, omitting any salt or oil. Drain and set aside.

2. In a large nonstick skillet, heat butter and oil and sauté mushrooms, green onions, parsley, and garlic over medium heat for about 5–7 minutes, or until tender.

3. In a bowl, combine cornstarch with about 1/2 cup milk, and mix until smooth. Add to the pan and stir continuously.

4. Gradually add wine and remaining milk, stirring until mixture thickens. Reduce heat and add spinach and crabmeat, stirring until spinach is wilted. Season to taste.

5. Toss with pasta and sprinkle with Parmesan cheese before serving, if desired.

NUTRITIONAL INFORMATION PER SERVING
Calories 252 | Calories from fat 16% | Fat 4 g
Saturated Fat 1 g | Cholesterol 49 mg | Sodium 290 mg
Carbohydrate 30 g | Dietary Fiber 1 g | Sugars 7 g | Protein 21 g

DIABETIC EXCHANGES
1 1/2 starch | 1/2 fat-free milk | 2 very lean meat

TERRIFIC TIDBIT

Did you know that 12 cups raw spinach yields 2 cups cooked? That's 12 cups of nutrients packed into 2!

190

Crabmeat Angel Hair Pasta pg. 190

SCALLOPS WITH ANGEL HAIR

MAKES 6–8 SERVINGS

Mild seared scallops, a light spunky tomato sauce, and crunchy bacon make up this unique dish that's guaranteed to be noticed. Be prepared to share the recipe with everyone who tries it!

12 ounces angel hair pasta

4 strips center-cut bacon

1 pound sea scallops

2 cups fat-free half-and-half

1 teaspoon paprika

1/2 teaspoon chili powder

1/4 teaspoon ground ginger

1/2 cup finely chopped tomatoes

1. Cook pasta according to package directions, omitting any salt or oil. Drain and set aside.

2. Cook bacon in microwave until crisp. Crumble, and set aside.

3. In a nonstick skillet coated with nonstick cooking spray, sear scallops on both sides over medium heat. Cook in batches if necessary. Remove scallops to a plate.

4. Pour half-and-half into pan, scraping up any bits, and cook over low heat. Reduce sauce by one-third, stirring frequently. Stir in remaining ingredients.

5. Add scallops and cook until heated. Serve scallops and sauce over angel hair pasta and sprinkle with bacon.

NUTRITIONAL INFORMATION PER SERVING
Calories 266 | Calories from fat 8% | Fat 2 g
Saturated Fat 1 g | Cholesterol 22 mg | Sodium 220 mg
Carbohydrate 42 g | Dietary Fiber 1 g | Sugars 6 g | Protein 20 g

DIABETIC EXCHANGES
3 starch | 2 very lean meat

TERRIFIC TIDBIT

The secret for crispy seared scallops is to make sure the scallops are completely dry before cooking.

trim&TERRIFIC™ GULF COAST FAVORITES

OYSTERS AND ANGEL HAIR

MAKES 6 SERVINGS

Angel hair in a light garlic olive oil with crispy oysters will alert the taste buds of any oyster fan.

12 ounces angel hair pasta, reserving 1/2 cup pasta water

1 (8-ounce) container small oysters

1/2 cup Italian breadcrumbs

1/4 cup olive oil

1 tablespoon minced garlic

1/2 cup chopped fresh parsley

1 bunch green onions, chopped

Dash cayenne

Salt and pepper to taste

1. Cook pasta according to package directions. Drain, reserving 1/2 cup pasta water, and set aside

2. Drain oysters and roll in breadcrumbs. In a large nonstick skillet coated with nonstick cooking spray, cook oysters over medium heat until browned. Remove to a plate.

3. In the same pan, heat oil and sauté garlic, parsley, and green onions until tender, scraping bottom of pan to get bits, about 5 minutes. Add reserved pasta liquid and oysters, heating.

4. Toss pasta with sautéed mixture. Add cayenne and season to taste.

NUTRITIONAL INFORMATION PER SERVING
Calories 370 | Calories from fat 26% | Fat 11 g
Saturated Fat 2 g | Cholesterol 20 mg | Sodium 237 mg
Carbohydrate 54 g | Dietary Fiber 3 g | Sugars 4 g | Protein 12 g

DIABETIC EXCHANGES
3 1/2 starch | 1/2 very lean meat | 1 1/2 fat

TERRIFIC TIDBIT

When a recipe calls for chopped parsley, I recommend using fresh chopped parsley for any amount over a few tablespoons. Dried parsley flakes may be used for smaller amounts.

PASTA

THAI CHICKEN WITH LINGUINE

MAKES 4–6 SERVINGS

Introduce yourself to Thai food with this popular dish featuring fresh ginger (a must), peanut butter, coconut milk, and chicken. If you are in a rush, use rotisserie chicken in the cooked sauce.

1 (8-ounce) package linguine

1 teaspoon minced garlic

1/2 cup chopped green bell pepper

1/2 cup sliced mushrooms

1 tablespoon finely chopped fresh jalapeño pepper

1 pound boneless, skinless, chicken breasts, cut into thin strips, or 1 1/2 cups skinless, chopped rotisserie chicken

1 1/2 cups canned light coconut milk

1/4 cup peanut butter

2 tablespoons low-sodium soy sauce

1 tablespoon lime juice

2 tablespoons peeled, minced fresh ginger

1 tablespoon honey

Dash hot sauce

Salt and pepper to taste

1/2 cup chopped green onions

1. Prepare linguine according to package directions, drain well and set aside.

2. In a large nonstick skillet coated with nonstick cooking spray, sauté garlic, green pepper, mushrooms, and jalapeño for a few minutes.

3. Add chicken and continue cooking until chicken is almost done, about 5 minutes. Add remaining ingredients, except salt, pepper, and green onions.

4. Bring to a boil, reduce heat, and cook for several minutes. Season to taste. Serve chicken mixture over linguine and sprinkle with green onions.

NUTRITIONAL INFORMATION PER SERVING
Calories 348 | Calories from fat 26% | Fat 10 g
Saturated Fat 3 g | Cholesterol 44 mg | Sodium 330 mg
Carbohydrate 38 g | Dietary Fiber 2 g | Sugars 7 g | Protein 26 g

DIABETIC EXCHANGES
2 1/2 starch | 3 lean meat

TERRIFIC TIDBIT

Coconut milk may be found in the grocery store where Asian ingredients are located.

MEATY EGGPLANT SAUCE WITH RIGATONI

MAKES 4–6 SERVINGS

Rustic in texture and bold in flavors, this combination is an unassuming way of using nutritious eggplant in a hearty meat dish. The crunchy pine nuts and mild feta topping flawlessly enhances the bold red wine sauce.

1 (8-ounce) package rigatoni or penne pasta

1/2 pound ground sirloin

1 teaspoon minced garlic

3 cups peeled, diced eggplant

1 (15-ounce) can tomato sauce

1/2 cup red wine or cooking wine

1 teaspoon dried oregano leaves

Salt and pepper to taste

2 teaspoons pine nuts, toasted (optional)

1/4 cup crumbled reduced-fat feta cheese (optional)

1. Cook pasta according to package directions, omitting any oil. Drain and set aside.

2. In a large nonstick skillet, cook meat and garlic until meat begins to brown. Add eggplant and cook until eggplant begins to soften, about 5–7 minutes.

3. Add tomato sauce and wine. Cook for about 10 minutes or until the sauce thickens and the eggplant is tender.

4. Add oregano and season to taste. Serve the meaty eggplant sauce over pasta. Sprinkle with pine nuts and feta, if desired.

NUTRITIONAL INFORMATION PER SERVING
Calories 227 | Calories from fat 10% | Fat 3 g
Saturated Fat 1 g | Cholesterol 21 mg | Sodium 444 mg
Carbohydrate 35 g | Dietary Fiber 2 g | Sugars 5 g | Protein 15 g

DIABETIC EXCHANGES
2 starch | 1 vegetable | 1 very lean meat

TERRIFIC TIDBIT

Make extra sauce to freeze and pull out on those busy nights. After removing from freezer, serve with pasta and condiments.

PASTA

GARDEN FRESH PENNE

MAKES 4–6 SERVINGS

Ripe juicy tomatoes and mild avocados make an ideal light vegetarian pasta dinner. This also works as an awesome side dish.

1 (8-ounce) package penne pasta

2 tablespoons olive oil

1 teaspoon minced garlic

1/3 cup chopped red onion

2 cups coarsely chopped tomatoes

1 tablespoon balsamic vinegar

1 (14-ounce) can quartered artichoke hearts, drained

1 cup coarsely chopped avocado

Salt and pepper to taste

1/3 cup crumbled reduced-fat feta (or goat cheese)

1. Cook pasta according to package directions. Drain and set aside.

2. In a large nonstick skillet coated with nonstick cooking spray, heat oil and sauté garlic, onion, and tomatoes over medium heat for 5 minutes.

3. Add vinegar, artichoke hearts, and avocado. Cook until well heated. Season to taste.

4. Add pasta and toss. Sprinkle with cheese.

NUTRITIONAL INFORMATION PER SERVING
Calories 267 | Calories from fat 32% | Fat 10 g
Saturated Fat 2 g | Cholesterol 3 mg | Sodium 236 mg
Carbohydrate 37 g | Dietary Fiber 4 g | Sugars 4 g | Protein 8 g

DIABETIC EXCHANGES
2 starch | 1 vegetable | 1 1/2 fat

PASTA WITH PROSCIUTTO AND PARMESAN

MAKES 6–8 SERVINGS

After my visit to Italy, I created this simple winning combination featuring very Italian ingredients, such as olive oil, garlic, prosciutto, fresh basil, and Parmesan cheese.

12 ounces spiral shaped pasta, reserving 2 tablespoons pasta water

3 tablespoons olive oil

1/3 cup breadcrumbs

1 teaspoon minced garlic

1/4 cup chopped prosciutto

2 tablespoons coarsely chopped fresh basil

1/4 cup grated Parmesan cheese

Salt and pepper to taste

1. Prepare pasta according to package directions. Drain, reserving 2 tablespoons pasta water, and set aside.

2. In a nonstick skillet, heat oil and sauté breadcrumbs and garlic over medium heat, stirring until golden brown.

3. Stir in prosciutto and basil. Add pasta, pasta water, and cheese. Season to taste and serve.

NUTRITIONAL INFORMATION PER SERVING
Calories 240 | Calories from fat 27% | Fat 7 g
Saturated Fat 1 g | Cholesterol 5 mg | Sodium 138 mg
Carbohydrate 35 g | Dietary Fiber 1 g | Sugars 2 g | Protein 8 g

DIABETIC EXCHANGES
2 1/2 starch | 1 fat

SQUASH AND SAUSAGE RIGATONI WITH GOAT CHEESE

MAKES 8 SERVINGS

This simple summer medley of spicy sausage, squash, tomatoes, and goat cheese presents an array of fantastic dominant flavors in every bite.

1 (16-ounce) package small tubular pasta (rigatoni), reserving 1 cup pasta water

3/4 pound ground lean Italian sausage (or if links, remove casing and crumble)

3 tablespoons olive oil

1 cup chopped red onion

6 cups diced yellow squash

1 pint cherry or grape tomatoes, halved

3 ounces goat cheese or reduced-fat feta, crumbled

1. Cook pasta according to package directions, omitting any salt or oil. Drain, reserving 1 cup pasta water, and set aside.

2. In a large nonstick pan, cook sausage, crumbling, until done, about 5 minutes. Remove from pan and drain any excess fat. Set aside.

3. In the same pan, heat oil and sauté onion, squash, and tomatoes over medium heat until tender, about 7 minutes. Return sausage to pan, add reserved pasta water, and continue cooking for 5 minutes.

4. Toss with rigatoni, sprinkle with goat cheese, and serve.

NUTRITIONAL INFORMATION PER SERVING
Calories 371 | Calories from fat 27% | Fat 11 g
Saturated Fat 3 g | Cholesterol 17 mg | Sodium 395 mg
Carbohydrate 51 g | Dietary Fiber 3 g | Sugars 6 g | Protein 18 g

DIABETIC EXCHANGES
3 starch | 1 vegetable | 1 lean meat | 1 fat

TERRIFIC TIDBIT

Look for all the new fun varieties of sausage available, from chicken to vegetable, to us instead of pork sausage. Or, omit the sausage for a vegetarian dish.

PASTA

ROASTED SUMMER VEGETABLES AND PASTA

MAKES 8 (1-CUP) SERVINGS

This easy recipe captures the essence of summer. Fresh basil is a key ingredient, while roasted garlic adds a truly intensive flavor.

1 (8-ounce) package small tubular pasta

3 large yellow squash, about 4 cups, halved and sliced 1-inch thick crosswise

1 pint grape or cherry tomatoes

1 red onion, halved and sliced 1/2-inch thick

6 cloves garlic, sliced

3 tablespoons olive oil

Salt and pepper to taste

3 tablespoons grated Parmesan cheese

1/2 cup torn fresh basil leaves

1. Preheat oven to 450°F. Line a baking sheet with foil. Cook pasta according to package directions, omitting any salt or oil. Drain and set aside.

2. Spread squash, tomatoes, onion, and garlic on prepared baking sheet. Toss with oil and season to taste. Roast in oven for 35–40 minutes.

3. Add pasta to pan, mixing with vegetables. Sprinkle with Parmesan cheese, add basil, and toss well.

NUTRITIONAL INFORMATION PER SERVING
Calories 189 | Calories from fat 29% | Fat 6 g
Saturated Fat 1 g | Cholesterol 2 mg | Sodium 38 mg
Carbohydrate 28 g | Dietary Fiber 2 g | Sugars 5 g | Protein 6 g

DIABETIC EXCHANGES
1 1/2 starch | 1 vegetable | 1 fat

FETTUCCINE ALFREDO

MAKES 8 SERVINGS

This favorite classic Italian dish is quick to whip up and beloved by all alfredo fans. This recipe also makes a great side.

1 (16-ounce) package fettuccine

2 tablespoons butter

2 tablespoons all-purpose flour

1 cup nonfat sour cream

1 1/2 cups fat-free half-and-half

1 cup grated Parmesan cheese

Salk and pepper to taste

1. Cook pasta according to directions on package, omitting any salt or oil. Drain and set aside.

2. In a small nonstick pot, melt butter over low heat. Add flour, stirring until bubbly, for two minutes. Stir in sour cream and heat until hot.

3. Add cheese and stir until melted. Do not boil. Season to taste.

4. Toss with pasta and serve immediately.

NUTRITIONAL INFORMATION PER SERVING
Calories 346 | Calories from fat 17% | Fat 7 g
Saturated Fat 4 g | Cholesterol 21 mg | Sodium 247 mg
Carbohydrate 55 g | Dietary Fiber 1 g | Sugars 7 g | Protein 16 g

DIABETIC EXCHANGES
3 1/2 starch | 1 lean meat

trim&TERRIFIC™ **GULF COAST FAVORITES**

MEXICAN LASAGNA

MAKES 10–12 SERVINGS

Chili powder, pinto beans, and Monterey Jack cheese give a traditional lasagna south-western style for a truly one-of-a-kind flavor.

1 pound ground sirloin

1/2 cup chopped onion

1 (14 1/2-ounce) can chopped tomatoes with juice

2 (8-ounce) cans tomato sauce

1 tablespoon dried oregano leaves

1/4 teaspoon crushed red pepper flakes

2 tablespoons chili powder

1 (15-ounce) can pinto beans, rinsed and drained

1 cup reduced-fat ricotta cheese

1 egg white

2 tablespoons chopped green chilies

1 (8-ounce) package no-boil lasagna noodles

2 cups shredded, reduced-fat Monterey Jack cheese, divided

1. Preheat oven to 375°F. Coat a 13 × 9 × 2-inch baking dish with nonstick cooking spray.

2. In a large nonstick skillet, cook meat and onion until meat is done, about 7 minutes. Drain any excess fat. Add tomatoes, tomato sauce, oregano, red pepper flakes, chili powder, and pinto beans. Simmer, uncovered, for 10 minutes.

3. In a small bowl, mix ricotta cheese, egg white, and green chilies and set aside.

4. Spread a thin layer of meat sauce in the bottom of prepared pan. Top with half the noodles, overlapping, and half the remaining meat sauce. Spoon all the ricotta cheese mixture over the meat mixture and sprinkle with half the shredded cheese. Top with remaining noodles, meat sauce, and shredded cheese.

5. Bake, covered with foil, for 50 minutes. Uncover and bake 10 more minutes or until bubbly.

NUTRITIONAL INFORMATION PER SERVING
Calories 249 | Calories from fat 25% | Fat 7 g
Saturated Fat 3 g | Cholesterol 36 mg | Sodium 574 mg
Carbohydrate 25 g | Dietary Fiber 3 g | Sugars 4 g | Protein 21 g

DIABETIC EXCHANGES
1 1/2 starch | 1 vegetable | 2 lean meat

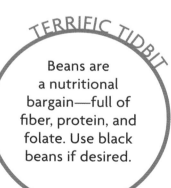

TERRIFIC TIDBIT

Beans are a nutritional bargain—full of fiber, protein, and folate. Use black beans if desired.

PASTA

Meaty White Lasagna pg. 201

MEATY WHITE LASAGNA
MAKES 10 SERVINGS

Creating the ultimate lasagna, a robust meat sauce boasts Italian sausage, layered with a creamy white sauce and two types of cheese!

1 pound ground sirloin

1/2 pound ground Italian sausage

1 cup chopped onion

2 teaspoons minced garlic

1 cup dry white wine or cooking wine

2 tablespoons tomato paste

3 tablespoons chopped parsley

1 (28-ounce) can crushed tomatoes in purée

1/4 cup all-purpose flour

3 cups skim milk

Dash nutmeg

Salt and pepper to taste

1/2 pound no-boil lasagna noodles

1 cup shredded, reduced-fat sharp Cheddar cheese

1 cup shredded, part-skim mozzarella cheese

1. Preheat oven to 350°F.

2. In a large nonstick skillet, cook meat and sausage over medium heat for about 5 minutes. Add onion and garlic. Continue cooking until meat is done. Drain any excess fat.

3. Add wine and bring to a boil. Continue boiling until wine is reduced by half. Stir in tomato paste, parsley, and tomatoes in pureé. Bring to a boil, reduce heat, and cook for another 10 minutes or until sauce thickens.

4. In a medium pot, whisk together flour and milk. Cook over medium heat, stirring, until mixture comes to a boil and sauce is bubbly and thickens. Add nutmeg, season to taste, and set aside.

5. Spread a thin layer of meat sauce in the bottom of a 13 × 9 × 2-inch baking pan. Cover with one-third each of the noodles, and layer with one-third each of the meat sauce, white sauce, and cheeses. Repeat layers, with remaining noodles, meat sauce, white sauce, and cheeses.

6. Bake, covered with foil, for 45–50 minutes. Uncover and continue baking for another 5–10 minutes. Let stand for 10 minutes before cutting.

NUTRITIONAL INFORMATION PER SERVING
Calories 313 | Calories from fat 24% | Fat 8 g
Saturated Fat 4 g | Cholesterol 46 mg | Sodium 618 mg
Carbohydrate 30 g | Dietary Fiber 3 g | Sugars 7 g | Protein 27 g

DIABETIC EXCHANGES
1 1/2 starch | 1 vegetable | 3 lean meat

PASTA

SEAFOOD LASAGNA

MAKES 8–10 SERVINGS

Seafood fans will be mesmerized with layers of shrimp, crabmeat, and cheese, in a tantalizing white sauce.

1 tablespoon butter

1/2 cup chopped onion

1/2 cup chopped green bell pepper

1 teaspoon minced garlic

4 tablespoons all-purpose flour

3 1/2 cups skim milk

1 pound small peeled shrimp

1/3 cup grated Parmesan cheese

Salt and pepper to taste

1/2 pound no-boil lasagna noodles

1 pound white or lump crabmeat, picked through for shells

1 cup shredded, part-skim mozzarella cheese

Grated Romano cheese (optional)

1. Preheat oven to 350°F. Coat a 13 × 9 × 2-inch baking dish with nonstick cooking spray.

2. In a nonstick pot coated with nonstick cooking spray, melt butter and sauté onion, green pepper, and garlic until tender, about 5 minutes.

3. Add flour and stir for 30 seconds. Gradually stir in milk and cook until sauce is thick and bubbly. Add shrimp and cook until shrimp are done, about 5 minutes. Stir in Parmesan cheese and season to taste.

4. Spread a thin layer of sauce in the bottom of prepared pan. Top with a layer of noodles and layer with half the crabmeat, one-third the shrimp sauce, and half the mozzarella cheese. Repeat layers ending by topping with shrimp sauce.

5. Cover tightly with foil and bake for 45–55 minutes until bubbly and lasagna noodles are done. If desired, top with Romano cheese. Let sit 10 minutes before cutting.

NUTRITIONAL INFORMATION PER SERVING
Calories 260 | Calories from fat 16% | Fat 5 g
Saturated Fat 2 g | Cholesterol 115 mg | Sodium 387 mg
Carbohydrate 25 g | Dietary Fiber 1 g | Sugars 5 g | Protein 27 g

DIABETIC EXCHANGES
1 1/2 starch | 3 very lean meat

TERRIFIC TIDBIT

Use any seafood combination depending on accessibility. Canned crabmeat may be used as well.

trim&TERRIFIC™ GULF COAST FAVORITES

SALMON AND SPINACH LASAGNA

MAKES 8–10 SERVINGS

A nutrition-packed dish with fresh salmon and accents of dill, spinach and tomatoes is easily assembled, innovative and out-of this-world.

1/3 cup all-purpose flour

3 1/3 cups skim milk

2 tablespoons sherry or cooking sherry

1 1/2 pounds salmon fillets, skin removed, cut into small chunks

1 1/2 teaspoons dried dill weed leaves

Salt and pepper to taste

1 (8-ounce) package no-boil lasagna noodles

2 cups chopped tomatoes

1 cup chopped red onion

3 cups fresh baby spinach

2 cups shredded, part-skim mozzarella cheese

1/4 cup chopped green onion stems or chives

1. Preheat oven to 350°F.

2. In a medium nonstick pot, whisk together flour and milk. Cook over medium heat, whisking constantly, until mixture is bubbly and thickens. Remove from heat. Stir in sherry and set aside. Sprinkle salmon with dill and season to taste.

3. Spread a thin layer of the sauce in the bottom of a 13 × 9 × 2-inch baking pan. Top with one-third of the noodles and cover with one-third of the sauce. Layer with half each of the salmon, tomatoes, red onions, spinach and cheese. Repeat layers ending with noodles and sauce.

4. Cover with foil and bake for 50-60 minutes or until pasta is done. Sprinkle with green onions or chives. Let sit 10 minutes before cutting.

NUTRITIONAL INFORMATION PER SERVING
Calories 283 | Calories from fat 21% | Fat 7 g
Saturated Fat 3 g | Cholesterol 51 mg | Sodium 231 mg
Carbohydrate 28 g | Dietary Fiber 2 g | Sugars 7 g | Protein 26 g

DIABETIC EXCHANGES
2 starch | 3 lean meat

TERRIFIC TIDBIT

For a twist, substitute won ton wrappers for lasagna noodles to create a light and tasty lasagna with interesting flavor and texture.

PASTA

Key Lime Cheesecake pg. 235; Lemon Cheesecake Squares pg. 236

SWEET TREATS

CHOCOLATE ESPRESSO COOKIES

MAKES 3 DOZEN COOKIES

Attention coffee and chocolate addicts! Perk up with this simple recipe of multifaceted tastes. Walnuts add crunch, and nutrition!

1 (1 pound 1.5-ounce) bag chocolate chip cookie mix
1/4 cup butter, melted
1 egg, beaten
1/4 cup coffee liqueur
1 tablespoon instant espresso coffee
1/3 cup bittersweet or dark chocolate chips
1/2 cup chopped walnuts (optional)

1. Preheat oven to 375°F. Coat a baking sheet with nonstick cooking spray.

2. Place cookie mix in a bowl and make a well in the center. Add all remaining ingredients, including walnuts if desired, and stir to combine.

3. Drop by teaspoonfuls onto prepared baking sheet. Bake for 9–11 minutes or until crisp. Transfer to a wire rack to cool.

NUTRITIONAL INFORMATION PER SERVING
Calories 107 | Calories from fat 39% | Fat 5 g
Saturated Fat 2 g | Cholesterol 9 mg | Sodium 63 mg
Carbohydrate 14 g | Dietary Fiber 0 g | Sugars 10 g | Protein 1 g

DIABETIC EXCHANGES
1 carbohydrate | 1 fat

RANGER COOKIES

MAKES 4 DOZEN COOKIES

I trimmed up this popular cookie recipe made with oatmeal, cereal, and coconut— for a fantastic crackle and crunch cookie.

1/3 cup canola oil
3/4 cup light brown sugar
1/3 cup sugar
1 egg
1 egg white
1 teaspoon vanilla extract
1 1/2 cups all-purpose flour
1 teaspoon baking soda
1 1/2 cups old-fashioned oatmeal
1 1/2 cups crisp rice cereal
1/3 cup flaked coconut

1. Preheat oven to 350°F. Coat a baking sheet with nonstick cooking spray.

2. In a mixing bowl, blend together oil, brown sugar, and sugar. Add egg, egg white, and vanilla, and mix well.

3. In a small bowl, combine flour and baking soda. Gradually add to mixing bowl. Stir in oatmeal, cereal, and coconut.

4. Drop by tablespoonfuls onto prepared baking sheet. Bake for 10–12 minutes or until lightly browned.

NUTRITIONAL INFORMATION PER SERVING
Calories 66 | Calories from fat 27% | Fat 2 g
Saturated Fat 0 g | Cholesterol 4 mg | Sodium 40 mg
Carbohydrate 11 g | Dietary Fiber 0 g | Sugars 6 g | Protein 1 g

DIABETIC EXCHANGES
1/2 carbohydrate | 1/2 fat

CRISPY OATMEAL COOKIES

MAKES 4 DOZEN COOKIES

Using oil for crispiness and butter for chewiness, this slightly more delicate oatmeal cookie has a light maple undertone.

3 tablespoons butter

1/4 cup canola oil

1/2 cup light brown sugar

1/2 cup sugar

1 egg

1/4 cup pure maple syrup

1 teaspoon vanilla extract

1 cup all-purpose flour

1/2 teaspoon baking powder

1/2 teaspoon baking soda

1 teaspoon ground cinnamon

2 cups old-fashioned oatmeal

1/2 cup chopped pecans

1. Preheat oven to 350°F. Coat a baking sheet with nonstick cooking spray.

2. In a large mixing bowl, beat butter, oil, brown sugar, sugar, egg, maple syrup, and vanilla until light.

3. In a small bowl, combine flour, baking powder, baking soda, and cinnamon. Add to the mixing bowl. Stir in oatmeal and pecans, and mix well.

4. Drop by rounded teaspoonfuls onto prepared baking sheet. Bake for 10–12 minutes or until lightly browned. Remove and let cool on wax paper.

NUTRITIONAL INFORMATION PER SERVING
Calories 67 | Calories from fat 40% | Fat 3 g
Saturated Fat 1 g | Cholesterol 6 mg | Sodium 25 mg
Carbohydrate 9 g | Dietary Fiber 1 g | Sugars 5 g | Protein 1 g

DIABETIC EXCHANGES
1/2 carbohydrate | 1/2 fat

TERRIFIC TIDBIT

Try adding white chocolate chips and dried apricots or cranberries for an added bonus!

DOUBLE CHOCOLATE BROWNIES

MAKES 4 DOZEN BROWNIES

My version of Carolyn Winder's ultimate brownies—dark chocolate brownies with a sweet chocolate-almond icing.

1 (18.4 ounce–21.5-ounce) box original brownie mix

2 eggs

1/3 cup canola oil

1/4 cup water

1/3 cup bittersweet or dark chocolate chips (1/2 cup for more chocolate)

3 tablespoons butter

2 tablespoons cocoa

2 cups confectioners sugar

2 tablespoons skim milk

1 teaspoon almond extract

1. Preheat oven to 350°F. Coat a 13 × 9 × 2-inch baking pan with nonstick cooking spray.

2. In a bowl, combine brownie mix, eggs, oil, and water until well mixed. Stir in chocolate chips.

3. Transfer to prepared pan. Bake for 23–25 minutes (do not overcook). Cool.

4. In a mixing bowl, combine remaining ingredients until creamy. Spread over brownies.

NUTRITIONAL INFORMATION PER SERVING
Calories 108 | Calories from fat 37% | Fat 4 g
Saturated Fat 1 g | Cholesterol 11 mg | Sodium 45 mg
Carbohydrate 16 g | Dietary Fiber 0 g | Sugars 12 g | Protein 1 g

DIABETIC EXCHANGES
1 carbohydrate | 1 fat

MINT MERINGUES

MAKES 4 DOZEN MERINGUES

The leave-it-in-the-oven method makes baking meringues a simple job. Chopped mint adds a colorful and refreshing finish to these light treats.

4 egg whites, room temperature

3/4 cup sugar

1 teaspoon vanilla extract

1/2 cup chopped peppermint patties

1. Preheat oven to 350°F. Line a cookie sheet with foil or parchment paper.

2. In a mixing bowl, beat egg whites until stiff peaks begin to form. Gradually add sugar, continuing to beat until very stiff. Add vanilla and fold in chopped mint.

3. Drop by teaspoonfuls onto prepared pan. Place in oven and turn oven off. Leave in oven for at least 4 hours or overnight. Store in airtight container.

NUTRITIONAL INFORMATION PER SERVING
Calories 21 | Calories from fat 0% | Fat 0 g
Saturated Fat 0 g | Cholesterol 0 mg | Sodium 5 mg
Carbohydrate 5 g | Dietary Fiber 0 g | Sugars 4 g | Protein 0 g

DIABETIC EXCHANGES
1/2 carbohydrate

TERRIFIC TIDBIT

Another baking method is to preheat oven to 225°F and bake for 1 1/2 hours.

Mint Meringues pg. 208; Pecan Caramel Bars pg. 210;
German Chocolate Cream Cheese Bars pg. 210

GERMAN CHOCOLATE CREAM CHEESE BARS

MAKES 4 DOZEN SQUARES

This simple-to-make recipe combines two popular desserts in one.

1 (18.25-ounce) box German chocolate cake mix

1 egg

1/3 cup flaked coconut

1/3 cup butter, melted

1 (8-ounce) package reduced-fat cream cheese

1 (16-ounce) box confectioners sugar

3 egg whites

1 teaspoon coconut extract

1 teaspoon vanilla extract

1. Preheat oven to 350°F. Coat a 13 × 9 × 2-inch baking pan with nonstick cooking spray.

2. In a large bowl, combine cake mix, egg, coconut, and butter. Press into the bottom of prepared pan.

3. In a mixing bowl, beat all remaining ingredients until mixture is smooth and creamy. Pour over mixture in pan.

4. Bake for 35–40 minutes or until top is golden brown. Cool and cut into squares.

NUTRITIONAL INFORMATION PER SERVING
Calories 108 | Calories from fat 26% | Fat 3 g
Saturated Fat 2 g | Cholesterol 11 mg | Sodium 116 mg
Carbohydrate 19 g | Dietary Fiber 0 g | Sugars 15 g | Protein 1 g

DIABETIC EXCHANGES
1 1/2 carbohydrate | 1/2 fat

PECAN CARAMEL BARS

MAKES 25 SQUARES

Melt-in-your-mouth bars with decadent flair.

1/3 cup light brown sugar

1/4 cup butter

1 tablespoon water

1 teaspoon vanilla extract

1 cup all-purpose flour

40 caramels, unwrapped

3 tablespoons skim milk

1/2 cup coarsely chopped pecans

1. Preheat oven to 350°F. Coat a 9-inch square pan with nonstick cooking spray.

2. In a large mixing bowl, beat together brown sugar, butter, water, and vanilla. Gradually add flour and mix well. Press into the bottom of prepared pan. Bake for 7–9 minutes or until soft to touch.

4. Place caramels and milk in a microwave-safe bowl and microwave for one minute. Stir, and return to microwave for 30 seconds or until smooth and melted.

5. Remove pan from oven and pour caramel mixture evenly over crust. Sprinkle with pecans. Return to oven and continue baking for 8–10 minutes or until mixture is bubbly.

NUTRITIONAL INFORMATION PER SERVING
Calories 125 | Calories from fat 35% | Fat 5 g
Saturated Fat 2 g | Cholesterol 6 mg | Sodium 55 mg
Carbohydrate 20 g | Dietary Fiber 0 g | Sugars 14 g | Protein 2 g

DIABETIC EXCHANGES
1 1/2 carbohydrate | 1 fat

APPLE CARAMEL SPICE BARS

MAKES 2 DOZEN SERVINGS

A cross between an apple crumble pie and a spice cake, this mouthwatering treat with a crumbly oatmeal pecan topping is simple to make. Cut in bars or squares and serve warm with frozen vanilla yogurt for the ultimate treat!

1 (18.25-ounce) box spice cake mix

1 cup old-fashioned oatmeal

1 egg

1/2 cup butter, melted

1/3 cup chopped pecans

2 baking apples, peeled, cored, and thinly sliced

1 cup fat-free caramel flavored topping

2 tablespoons all-purpose flour

1. Preheat oven to 350°F. Coat a 13 × 9 × 2-inch baking pan with nonstick cooking spray

2. In a bowl, combine cake mix and oatmeal. Add egg and butter, and blend with pastry blender or fork until mixed and crumbly. Remove 1 cup crumb mixture to another bowl, add pecans, and set aside.

3. Pat remaining crumb mixture into prepared pan and bake for 6 minutes. Remove from oven and arrange apples evenly over crust.

4. In a small bowl, combine caramel topping and flour. Pour evenly over apples and sprinkle with reserved pecan-crumb mixture.

5. Bake for 30 minutes or until bubbly and sides pull away from edges. Don't overcook.

NUTRITIONAL INFORMATION PER SERVING
Calories 196 | Calories from fat 31% | Fat 7 g
Saturated Fat 3 g | Cholesterol 19 mg | Sodium 207 mg
Carbohydrate 32 g | Dietary Fiber 1 g | Sugars 18 g | Protein 2 g

DIABETIC EXCHANGES
2 carbohydrate | 1 1/2 fat

TERRIFIC TIDBIT

Granny Smith apples are available year-round and their tartness makes them good for cooking. Rome apples may also be used for cooking.

King Cake with Cream Cheese Cinnamon Filling pg. 213; Mini Muffalatos pg. 18

KING CAKE WITH CREAM CHEESE CINNAMON FILLING

MAKES 16 SERVINGS

Now, you can make a quick King Cake recipe in your own home any time, without worrying about a complicated yeast dough. Kids love helping with this cake year round—try red and pink colors for Valentine's Day, pastels for Easter, and red and green for Christmas!

2 (8-ounce) cans reduced-fat crescent rolls

4 ounces reduced-fat cream cheese

2 tablespoons confectioners sugar

1 teaspoon vanilla extract

2 tablespoons butter

1/3 cup light brown sugar

1 tablespoon ground cinnamon

Mardi Gras Icing (recipe to the right)

1. Preheat oven to 350°F. Coat a 10-inch round pizza pan with nonstick cooking spray.

2. Separate crescent rolls at perforations, into 16 slices. Place slices around prepared pan with points in the center. About halfway down from points, press seams together.

3. In a mixing bowl, beat cream cheese, confectioners sugar, and vanilla until creamy. Spread on dough in the center where seams have been pressed together.

4. In another small bowl, combine butter, brown sugar, and cinnamon with a fork until crumbly. Sprinkle over cream cheese. Fold dough points over filling, then fold bottom of triangle over points forming a circular roll like a king cake.

5. Bake for about 20–25 minutes or until golden brown. Cool slightly and drizzle with colored Mardi Gras Icing.

MARDI GRAS ICING

1 cup confectioners sugar

1–2 tablespoons skim milk

1/2 teaspoon vanilla extract

Yellow, green, red, and blue food coloring

1. In a small bowl, combine all ingredients, except food color. Divide mixture into three bowls.

2. In first bowl, add a few drops of yellow food coloring. In second bowl, add a few drops of green food coloring. In third bowl, add equal amounts of drops of red and blue food coloring (to create purple).

3. Drizzle over baked cake.

NUTRITIONAL INFORMATION PER SERVING
Calories 184 | Calories from fat 36% | Fat 7 g
Saturated Fat 3 g | Cholesterol 9 mg | Sodium 275 mg
Carbohydrate 26 g | Dietary Fiber 0 g | Sugars 16 g | Protein 3 g

DIABETIC EXCHANGES
1 1/2 carbohydrate | 1 1/2 fat

TERRIFIC TIDBIT

The icing colors represent power (yellow), faith (green), justice (purple).

BANANA WALNUT UPSIDE DOWN CAKE

MAKES 6–8 SERVINGS

Maple syrup, bananas, and walnuts turn this classic cake into a decadent, moist dessert. Hot out of oven this cake is irresistible.

1/3 cup light brown sugar

5 tablespoons butter, divided

3 tablespoons pure maple syrup

1/4 cup coarsely chopped walnuts

3 medium bananas, peeled and cut into 1/4-inch slices

1 cup all-purpose flour

2 teaspoons baking powder

1/4 teaspoon baking soda

1 teaspoon ground cinnamon

1/2 cup sugar

1 egg

1 teaspoon vanilla extract

1/3 cup buttermilk

1. Preheat oven to 350°F.

2. In a microwave-safe dish, combine brown sugar, 2 tablespoons butter, and maple syrup. Microwave for 1 minute, or until mixture is melted together.

3. Pour evenly into the bottom of a 9-inch round cake pan. Sprinkle with walnuts, and arrange banana slices on top.

4. In a small bowl, combine flour, baking powder, baking soda, and cinnamon. Set aside.

5. In a mixing bowl, beat sugar and remaining 3 tablespoons butter until creamy. Add egg and vanilla, and beat until light and fluffy.

6. Add flour mixture to mixing bowl, alternating with buttermilk, and ending with flour. Carefully spoon batter over bananas in pan. Bake for 30–35 minutes or until a wooden pick inserted comes out clean. Run knife around pan sides and immediately invert onto serving plate.

NUTRITIONAL INFORMATION PER SERVING
Calories 301 | Calories from fat 31% | Fat 11 g
Saturated Fat 5 g | Cholesterol 46 mg | Sodium 214 mg
Carbohydrate 50 g | Dietary Fiber 2 g | Sugars 32 g | Protein 4 g

DIABETIC EXCHANGES
3 1/2 carbohydrate | 2 fat

TERRIFIC TIDBIT

This cake is best eaten immediately, or at least the same day, as bananas will brown.

CARROT CAKE WITH CREAM CHEESE FROSTING

MAKES 16–20 SERVINGS

This moist, fabulous three-layer cake iced with a velvety Cream Cheese Frosting is "one of the best!" Purchase pre-shredded, bagged carrots for a great short cut.

2 cups all-purpose flour

1 1/2 teaspoons baking soda

1 teaspoon baking powder

2 teaspoons ground cinnamon

2 eggs

1 egg white

1/4 cup canola oil

1 cup sugar

3/4 cup buttermilk

1 teaspoon vanilla extract

2 cups shredded carrots

1 (8-ounce) can crushed pineapple in juice, drained or 1/2 cup drained, crushed pineapple

1/3 cup flaked coconut

1/2 cup chopped pecans

Cream Cheese Frosting (recipe below)

1. Preheat oven to 350°F. Coat three 9-inch round cake pans with nonstick cooking spray.

2. In a bowl, combine flour, baking soda, baking powder, and cinnamon. Set aside.

3. In a mixing bowl, beat together eggs, egg white, oil, sugar, buttermilk, and vanilla. Gradually add flour mixture and mix until blended. Stir in remaining ingredients, and mix well.

4. Pour batter into prepared pans. Bake for 17–20 minutes or until tops spring back when lightly touched.

5. Cool cakes in pans for 10 minutes. Turn out onto racks to cool. Frost layers and sides with Cream Cheese Frosting.

CREAM CHEESE FROSTING

1 (8-ounce) package reduced-fat cream cheese

3 tablespoons butter

1 teaspoon grated orange rind (optional)

1 teaspoon vanilla extract

1 (16-ounce) box confectioners sugar

1. In a mixing bowl, beat together cream cheese and butter until smooth.

2. Add orange rind and vanilla. Gradually add confectioners sugar, stirring, until light and creamy.

NUTRITIONAL INFORMATION PER SERVING
Calories 291 | Calories from fat 31% | Fat 10 g
Saturated Fat 4 g | Cholesterol 34 mg | Sodium 206 mg
Carbohydrate 47 g | Dietary Fiber 1 g | Sugars 35 g | Protein 4 g

DIABETIC EXCHANGES
3 carbohydrate | 2 fat

SWEET TREATS

LEMON BLUEBERRY POUND CAKE

MAKES 16–20 SERVINGS

A lemon cake and fresh blueberries pair up for a simple, delectable cake.

1 (18.25-ounce) box lemon cake mix

1 (8-ounce) package reduced-fat cream cheese

2 eggs

1 1/3 cups water

1 teaspoon vanilla extract

2 cups blueberries

1/2 cup chopped pecans

3 tablespoons lemon juice

1 cup confectioners sugar

1. Preheat oven to 350°F. Coat a Bundt pan with nonstick cooking spray.

2. In a mixing bowl, beat together cake mix, cream cheese, eggs, water, and vanilla until creamy. Fold in blueberries and pecans.

3. Pour batter into prepared pan. Bake for 40 minutes or until a toothpick inserted comes out clean. Do not overcook. Cool in pan for 10 minutes and invert onto serving dish.

4. In a small bowl, combine lemon juice and confectioners sugar. Drizzle over warm cake.

NUTRITIONAL INFORMATION PER SERVING
Calories 191 | Calories from fat 32% | Fat 7 g
Saturated Fat 3 g | Cholesterol 29 mg | Sodium 225 mg
Carbohydrate 30 g | Dietary Fiber 1 g | Sugars 20 g | Protein 3 g

DIABETIC EXCHANGES
2 carbohydrate | 1 1/2 fat

ORANGE MARMALADE BUNDT CAKE

MAKES 16 SERVINGS

Orange glaze soaks into the cake to make a moist and fruity wonderful dessert.

1 (18.25-ounce) box yellow cake mix

1 cup orange juice

1/3 cup canola oil

1 (6-ounce) container nonfat orange yogurt

1 teaspoon grated orange rind

1 egg

2 egg whites

1/4 cup plus 1 tablespoon orange liqueur or orange juice

1/2 cup orange marmalade, apricot, or peach preserves

1. Preheat oven to 350°F. Coat a Bundt pan with nonstick cooking spray.

2. In a mixing bowl, beat together all ingredients, except 1 tablespoon liqueur and preserves. Mix until well blended.

3. Pour batter into prepared pan. Bake for 40–45 minutes or until center of cake bounces back when touched. Let sit for 5 minutes and invert to serving plate.

4. In a microwave-safe bowl, combine remaining liqueur and preserves. Microwave for 45 seconds. Pour over warm cake.

NUTRITIONAL INFORMATION PER SERVING
Calories 231 | Calories from fat 28% | Fat 7 g
Saturated Fat 2 g | Cholesterol 14 mg | Sodium 233 mg
Carbohydrate 38 g | Dietary Fiber 0 g | Sugars 26 g | Protein 2 g

DIABETIC EXCHANGES
2 1/2 carbohydrate | 1 1/2 fat

trim&TERRIFIC™ **GULF COAST FAVORITES**

Orange Marmalade Bundt Cake pg. 216

SWEET POTATO CINNAMON BUNDT CAKE WITH ORANGE GLAZE

MAKES 16–20 SERVINGS

The natural sweetness of sweet potatoes with a cinnamon streusel and citrus glaze creates one amazing cake. I was bombarded with requests for the recipe!

1/2 cup butter

1/2 cup sugar

2/3 cup light brown sugar, divided

1 egg

2 egg whites

1 (15-ounce) can sweet potatoes (yams), drained and mashed or 1 cup cooked, mashed fresh sweet potatoes

2 1/2 cups all-purpose flour

1 1/2 teaspoons baking powder

1 teaspoon baking soda

3 1/2 teaspoons ground cinnamon, divided

1 cup nonfat plain yogurt

1 teaspoon vanilla extract

1/2 cup chopped pecans

1 cup confectioners sugar

2 tablespoons orange juice

1 teaspoon lemon juice

1. Preheat oven to 350°F. Coat a nonstick Bundt pan with nonstick cooking spray.

2. In a mixing bowl, beat together butter, sugar, 1/3 cup brown sugar, egg, and egg whites until light and fluffy. Add sweet potatoes and mix well.

3. In another bowl, combine flour, baking powder, baking soda, and 2 teaspoons cinnamon. Gradually add flour mixture to mixing bowl alternating with yogurt, beginning and ending with flour mixture. Add vanilla.

4. In another bowl, combine pecans with remaining 1/3 cup brown sugar and 1 1/2 teaspoons cinnamon.

5. Spread one-third of the batter into prepared pan. Sprinkle with half the pecan topping. Repeat layers ending with final one-third of the batter. Bake for 40–45 minutes or until a toothpick inserted comes out clean.

6. Cool in pan for 10 minutes. Invert onto serving plate. In a small bowl, whisk together remaining ingredients. Drizzle over warm cake.

NUTRITIONAL INFORMATION PER SERVING
Calories 225 | Calories from fat 28% | Fat 7 g
Saturated Fat 3 g | Cholesterol 23 mg | Sodium 155 mg
Carbohydrate 37 g | Dietary Fiber 2 g | Sugars 20 g | Protein 4 g

DIABETIC EXCHANGES
2 12 carbohydrate | 1 1/2 fat

TERRIFIC TIDBIT

When a recipe calls for canned sweet potatoes, fresh may also be used.

trim&TERRIFIC™ **GULF COAST FAVORITES**

EASY RED VELVET CAKE

MAKES 16–20 SERVINGS

Perfect for Christmas, Valentine's Day, or any special occasion, this southern classic never goes out of style. Take a short cut by using cake mix to effortlessly prepare a beautiful and deliciously rich luscious cake.

1 (18.25-ounce) box yellow cake mix

2 tablespoons cocoa

1/4 cup canola oil

1 egg

3 egg whites

1 (1-ounce) bottle red food coloring

1 cup skim milk

1 tablespoon vinegar

Cream Cheese Icing (recipe to the right)

1. Preheat oven to 350°F. Coat three 9-inch round cake pans with nonstick cooking spray.

2. In a mixing bowl, combine cake mix, cocoa, oil, egg, egg whites, and food coloring. In a small bowl, combine milk and vinegar, and add to mixing bowl. Mix until well combined.

3. Pour batter into prepared pans and bake for 15–20 minutes or until a toothpick inserted comes out clean. Cool layers on a rack and ice with Cream Cheese Icing.

CREAM CHEESE ICING

1 (8-ounce) package reduced-fat cream cheese, softened

3 tablespoons butter

1 (16-ounce) box confectioners sugar

1 teaspoon vanilla extract

1. In a mixing bowl, beat cream cheese and butter until smooth. Add confectioners sugar and beat until light. Add vanilla.

NUTRITIONAL INFORMATION PER SERVING
Calories 272 | Calories from fat 29% | Fat 9 g
Saturated Fat 4 g | Cholesterol 23 mg | Sodium 246 mg
Carbohydrate 45 g | Dietary Fiber 0 g | Sugars 35 g | Protein 3 g

DIABETIC EXCHANGES
3 carbohydrate | 2 fat

TERRIFIC TIDBIT

For another fantastic dessert option, turn this cake into a trifle by layering cake, cream cheese icing, and nonfat whipped topping in a trifle or glass bowl. One time, the layers fell apart and I turned it into a trifle and now I make the cake both ways and can't decide which is the most popular!

SWEET TREATS

White Chocolate Cake with White Chocolate Cream Cheese Frosting pg. 221

WHITE CHOCOLATE CAKE WITH WHITE CHOCOLATE CREAM CHEESE FROSTING

MAKES 16–20 SERVINGS

A moist, magnificent cake with the ultimate White Chocolate Cream Cheese Frosting. Splurge!

4 ounces white chocolate

1/3 cup boiling water

6 tablespoons butter

2 tablespoons canola oil

2 cups sugar

2 eggs, separated

1 teaspoon vanilla extract

2 cups all-purpose flour

1 teaspoon baking soda

1 cup buttermilk

1/2 cup chopped pecans

1/2 cup flaked coconut (optional)

2 egg whites

White Chocolate Cream Cheese Frosting (recipe below)

1. Preheat oven to 350°F. Coat three 9-inch round pans with nonstick cooking spray.

2. In a small bowl, stir white chocolate in boiling water until melted. Cool slightly.

3. In a mixing bowl, beat together butter, oil, and sugar until creamy. Add egg yolks and mix well. Add vanilla. Gradually add white chocolate.

4. In a another bowl, combine flour and baking soda. Gradually add to mixing bowl, alternating with buttermilk, ending with flour mixture. Stir in pecans and coconut, if desired.

5. In another bowl, beat 4 egg whites until stiff peaks form. Gradually fold into batter in mixing bowl.

6. Pour batter into prepared pans. Bake for 20–25 minutes or until a toothpick inserted comes out clean. Cool in pans 10 minutes and remove to wire racks.

7. Frost layers and sides with White Chocolate Cream Cheese Frosting.

WHITE CHOCOLATE CREAM CHEESE FROSTING

1 (8-ounce) package reduced-fat cream cheese

1 tablespoon butter

1 ounce white chocolate, melted in 2 tablespoons boiling water

1 (16-ounce) box confectioners sugar

1 teaspoon lemon juice

1 teaspoon vanilla extract

1. In a mixing bowl, beat cream cheese and butter until creamy. Add white chocolate mixing well. Add confectioners sugar and lemon juice. Beat until light. Add vanilla.

NUTRITIONAL INFORMATION PER SERVING
Calories 360 | Calories from fat 32% | Fat 13 g
Saturated Fat 6 g | Cholesterol 43 mg | Sodium 173 mg
Carbohydrate 58 g | Dietary Fiber 1 g | Sugars 48 g | Protein 5 g

DIABETIC EXCHANGES
4 carbohydrate | 2 1/2 fat

SWEET TREATS

HEAVENLY HASH CAKE

MAKES 28 SERVINGS

Rich chocolate cake with a gooey marshmallow layer and chocolate icing with toasted pecans epitomizes southern indulgence and chocoholic perfection.

1/3 cup canola oil
1 teaspoon vanilla extract
3/4 cup sugar
2 eggs
3/4 cup boiling water
1/2 cup cocoa
1 1/3 cups all-purpose flour

1 teaspoon baking soda
1/2 teaspoon baking powder
1/2 cup buttermilk
1 (7-ounce) jar marshmallow crème
Chocolate Icing (recipe below)
1/2 cup chopped pecans, toasted

1. Preheat oven to 350°F. Coat a 13 × 9 × 2-inch baking pan with nonstick cooking spray.

2. In a mixing bowl, beat together oil, vanilla, and sugar until creamy. Add eggs and beat well.

3. In a small bowl, combine water and cocoa. Add to mixing bowl and mix well.

4. In another bowl, combine flour, baking soda, and baking powder. Add to mixing bowl alternating with buttermilk, beginning and ending with flour mixture.

5. Pour batter into prepared pan. Bake for 15–20 minutes or until top springs back when lightly touched.

6. Carefully spread marshmallow crème over hot cake. Pour Chocolate Icing evenly over marshmallow layer. Sprinkle with pecans. Cool and cut into squares.

CHOCOLATE ICING

A thick chocolate glaze.

3 tablespoons butter
1/4 cup evaporated skim milk
1/4 cup cocoa
2 cups confectioners sugar
1 teaspoon vanilla extract

1. In a medium nonstick pot, cook butter, milk, and cocoa over medium heat for several minutes. Bring to a boil.

2. Add confectioners sugar and vanilla, blending well. Cook for several more minutes. Drizzle over warm cake.

NUTRITIONAL INFORMATION PER SERVING
Calories 167 | Calories from fat 32% | Fat 6 g
Saturated Fat 1 g | Cholesterol 19 mg | Sodium 77 mg
Carbohydrate 27 g | Dietary Fiber 1 g | Sugars 18 g | Protein 2 g

DIABETIC EXCHANGES
2 carbohydrate | 1 fat

CHOCOLATE MOUNDS LAYERED CAKE

MAKES 16–20 SERVINGS

Every bite of this three-layer chocolate cake tastes like a rich candy bar. Oatmeal keeps it moist and the mix of chocolate, coconut, and pecans make it undeniably delicious.

2 cups boiling water

1 cup old-fashioned oatmeal

1 (18.25-ounce) box German chocolate cake mix

3 egg whites

1 (14-ounce) can fat-free sweetened condensed milk, divided

1/3 cup flaked coconut

1/3 cup chopped pecans

3 tablespoons butter

1/3 cup cocoa

1 (16-ounce) box confectioners sugar

1 teaspoon vanilla extract

3-4 tablespoons skim milk

1. Preheat oven to 350°F. Coat three 9-inch round cake pans with nonstick cooking spray.

2. In a small bowl, combine boiling water and oatmeal. Let sit for 10 minutes. In a mixing bowl, beat together cake mix, egg whites, 1/2 cup condensed milk, and oatmeal until well combined.

3. Pour batter into prepared pans and bake for 12–15 minutes or until cake springs back when lightly touched. Remove from pans and cool completely on wire racks.

4. In a small bowl, combine coconut and pecans with remaining condensed milk. Set aside.

5. In a mixing bowl, beat together butter, cocoa, confectioners sugar, and vanilla. Gradually add skim milk until frosting reaches a spreadable consistency.

6. Lay bottom layer of cake on a serving plate and spread with a thin layer of half of the coconut mixture. Repeat layers, and top with final cake layer. Frost sides and top with prepared chocolate frosting.

NUTRITIONAL INFORMATION PER SERVING
Calories 305 | Calories from fat 16% | Fat 5 g
Saturated Fat 2 g | Cholesterol 7 mg | Sodium 239 mg
Carbohydrate 61 g | Dietary Fiber 1 g | Sugars 48 g | Protein 4 g

DIABETIC EXCHANGES
4 carbohydrate | 1 fat

TERRIFIC TIDBIT

I used dark cocoa to make the frosting for more contrast with the chocolate cake.

SWEET TREATS

SHORT-CUT REFRIGERATED COCONUT CAKE

MAKES 28 SERVINGS

Homemade coconut syrup makes a rich moist cake and whipped topping adds a light touch to this refreshing divine dessert. Preparation gets a speed boost with yellow cake mix.

1 (18.25-ounce) box yellow cake mix

1 egg

3 egg whites

1/4 cup canola oil

1 1/2 teaspoons coconut extract

1 cup nonfat sour cream

1/2 cup water

1/3 cup flaked coconut

Coconut Syrup (recipe to the right)

1 (8-ounce) container frozen fat-free whipped topping, thawed

1. Preheat oven to 350°F. Coat a 13 × 9 × 2-inch baking pan with nonstick cooking spray.

2. In a large mixing bowl, beat together all ingredients except coconut and whipped topping, until well mixed. Stir in coconut.

3. Pour batter into prepared pan. Bake for 25–30 minutes, or until a toothpick inserted comes out clean.

4. Remove from oven and poke holes in top of cake with fork. Pour Coconut Syrup evenly over top. Cool and spread with whipped topping.

COCONUT SYRUP

1 cup skim milk

1/2 cup sugar

1/3 cup flaked coconut

1. In a small pot, combine all ingredients and bring to a boil. Boil for 5 minutes, stirring continuously. Pour over warm cake.

NUTRITIONAL INFORMATION PER SERVING
Calories 143 | Calories from fat 24% | Fat 4 g
Saturated Fat 1 g | Cholesterol 9 mg | Sodium 149 mg
Carbohydrate 24 g | Dietary Fiber 0 g | Sugars 15 g | Protein 2 g

DIABETIC EXCHANGES
1 1/2 carbohydrate | 1 fat

TERRIFIC TIDBIT

Coconut extract, which is found in the spice section, gives a recipe coconut flavor without the added fat. When I use coconut extract, I reduce the amount of flaked coconut.

YAM PECAN PIE IN GINGERSNAP CRUST

MAKES 8–10 SERVINGS

When you can't decide between a pecan or sweet potato pie, have them both! A gingersnap crust sets the stage for a perfect blend of pecan and sweet potato, capturing the best of what Louisiana has to offer.

1 1/4 cups gingersnap cookie crumbs

2 tablespoons butter, melted

1 1/2 teaspoons vanilla

1 (15-ounce) can sweet potatoes (yams), drained and mashed, or 1 cup fresh mashed cooked sweet potatoes

2 eggs, divided

1/4 cup light brown sugar

1/2 teaspoon ground cinnamon

1/4 teaspoon ground nutmeg

3 egg whites

2/3 cup dark corn syrup

1/2 cup sugar

2 teaspoons vanilla extract

2/3 cup pecans, chopped

1. Preheat oven to 350°F.

2. In a bowl, combine gingersnap crumbs, butter, and vanilla. Press onto bottom and sides of a pie plate. Bake for 10 minutes and remove from oven.

3. In a mixing bowl, blend together sweet potatoes, 1 egg, brown sugar, cinnamon, and nutmeg. Spread evenly in pie crust.

4. In a mixing bowl, beat together egg whites, corn syrup, sugar, vanilla, and remaining egg until mixture is creamy. Stir in pecans.

5. Carefully spoon over sweet potato layer. Bake for 50–60 minutes until filling is set around edges, or until a knife inserted comes out clean. Cool and serve.

NUTRITIONAL INFORMATION PER SERVING
Calories 311 | Calories from fat 28% | Fat 10 g
Saturated Fat 3 g | Cholesterol 48 mg | Sodium 168 mg
Carbohydrate 53 g | Dietary Fiber 2 g | Sugars 26 g | Protein 4 g

DIABETIC EXCHANGES
3 1/2 carbohydrate | 2 fat

TERRIFIC TIDBIT

Ginger-snaps may also be put in a plastic bag and crushed into crumbs.

HONEY PECAN TOPPING

MAKES 8–10 SERVINGS

Jazz up your favorite pecan or sweet potato pie with this topping.

1/4 cup light brown sugar

2 tablespoons butter

2 tablespoons honey

1 cup pecan halves

1. Preheat broiler. Prepare a baked pie.

2. In a nonstick pot, combine brown sugar, butter, and honey. Cook over low heat until sugar dissolves, stirring constantly. Add pecans and stir until well coated.

3. Spread topping evenly over pie. Place pie in broiler and broil until topping is bubbly and golden brown. Watch carefully.

———————————

NUTRITIONAL INFORMATION PER SERVING
Calories 128 | Calories from fat 67% | Fat 10 g
Saturated Fat 2 g | Cholesterol 6 mg | Sodium 18 mg
Carbohydrate 10 g | Dietary Fiber 1 g | Sugars 9 g | Protein 1 g

DIABETIC EXCHANGES
1/2 carbohydrate | 2 fat

TERRIFIC TIDBIT

When a refrigerated pie crust is called for, I prefer the type that you unfold and place in a pie plate. I always keep one in the refrigerator to pull out for a "pie on demand."

CHOCOLATE PECAN PIE

MAKES 8–10 SERVINGS

Combining a rich pecan filling with a hint of chocolate makes this incredible pie a snap to prepare thanks to a store-bought pie shell.

2 eggs

2 egg whites

1 cup light corn syrup

1 tablespoon butter, melted

1/4 cup sugar

1/4 cup light brown sugar

1 tablespoon all-purpose flour

1 tablespoon vanilla extract

1 cup coarsely chopped pecans

1/3 cup semi-sweet chocolate chips

1 (9-inch) unbaked pie shell

1. Preheat oven to 350°F.

2. In a bowl, whisk together eggs, egg whites, corn syrup, butter, sugar, brown sugar, flour and vanilla. Stir in pecans and chocolate chips.

3. Pour into pie shell. Bake for 45–50 minutes or until set. Cool completely.

———————————

NUTRITIONAL INFORMATION PER SERVING
Calories 383 | Calories from fat 42% | Fat 19 g
Saturated Fat 5 g | Cholesterol 49 mg | Sodium 136 mg
Carbohydrate 53 g | Dietary Fiber 2 g | Sugars 25 g | Protein 5 g

DIABETIC EXCHANGES
3 1/2 carbohydrate | 4 fat

BANANA CREAM SURPRISE PIE

MAKES 8–10 SERVINGS

Cool layers of a thin chocolate custard, bananas, and vanilla pudding take this extraordinary pie to new heights. I thought the result was so exceptional, I whipped up a second pie the next day with my leftover bananas.

1 cup reduced-fat vanilla wafer crumbs

2 tablespoons butter, melted

1 teaspoon vanilla extract

1 tablespoon cornstarch

2 tablespoons cocoa

1/3 cup plus 1 3/4 cups skim milk, divided

2 large bananas, sliced

1 (4-serving) package instant French vanilla pudding and pie filling mix

1 (8-ounce) container frozen fat-free whipped topping, thawed

Chocolate shavings for garnish (optional)

1. Preheat oven to 375°F.

2. In a bowl, combine vanilla wafer crumbs, butter, and vanilla. Press onto bottom and sides of a pie plate. Bake for 5–7 minutes or until lightly browned.

3. In a small pot, combine cornstarch, cocoa, and 1/3 cup milk. Cook over medium heat, stirring constantly, until mixture thickens and is bubbly, about 3 minutes. Carefully spread over baked crust. Arrange sliced bananas on top.

4. Prepare pudding according to package directions, using 1 3/4 cups milk. Spread over bananas. Top with whipped topping and chocolate shavings, if desired. Refrigerate 2–3 hours before serving.

NUTRITIONAL INFORMATION PER SERVING
Calories 181 | Calories from fat 16% | Fat 3 g
Saturated Fat 2 g | Cholesterol 7 mg | Sodium 224 mg
Carbohydrate 34 g | Dietary Fiber 1 g | Sugars 21 g | Protein 3 g

DIABETIC EXCHANGES
2 1/2 carbohydrate | 1/2 fat

SWEET TREATS

BUTTERMILK STREUSEL PIE

MAKES 8–10 SERVINGS

A crunchy brown sugar topping over a light custard pie is remenescent of a Crème Brûlée, but minus all the effort. I like to serve this pie with fresh berries.

2 eggs
3/4 cup sugar
2 tablespoons all-purpose flour
1 3/4 cups buttermilk
1 teaspoon vanilla extract
1 (9-inch) unbaked pie shell
Streusel Topping (recipe to the right)

1. Preheat oven to 325°F.

2. In a mixing bowl, beat together eggs, sugar, flour, buttermilk, and vanilla. Pour into pie shell.

3. Bake for 30 minutes. Reduce oven temperature to 300°F. Sprinkle with Streusel Topping, and bake for 50-55 minutes or until set.

4. Turn oven to broil and broil for about 2 minutes. Watch carefully. Let stand 20 minutes before serving.

STREUSEL TOPPING

1/4 cup all-purpose flour
1/3 cup light brown sugar
1/2 teaspoon ground cinnamon
1 tablespoon butter, melted
1 teaspoon vanilla extract

1. In a small bowl, combine all ingredients until mixture is crumbly.

_____

NUTRITIONAL INFORMATION PER SERVING
Calories 243 | Calories from fat 30% | Fat 8 g
Saturated Fat 4 g | Cholesterol 51 mg | Sodium 150 mg
Carbohydrate 38 g | Dietary Fiber 0 g | Sugars 25 g | Protein 4 g

DIABETIC EXCHANGES
2 1/2 carbohydrate | 1 1/2 fat

TERRIFIC TIDBIT

If you don't have buttermilk, mix 1 tablespoon vinegar or lemon juice with 1 cup milk. Crème Brûlèe consists of a custard base, topped with a hard caramel—this desert has crème brûlèe components and flavor.

TROPICAL YAM TRIFLE
MAKES 16–20 SERVINGS

An explosion of tropical flavors comes together for a spectacular finish with the show-stopper trifle that is light, refreshing and absolutely marvelous. I promise one taste of this dessert will "wow" you.

1 (8-ounce) package reduced-fat cream cheese

1/2 cup sugar

2 1/4 cups skim milk, divided

1 teaspoon coconut extract

2 (15-ounce) cans sweet potatoes (yams), drained and mashed, or 2 cups fresh sweet potatoes, cooked and mashed

1 teaspoon vanilla extract

1 (4-serving) packages instant coconut or vanilla pudding and pie filling mix

1 (16-ounce) store-bought angel food cake, cut into cubes

1 (8-ounce) can crushed pineapple in juice

1/3 cup flaked coconut, divided

1 (8-ounce) container frozen fat free whipped topping, thawed

Fresh berries, toasted coconut to garnish (optional)

1. In a large bowl, beat together cream cheese and sugar. Gradually add 1/2 cup milk and coconut extract, mixing until creamy. Add sweet potatoes and vanilla, mixing until smooth. Set aside

2. In another bowl, mix pudding with remaining 1 3/4 cups milk until thickened.

3. In a trifle bowl or large glass bowl, layer half each of the angel food cake, pineapple with juice, cream cheese mixture, pudding, coconut, and whipped topping. Repeat layers with remaining half of ingredients. Refrigerate. Garnish, if desired, and serve.

NUTRITIONAL INFORMATION PER SERVING
Calories 213 | Calories from fat 15% | Fat 4 g
Saturated Fat 3 g | Cholesterol 9 mg | Sodium 233 mg
Carbohydrate 41 g | Dietary Fiber 2 g | Sugars 23 g | Protein 4 g

DIABETIC EXCHANGES
2 1/2 carbohydrate | 1 fat

TERRIFIC TIDBIT

Look for Louisiana yams in the grocery to insure the sweetest of sweet potatoes.

RASPBERRY TRIFLE LACED WITH CHOCOLATE SAUCE

MAKES 16 SERVINGS

Layers of cake, pudding, chocolate sauce, and raspberries create a stunning dessert.

3 (4-serving) packages instant vanilla pudding and pie filling mix

4 cups cold skim milk

1 (10-ounce) jar seedless raspberry jam

1/4 cup orange juice or orange liqueur

2 (3-ounce) packages ladyfingers (about 24), separated lengthwise into halves

3 cups fresh raspberries

Chocolate Sauce (recipe to the right)

1 (8-ounce) container frozen fat-free whipped topping, thawed

Raspberries and fresh mint for garnish (optional)

1. In a mixing bowl, beat or whisk pudding mix and milk until thick. Set aside. In a small bowl, combine raspberry jam and orange juice or liqueur.

2. Place one-fourth of the ladyfingers (12 halves) cut side up along the bottom of a trifle bowl or large glass bowl.

3. Spoon about one-fourth each of the raspberry jam mixture over ladyfingers, top with one-fourth of the pudding and one-fourth of the raspberries. Drizzle with Chocolate Sauce. Repeat layers three more times.

4. Spread whipped topping over last layer. Refrigerate at least 4 hours before serving. Garnish with raspberries, mint, and any extra chocolate sauce, if desired.

CHOCOLATE SAUCE

This chocolate sauce is my favorite recipe. Try it over ice cream as well!

2/3 cup sugar

1/3 cup cocoa

3 tablespoons butter

1/3 cup fat-free half-and-half

1 teaspoon vanilla extract

1. In a small pot, combine sugar, cocoa, butter, and half-and-half.

2. Bring to a boil, stirring continuously. Remove from heat and add vanilla.

NUTRITIONAL INFORMATION PER SERVING
Calories 290 | Calories from fat 10% | Fat 3 g
Saturated Fat 1 g | Cholesterol 9 mg | Sodium 357 mg
Carbohydrate 61 g | Dietary Fiber 2 g | Sugars 48 g | Protein 4 g

DIABETIC EXCHANGES
4 carbohydrate | 1/2 fat

TERRIFIC TIDBIT

In a pinch, strawberries may be substituted for raspberries and store-bought chocolate sauce for homemade.

trim&TERRIFIC™ **GULF COAST FAVORITES**

Raspberry Trifle Laced with Chocolate Sauce pg. 230

TIRAMISU TRIFLE
MAKES 16 SERVINGS

Layers of ladyfingers doused with espresso syrup, lightly coffee-flavored pudding, and a whipped creamy layer make a terrific Tiramisu presentation.

1 cup water

1 tablespoon sugar

2 teaspoons instant espresso coffee

4 ounces reduced-fat cream cheese

2 cups fat-free half-and-half

2 (4-serving) packages instant French vanilla pudding and pie filling mix

1/3 cup coffee liqueur

2 (3-ounce) packages ladyfingers (about 24), separated lengthwise into halves

1 (8-ounce) container frozen fat-free whipped topping, thawed

Cocoa for garnish

1. In a microwave-safe bowl, combine water, sugar, and instant espresso coffee. Microwave 30 seconds or until sugar is dissolved. Set aside to cool.

2. In a mixing bowl, beat cream cheese, gradually adding half-and-half and pudding mix, mixing until thick. Add coffee liqueur, mix well, and set aside.

3. Arrange half of the ladyfingers (24 halves) in the bottom of a trifle bowl. Drizzle with half of the espresso mixture, and spread with half of the pudding mixture and about one-third of the whipped topping. Top with remaining ladyfingers, espresso mixture, and pudding mixture. Top with remaining whipped topping.

4. Sprinkle with cocoa and refrigerate until well chilled.

NUTRITIONAL INFORMATION PER SERVING
Calories 184 | Calories from fat 10% | Fat 2 g
Saturated Fat 1 g | Cholesterol 8 mg | Sodium 278 mg
Carbohydrate 35 g | Dietary Fiber 0 g | Sugars 24 g | Protein 4 g

DIABETIC EXCHANGES
2 1/2 carbohydrate | 1/2 fa

TERRIFIC TIDBIT

Strong coffee may be used for the coffee mixture if instant espresso coffee is not available. I like to top the trifle with shaved chocolate and a strawberry or raspberry garnish.

232

BREAD PUDDING
MAKES 16 SERVINGS

Semi-sweet chocolate mingles with rich white chocolate in this magnificent dessert.

16 ounces whole-wheat Hawaiian bread, or French bread

1/2 cup white chocolate chips

1/3 cup semi-sweet chocolate chips

1/3 cup flaked coconut (optional)

2 eggs

4 egg whites

3/4 cup sugar

1 tablespoon vanilla extract

1 (12-ounce) can evaporated skim milk

2 cups skim milk

1. Preheat oven to 350°F. Coat a 13 × 9 × 2-inch baking dish with nonstick cooking spray.

2. Cut bread into 1-inch squares and arrange in prepared baking dish. Sprinkle with white chocolate and semi-sweet chocolate chips. Top with coconut, if desired.

3. In a large bowl, whisk together remaining ingredients, and mix well. Pour mixture evenly over bread. Let stand 10 minutes to allow liquid to soak in.

4. Bake for 40–50 minutes or until light brown and center is done. Let sit for 10 minutes and cut into squares.

NUTRITIONAL INFORMATION PER SERVING
Calories 224 | Calories from fat 23% | Fat 6 g
Saturated Fat 3 g | Cholesterol 34 mg | Sodium 212 mg
Carbohydrate 35 g | Dietary Fiber 1 g | Sugars 24 g | Protein 8 g

DIABETIC EXCHANGES
2 1/2 carbohydrate | 1 very lean meat | 1 fat

APPLE CRISP CRUMBLE
MAKES 8 SERVINGS

A crumbly topping baked atop warm maple-flavored apples is scandalously delicious.

6 cups baking apples, peeled, cored, and sliced (about 4)

1/3 cup plus 2 tablespoons pure maple syrup

2 teaspoons lemon juice

1/2 cup all-purpose flour

1/2 cup light brown sugar

1 teaspoon ground cinnamon

1 cup old-fashioned oatmeal

1 teaspoon vanilla extract

2 tablespoons orange juice

4 tablespoons butter, softened

1/3 cup chopped pecans

1. Preheat oven to 350°F. Coat a 9 × 9 × 2-inch baking dish with nonstick cooking spray.

2. In a bowl, combine apples with 1/3 cup maple syrup and lemon juice. Arrange apples in prepared pan.

3. In a small bowl, combine flour, brown sugar, cinnamon, oatmeal, and vanilla. Add orange juice and butter, and mix until crumbly. Stir in pecans. Sprinkle mixture over apples.

4. Bake for 40–50 minutes or until apples are tender.

NUTRITIONAL INFORMATION PER SERVING
Calories 294 | Calories from fat 30% | Fat 10 g
Saturated Fat 4 g | Cholesterol 15 mg | Sodium 48 mg
Carbohydrate 50 g | Dietary Fiber 3 g | Sugars 33 g | Protein 3 g

DIABETIC EXCHANGES
3 1/2 carbohydrate | 2 fat

SWEET TREATS

WHITE CHOCOLATE CHEESECAKE

MAKES 16 SERVINGS

White chocolate and cheesecake are outrageously delicious when combined in one dazzling dessert. You will be begging for a second piece. Serve with raspberries.

1 cup graham cracker crumbs

1/2 cup old-fashioned oatmeal

2 tablespoons plus 2/3 cup sugar

1 teaspoon almond extract

2 tablespoons butter, melted

2 (8-ounce) packages reduced-fat cream cheese

2 eggs

2 egg whites

1/4 cup all-purpose flour

3 ounces white chocolate, melted

1 cup nonfat sour cream

2 teaspoons vanilla extract

1. Preheat oven to 325°F.

2. In a bowl, combine graham cracker crumbs, oatmeal, 2 tablespoons sugar, almond extract, and butter. Press onto the bottom and sides of a spring-form pan.

3. In a mixing bowl, beat together cream cheese and 2/3 cup sugar until light. Add eggs and egg whites, one at a time, beating well after each addition. Add flour and white chocolate, mixing well. Add sour cream and vanilla and mix well.

4. Pour into prepared crust and bake for 55 minutes. Remove from oven, cool to room temperature, and refrigerate until well chilled. Remove from pan and serve.

NUTRITIONAL INFORMATION PER SERVING
Calories 217 | Calories from fat 44% | Fat 11 g
Saturated Fat 6 g | Cholesterol 55 mg | Sodium 197 mg
Carbohydrate 23 g | Dietary Fiber 0 g | Sugars 16 g | Protein 7 g

DIABETIC EXCHANGES
1 1/2 carbohydrate | 1 lean meat | 2 fat

TERRIFIC TIDBIT

If desired, more white chocolate may be added a richer cheesecake.

trim&TERRIFIC™ GULF COAST FAVORITES

KEY LIME CHEESECAKE

MAKES 16– 20 SERVINGS

Florida is infamous for its Key limes, but you can purchase a bottle of Key lime juice to make this dessert any time. A light lime flavor with a chocolate crust creates a refreshing cheesecake. Drizzle with chocolate syrup for a fancy finish.

1 1/4 cups chocolate wafer crumbs

2 tablespoons butter, melted

2 teaspoons vanilla extract, divided

3 (8-ounce) packages reduced-fat cream cheese

1 cup sugar

3 tablespoons all-purpose flour

2 eggs

2 egg whites

1/3 cup Key lime juice

1 cup nonfat sour cream

1. Preheat oven to 350°F. Coat a 9-inch spring form pan with nonstick cooking spray.

2. In a small bowl, combine chocolate crumbs, butter, and 1 teaspoon vanilla. Press onto the bottom and sides of prepared pan.

3. In a mixing bowl, beat together cream cheese, sugar, and flour until creamy. Add eggs and egg whites, one at a time, beating well after each addition. Add Key lime juice, sour cream, and remaining 1 teaspoon vanilla. Mix well.

4. Pour into prepared crust and bake for 1 hour, or until the center of cake is just about set. Remove from oven and transfer pan to a wire rack to cool completely at room temperature. Refrigerate until well chilled.

NUTRITIONAL INFORMATION PER SERVING
Calories 190 | Calories from fat 46% | Fat 10 g
Saturated Fat 6 g | Cholesterol 50 mg | Sodium 215 mg
Carbohydrate 20 g | Dietary Fiber 0 g | Sugars 14 g | Protein 6 g

DIABETIC EXCHANGES
1 1/2 carbohydrate | 2 fat

TERRIFIC TIDBIT

For a Key Lime Marble Cheesecake: Melt 1/2 cup semi-sweet chocolate chips and blend well with half of the cream cheese mixture. Add lime juice to other half, and alternately spoon batters into crust. Gently swirl with a knife to marble.

LEMON CHEESECAKE SQUARES

MAKES 25 SQUARES

Light lemon cheesecake and tart lemon curd creates the ultimate lemon lover's dessert!

1 cup graham cracker crumbs

1 tablespoon plus 3/4 cup sugar

2 tablespoons butter, melted

2 (8-ounce) packages reduced-fat cream cheese

1 egg

2 egg whites

1/4 cup lemon juice

1 tablespoon grated lemon rind

1 cup lemon curd (found in jar)

1. Preheat oven to 350°F. Coat a 9 × 9 × 2-inch baking dish with nonstick cooking spray.

2. In a small bowl, combine graham cracker crumbs, 1 tablespoon sugar, and butter. Press into bottom of prepared pan.

3. In a mixing bowl, beat cream cheese and remaining sugar, until creamy. Add egg, egg whites, lemon juice, and lemon rind. Mix well.

4. Pour into prepared crust and bake for 40 minutes, until center is set. Remove and carefully spread with lemon curd. Cool completely and refrigerate. Cut into squares.

NUTRITIONAL INFORMATION PER SERVING
Calories 113 | Calories from fat 44% | Fat 6 g
Saturated Fat 3 g | Cholesterol 24 mg | Sodium 126 mg
Carbohydrate 13 g | Dietary Fiber 0 g | Sugars 10 g | Protein 3 g

DIABETIC EXCHANGES
1 carbohydrate | 1 fat

OATMEAL CHOCOLATE PIZZA

MAKES 12–16 SLICES

A giant indulgent oatmeal cookie topped with chocolate chips and marshmallows.

1 cup light brown sugar

1 1/2 cups all-purpose flour

1 teaspoon baking soda

1 cup old-fashioned oatmeal

1/2 cup butter, melted

1 teaspoon vanilla extract

1 egg

1/3 cup semi-sweet chocolate chips

1/4 cup flaked coconut

1 1/2 cups miniature marshmallows

1/2 cup chopped pecans, optional

1. Preheat oven to 350°F. Coat a 12–14-inch pizza pan with nonstick cooking spray.

2. In a large bowl, combine brown sugar, flour, baking soda, and oatmeal. Add butter, vanilla, and egg. Mix well.

3. Press onto prepared pan, keeping dough 1 inch from edge of pan.

4. Sprinkle with chocolate chips, coconut, marshmallows, and pecans, if desired. Bake 10–12 minutes or until edges are set. Don't overbake.

NUTRITIONAL INFORMATION PER SERVING
Calories 212 | Calories from fat 34% | Fat 8 g
Saturated Fat 5 g | Cholesterol 28 mg | Sodium 136 mg
Carbohydrate 33 g | Dietary Fiber 1 g | Sugars 19 g | Protein 3 g

DIABETIC EXCHANGES
2 carbohydrate | 1 1/2 fat

GLAZED FRESH STRAWBERRY PIZZA PIE

MAKES 12–16 SERVINGS

When strawberry season hits, have fun with this engaging and luscious take on a fresh strawberry pie. A giant sugar cookie crust with orange cream cheese filling and a strawberry glaze topping is enticing for all ages.

1 (16.5-ounce) roll refrigerated ready-to-slice sugar cookie dough

1 cup sugar

1/2 cup diet Sprite

1/4 cup cornstarch

1 quart strawberries, stemmed and sliced

1 tablespoon lemon juice

1/2 teaspoon vanilla extract

6 ounces reduced-fat cream cheese

1/4 cup confectioners sugar

2 tablespoons orange juice

1/2 teaspoon grated orange rind

Strawberry halves for garnish (optional)

Fat-free frozen whipped topping, thawed (optional)

1. Preheat oven to 350°F. Coat a 12- to 14-inch pizza pan with nonstick cooking spray.

2. Press sugar cookie dough onto prepared pan. Bake for about 12 minutes or until light brown. Cool completely.

3. In a small nonstick pot, combine sugar, Sprite, cornstarch, and strawberries. Mix well. Bring to a boil over a medium heat, and boil for about 3 minutes or until mixture thickens. Remove from heat, stir in lemon juice and vanilla, and set aside to cool.

4. In a mixing bowl, beat together cream cheese and confectioners sugar until creamy. Gradually add orange juice and mix well. Stir in orange rind.

5. Spread cream cheese mixture over baked sugar cookie. Carefully spread cooled strawberry mixture evenly over cream cheese layer. If desired, garnish with strawberry halves and serve with whipped topping. Refrigerate until serving.

NUTRITIONAL INFORMATION PER SERVING
Calories 211 | Calories from fat 28% | Fat 6 g
Saturated Fat 3 g | Cholesterol 10 mg | Sodium 148 mg
Carbohydrate 36 g | Dietary Fiber 1 g | Sugars 25 g | Protein 2 g

DIABETIC EXCHANGES
2 1/2 carbohydrate | 1 fat

TERRIFIC TIDBIT

For a "grown up" version, orange liqueur may be substituted for the orange juice.

SWEET TREATS

REFRIGERATOR STAPLES

Avocado
Bacon (center-cut)
Bell peppers (green, red, yellow)
Biscuits
Butter
Buttermilk
Celery
Cheese (reduced-fat)
Coleslaw (shredded cabbage mix)
Cream cheese (reduced-fat)
Cucumbers
Eggs
Frozen whipped topping, thawed (fat-free)
Fruit (assorted seasonal
Garlic (chopped in jar)
Half-and-half (fat-free)
Horseradish
Lemon juice
Lime juice
Milk (fat-free)
Mixed greens
Mushrooms
Onion (yellow, red, and green)
Orange juice
Parsley (flat leaf preferred)
Pie crust
Ricotta cheese (reduced-fat)
Sausage (reduced-fat)
Sour cream (nonfat)
Spinach (baby spinach)
Tortillas
Vegetables (assorted seasonal)
Yogurt (plain fat-free)

FREEZER STAPLES

Boneless, skinless chicken breasts
Crawfish
Edamame (shelled green soy beans)
Fish (assorted)
Fruit (including berries)
Game (duck, dove, venison)

Pork (cuts ending in "loin" or "round")
Salmon
Shrimp
Sirloin (ground, roast, cuts ending in "loin" or "round")
Vegetables (chopped spinach, corn, snow peas...)
Yogurt or ice cream (reduced-fat or fat-free)
Wild game (venison, dove, quail...)

BAKING STAPLES

Baking powder
Baking soda
All-purpose baking mix
Cake mixes (chocolate, brownie, German chocolate, yellow, white)
Chocolate (semi-sweet, white or dark chips)
Cocoa powder
Coconut (flaked)
Cornmeal
Cornstarch
Dried fruit (assorted)
Evaporated milk (fat-free)
Extracts (vanilla, almond, butter, and coconut)
Flour (all purpose, self-rising, whole wheat)
German chocolate bar
Graham crackers (reduced-fat)
Instant pudding and pie filling mix
Oatmeal (old-fashioned)
Sugar (granulated, brown, confectioners')
Sweetened condensed milk (fat-free)

SPICE AND SEASONING STAPLES

Basil leaves
Bay leaves
Chili powder
Cinnamon (ground)
Cumin (ground)
Curry (ground)

Dill weed leaves
Dry mustard powder
Garlic powder
Garlic bulbs
Ginger (ground)
Nutmeg (ground)
Oregano leaves
Paprika
Parsley flakes
Pepper (coarsely ground, red pepper flakes)
Rosemary leaves
Salt
Taco seasoning mix (low sodium)
Thyme leaves

PANTRY STAPLES

Artichoke hearts (canned in water)
Barley
Barbecue sauce
Bread (whole wheat or white)
Bread crumbs (Italian or plain)
Broth (reduced-sodium, fat-free; chicken, beef, vegetable)
Canned beans (assorted)
Canned corn
Canned diced tomatoes and green chilies
Canned fruit (water packed, including pineapple and mandarin oranges)
Canned green chilies (diced)
Canned sweet potatoes (yams)
Canned tomatoes (diced, whole, sauce, paste)
Canned water chestnuts (sliced)
Capers
Couscous
Enchilada Sauce
Grits (quick)
Honey
Hot sauce
Jams (all fruit)
Ketchup
Mayonnaise (light)
Marinara Sauce (jar)

Mustard (Dijon, Creole or grainy, yellow)
Nonstick cooking spray
Nuts (walnuts, pecans, almonds, pine nuts, peanuts)
Oils (canola, olive, sesame)
Olives (green, black)
Pasta (assorted, no boil lasagna noodles)
Peanut butter
Rice (white, yellow, wild, regular and quick-cooking brown)
Roasted red peppers (jar)
Salsa (assorted flavors)
Sliced jalapeño peppers (jar)
Soy sauce (low sodium)
Sun-dried tomatoes (dry packed)
Syrup (pure maple, white corn syrup)
Vinegar (balsamic, cider, red wine, raspberry, seasoned rice)
Wine (red, white, sherry, cooking)
Worcestershire sauce

LAGNIAPPE (EXTRAS)

Allspice (ground)
Chipotle chili powder
Coconut milk (light)
Cookies (vanilla wafers, gingersnaps)
Fresh herbs (basil, mint)
Garlic chili sauce
Ginger (fresh)
Hearts of Palm
Hoisin sauce
Lady fingers
Lentils
Molasses
Phyllo dough
Pizza crust
Poppy seeds
Sesame seeds
Thai peanut sauce
Wasabi powder
Won ton wrappers

JAZZ BRUNCH

Milk Punch, 45
Grillades and Cheese Grits, 43, 44
Apple, Brie, and Brown Sugar
 Pizza, 40
Sweet Potato, Orange and Cran-
 berry Muffins, 33
Fresh Berries

LADIES LAKE LUNCHEON

Mango Soup, 48
Shrimp Poppy Seed Pasta Salad, 85
Broccoli and Red Tip Lettuce
 Salad, 76
Bluebery Muffins with Streusel
 Topping, 34
German Chocolate Cream Cheese
 Bars, 210

LUNCHEON TRIO

Crawfish and Sweet Potato
 Bisque, 53
Festive Spinach Salad, 73
Shrimp Boat, 123
Pecan Caramel Bars, 210

CLASSY SASSY LUNCH

Gazpacho with Corn and Goat
 Cheese, 49
Tuna and Avocado Salad with
 Wasabi Vinaigrette, 87
Mango Bread, 38
White Chocolate Cheesecake, 234

SOUTHERN SUNDAYS

Beef Brisket, 172
One Step Macaroni and Cheese, 96
Butter Pecan Brussels Sprouts Stir-
 Fry, 94
Beer Bread, 26
Banana Walnut Upside Down
 Cake, 214

Creamy Cucumbers with Dill, 74
Ultimate Italian Meatloaf, 168
Roasted Garlic Mashed
 Potatoes, 99
Broccoli Pecans with Creamy
 Horseradish Sauce, 92
Italian Pull Aparts, 27
Buttermilk Streusel Pie, 228

SIMPLY SOUTHWESTERN

Crab Nachos, 18
Southwestern Guacamole, 8
Easy Chicken Enchiladas, 153
Chocolate Espresso Cookies, 206

BACKYARD BARBECUE

Oven Style Baby Back Barbecue
 Ribs, 177
Grilled Dove Breasts, 158
Maple Baked Beans, 91
Crunchy Fruity Coleslaw, 78
Double Roasted Potato Salad, 79
Glazed Fresh Strawberry Pizza
 Pie, 237

AT THE BEACH

Roasted Tomato Salsa, 8
Fish Soft Tacos, 119
Key Lime Cheesecake, 235

HUNTER'S CAMP SPECIAL

Ronnie's Venison Bites, 7
Pot Roasted Duck, 161
Barley Pilaf, 90
Best Cornbread, 31
Ranger Cookies (bring from
 home), 206

MARDI GRAS MADNESS

Louisiana Red Bean Dip, 10
Festive Spinach Salad, 69
Chicken and Sausage Gumbo, 60
King Cake with Cream Cheese Cin-
 namon Filling, 213

TIME TO TAILGATE

Mini Muffalettas, 18
Hamburger Dip, 7
Blackened Chicken Tenders, 142
Southwestern Roasted Hummus
 Dips, Pitas, 9
Simple Spicy Shrimp, 17
Double Chocolate Brownies, 208

DINNER ON THE BAYOU

Pear and Brie Mixed Green Salad
 with Orange Vinaigrette, 69
Spicy Fish with Shrimp Corn
 Sauté, 115

Bourbon Mashed Sweet
 Potatoes, 100
Speedy Savory Drop Biscuits, 28
Chocolate Pecan Pie, 226

LOUISIANA LAGNIAPPE

Quick Shrimp and Corn Soup, 50
Blackened Salmon, 121
Two Potato Roast, 101
Spinach Gratin, 105
Tropical Yam Trifle, 229

CAJUN CASUAL

Crawfish Dip, 11
Shrimp Creole with Rice, 126
Southern Okra Succotash, 95
Chocolate Mounds Layered
 Cake, 233

TROPICAL PARADISE

Exotic Shrimp Bundles, 15
Bourbon Glazed Pork
 Tenderloin, 177
Lemon Sweet Potato
 Casserole, 101
Black Bean and Mango Salad, 74
Short-Cut Refrigerated Coconut
 Cake, 224

SIMPLY SOUTHWESTERN

Southwestern Pork Chops, 179
Mexican Couscous Salad, 78
Southwestern Cornbread
 Muffins, 31
Apple Caramel Spice Bars, 211

ITALIAN IMPRESSIVE DINING

Minestrone, 59
Tomato and Mozzarella Salad, 72
Special Shrimp Scampi, 127
Pasta with Prosciutto and
 Parmesan, 196
Tiramisu Trifle, 232

ASIAN CAJUN

Beef Lettuce Wraps, 173
Crawfish and Eggplant Red
 Curry, 135
Coconut Rice, 174
Fortune Cookies (pick up)

MENU SUGGESTIONS

OUTSTANDING OYSTERS

Oyster Artichoke Soup, 55
Oyster and Angel Hair, 193
Oyster Rockefeller Dip (can also be a side), 13
Baked Italian Oysters, 139
Wild Rice and Oyster Dish, 107

LOUISIANA EXTRAVAGANZA

Marinated Crabmeat Mixed Green Salad, 83
Barbecue Shrimp, 122
Angel Hair Pasta
French Bread
Baked Italian Oysters, 139
Bread Pudding, 233

PUTTIN' ON THE RITZ

French Onion Soup, 58
Simple Sensational Fish Carlysle, 117
Asparagus with Lemon Caper Vinaigrette, 90
Poppy Seed Pull-Apart Bread, 28
Raspberry Trifle Laced with Chocolate Sauce, 230

COMPANY COCKTAIL PARTY

Baked Caramel Brie, 14
Marinated Shrimp, 6
Hot Crab Spinach Dip Baked in French Bread, 12
Stuffed Pesto Mushrooms, 20
Tomato and Goat Cheese Tarts, 16
Smoked Gouda Crawfish, Melba Rounds, 11

WARM ME UP DINNER

Ultimate Chili, 64, or Jane's "Throw It In" Vegetarian Chili, 62
Chicken and Dumplings, 154 (another option)
Best Cornbread, 31
Apple Crisp Crumble, 233

MAKE IT IN MINUTES

Beef Lettuce Wraps. 173
Crawfish Dip, 11
Chicken Tortilla Soup, 61
Glazed Mustard Salmon, 120
Quick Lemon Basil Shrimp, 129

Roasted Summer Vegetables with Pasta, 198
Chocolate Espresso Cookies, 206
Easy Red Velvet Cake, 219

FIX AND FORGET

Slow Cooked Greek Chicken, 152
Beef Brisket, 172
Venison Pot Roast, 183
Crock Pot Teal, 161

KID'S NIGHT IN ON PARENT'S NIGHT OUT

Blackened Chicken Fingers, 142
Green Bean Casserole, 96
Sweet Potato Fries, 97
Oatmeal Chocolate Pizza, 236

WEEKDAY WINNER DINNER

Herb Roasted Tenderloin, 178, or Baked Parmesan Trout, 112
Marinated Avocado, Tomato and Onion Salad, 68
Corn and Rice, 94
Southern Biscuits and Gravy, 29
Banana Cream Surprise Pie, 227

FAMILY BIRTHDAY DINNER

Chicken Parmesan. 146, or Shrimp Parmesan, 127
Fettuccine Alfredo, 198
Spinach Gratin, 105
White Chocolate Cake with White Chocolate Cream Cheese Frosting, 221

MAKE IT FROM LEFTOVERS

Seafood Cornbread, 32
Stuffed Louisiana Potatoes, 98
Fish Cakes, 118
Shrimp Deluxe Pizza, 130
Chicken Caesar Sandwich, 158
Chicken Tortilla Soup, 61
Easy Chicken Enchiladas, 153
Barbecue Chicken Bake with Cornbread Crust, 156
Steak Tacos with Cucumber Avocado Salsa, 175
Dirty Rice, 166
Roasted Summer Vegetables with Pasta, 198

ONE-DISH MEALS

Barbecue Chicken Bake with Cornbread Crust, 156
Crabmeat Angel Hair Pasta, 190
Greek Salad with Oregano Marinated Chicken, 81
Chicken and Wild Rice Casserole, 155
Chicken and Sausage Jambalaya, 144
Meaty Eggplant Sauce with Rigatoni, 195

CROWD PLEASERS

Fabulous French Bread Loaf, 27
Crawfish Fettuccine, 189
Chicken and Sausage Jambalaya, 144
Ultimate Chili, 62

FREEZE AND PLEASE

Exotic Shrimp Bundles, 15
Shrimp, Crab and Corn Soup, 51
Stuffed Louisiana Potatoes, 98
Crawfish Fettuccine, 189
Fish Cakes, 118
Meaty White Lasagna, 201
Jane's "Throw It In" Vegetarian Chili, 203
Fiesta Beef Enchiladas, 169

LIKE IT LIGHT DINNERS

Spinach Prosciutto Ravioli, 106
Beef Lettuce Wraps, 173
Shrimp Deluxe Pizza, 130
Crawfish Cakes with Horseradish Sauce, 136
Garden Fresh Penne, 196

HOLIDAY EXTRAS

Chicken, Brie, and Cranberry Chutney Quesadillas, 15
Lemon Sweet Potato Casserole, 101
Bourbon Mashed Sweet Potatoes with Praline Topping, 100
Yam Pecan Pie in Gingersnap Crust with Honey Pecan Topping, 225–226
Sweet Potato Cinnamon Bundt Cake with Orange Glaze, 218
Easy Red Velvet Cake, 219

AMANDINE The French term that means "with almonds." Fish is first cooked and then topped with toasted almonds.

ANDOUILLE A spicy and smoked Louisiana sausage of lean pork to add flavor to other Cajun dishes such as gumbos, red beans and rice, and jambalaya.

BARBEQUE SHRIMP Shrimp cooked in their shells with a blend of olive oil, butter or margarine seasoned with bay leaf, garlic, and herbs and spices.

BEIGNET A beignet is a rectangular puff of fried dough sprinkled with powdered sugar.

BISQUE A thick cream based soup, bisque is most often made with crawfish, crab or shrimp.

BLACKENED Fish or meat cooked in a cast iron skillet with butter at high heat with a heavy coating of spices and seasonings.

BREAD PUDDING Stale French bread is soaked in a custard, combined with other ingredients and baked.

CAYENNE A bright-red, moderately "hot" pepper that has been dried and used to season a variety of New Orleans-Creole dishes since the 18th century.

CORN MAQUE-CHOUX Corn is cooked down with tomato, peppers, onion, and spices. Meat or seafood may be added to serve as the main dish. This old Louisiana-Creole recipe dates back to the French settlers.

CREOLE MUSTARD A traditional brown whole-grain mustard that can contain other ingredients like horseradish and vinegar. Country or grainy mustard may be substituted.

CREOLE SEASONING A blend of cayenne, garlic, onion, pepper and salt—can be variation.

DIRTY RICE This traditional Cajun dish resembles jambalaya. The name comes from the tiny bits of meat, especially giblets or sausage, that are cooked with seasonings in white rice.

DRESSED A "dressed" po' boy sandwich with lettuce, tomato, mayonnaise or mustard.

ETOUFFEE The term literally means "cooked down" or "smothered," and refers to a thick stew of crawfish tails cooked with onions, celery and green pepper and served over rice.

FILÉ The Creole word for ground sassafras used to thicken and add a distinct flavor to gumbos.

GRILLADES Medallions of beef or veal. Grillades and grits is a popular breakfast, especially in New Orleans.

GUMBO From *quingombo*, an African word for okra, this Cajun/Creole creation can refer to any number of thick, robust soups made with a roux with seafood or meat, and flavored with okra and other seasonings. Gumbo is typically served over rice.

JAMBALAYA A Louisiana Creole dish of Spanish and French creation. Jambalaya is made in one pot with rice the indispensable ingredient with meat, vegetables and stock.

MEUNIÈRE This French method of preparing fish entails fish, coated with flour, and sautéed in brown butter, with lemon juice added to the sauce.

MUFFALETTA Originating in 1906 at the Central Grocery in New Orleans, this huge Italian sub-style sandwich is noted for the key ingredient, marinated olive salad, with slices of provolone, cheese, ham and salami.

OYSTERS ROCKEFELLER This renowned dish of baked oysters on the half shell was created at Antoine's Restaurant in New Orleans in 1899 by the proprietor, Jules Alciatore. The name honors John D. Rockefeller, at that time one of the world's richest men, because of the sauce's intense richness.

PO' BOY A hefty sandwich indigenous to southern Louisiana made with New Orleans-style French bread and any number of fillings.

REMOULADE The classic Creole dressing is a mixture of olive oil with mustard, green onions, cayenne, lemon, paprika and parsley, and is most often served con chilled boiled seafood.

ROUX Flour browned in fat until light brown to a rich nut color brown used as a base to thicken, color and flavor soups, stews, gravies and gumbos.

SAUCE PIQUANTE The literal translation is "peppery sauce." A hot spicy stew made with a roux, tomatoes and combined with alligator, chicken, pork, sausage, or game highly seasoned with herbs and peppers cooked for hours.

SWEET POTATO A root vegetable that is often called a yam. Sweet potatoes from Louisiana are referred to as "Louisiana yams" because of their orange flesh sweet moist inside due to the climate and soil.

TASSO A specialty Cajun dried piece of lean intensely seasoned pork used to give a distinct flavor to dishes

INDEX

trim&TERRIFIC™ GULF COAST FAVORITES

BOOKS BY HOLLY CLEGG

Holly Clegg's trim&TERRIFIC® Too Hot in the Kitchen: Secrets To Sizzle At Any Age

Holly Clegg's trim&TERRIFIC® Gulf Coast Favorites

The New Holly Clegg trim&TERRIFIC® Cookbook

Holly Clegg's trim&TERRIFIC® Home Entertaining The Easy Way

Holly Clegg's trim&TERRIFIC® Freezer Friendly Meals

Holly Clegg's trim&TERRIFIC® Diabetic Cooking

Eating Well Through Cancer: Easy Recipes & Recommendations Before & After Treatment

For more information, visit www.hollyclegg.com or call 1-800-88HOLLY